Music for Wales

Music for Wales

WALFORD DAVIES AND THE NATIONAL COUNCIL
OF MUSIC, 1918–1941

DAVID IAN ALLSOBROOK

CARDIFF
UNIVERSITY OF WALES PRESS
1992

British Library Cataloguing in Publication Data

Allsobrook, David Ian
   Music for Wales: Walford Davies and the National Council of Music, 1918-41
   I. Title
   780.9429

ISBN 0-7083-1135-0 hardback
     0-7083-1153-9 paperback

Typeset by Alden Multimedia, Northampton
Printed by Biddles Ltd., Guildford

In loving memory of two musical Welshmen,
Benjamin and Vyrnwy Jones

CONTENTS

ILLUSTRATIONS

Foreword

I am happy to welcome this account of the work of Walford Davies in Wales. It touches on my own childhood recollections and on the period at Gregynog when Sir Walford and my father, Thomas Jones, between them encouraged and sustained the venture on which the philanthropic sisters, Gwendoline and Margaret Davies, had embarked, following their return from wartime service in France.

For the majority of those who came to Gregynog from the mid-twenties to the outbreak of the Second World War, the focus of excellence was undoubtedly the music. In the later years, the main direction came from Sir Adrian Boult, but the standard had been firmly set by Walford Davies, who continued to be an inspiring and a most welcome guest in that hospitable establishment both during and after his university engagement at Aberystwyth.

Meanwhile, he had become a familiar voice to millions, at first through gramophone recordings and later as one of the most successful broadcasters of his generation. How far his influence extended over musical education and performance in Wales was at times controversial, but that we should have been far poorer without his creative enthusiasm I cannot doubt.

Eirene White

The Rt. Hon. Baroness White of Rhymney

Preface

This study of an important episode in the evolution of musical life in Wales has an objective intention. Its genesis, however, was subjective, a quality betrayed in the dedication. Ben Jones was my grandfather, for most of his life a first hand on furnaces in Welsh steelworks. In the early 1920s he moved from his birthplace, Gorseinon in Glamorgan, to spend the rest of his long working life at Shotton in Flintshire. He was a splendid singer, of the old rhetorical Welsh kind, who had received his vocal lessons in Sunday school and later in his father-in-law's male-voice choir. I still possess some of the printed tonic sol-fa anthems and hymn tunes which my great-grandfather composed for his choirs in south Wales before the First World War; and my earliest musical training took place in our Shotton front parlour. The last memory of my grandfather which I have was vividly recorded on tape in 1965 when he was eighty-six: three verses of a song he had learnt in Sunday school at the age of six. Growing up in his household and attending his chapel, I drank from the rapidly diminishing pool of a vocal tradition of Welsh communal music-making which has long since evaporated.

Ben Jones's son, Vyrnwy, who died in 1988, was my godfather and a remarkable musician. At the age of eight he went from Shotton to Chester, a few miles over the border, to be a treble in the Cathedral choir. Later he was a pupil at Hawarden County School under Arthur Lyon, uniquely musical and inspirational among Welsh headmasters in his generation. My uncle became a student of E. T. Davies at Bangor, and there developed considerable skills as pianist, composer and leader of College musical activities.

Those reminiscences hardly comprise a distinguished personal story. But they do reflect some facets of Welsh musical evolution over the past hundred years. One of Vyrnwy's chief musical memories was of a school performance at Hawarden of Bach's B-minor Mass in 1929, presided over by Sir Walford Davies, and prepared by Lyon. Vyrnwy Jones encouraged all my musical endeavours. With the help, also, of a splendid piano-teacher from the Swansea Valley, trained at the Royal

Academy, I won piano prizes at the National Eisteddfod in the 1950s. The adjudicators, on one of those occasions, were Alun Hoddinott and Meirion Williams.

Once the idea of this book was under way, three people in particular spurred me forward. Heward Rees, at the Welsh Music Archive in Cardiff, has offered encouragement, detailed knowledge and essential technical advice. Gethin Jones, who grew up amid the fervid musical activity of the Cynon Valley in the 1920s and 1930s, provided a rich seam of information about the quality and quantity of music-making in his youth. The late Leslie Tussler, one of Walford Davis's amanuenses in south Wales, and a conductor of the old school, gave generously of his time and experience. His articles in *Welsh Music* are most useful sources for the study of major aspects of Welsh musical development in the inter-War years.

I must also thank the staffs of the University Library in Cardiff, of the National Library in Aberystwyth, of Cardiff Central Library, and of the Public Record Office at Kew for all their patient help. My immediate family – Marian, Daniel and Gudrun – know precisely how often I have stretched their tolerance during the past two years. They have my undying gratitude.

DAVID IAN ALLSOBROOK

University of Wales College of Cardiff

PROLOGUE

...Are the Welsh – we Welsh – afraid of excellence? Did we, in some dark mediaeval moment, fall in love with defeat? We are, we allow ourselves to be assured, 'a musical nation', but we are rotten composers of our individual destinies. Brilliant first movements, yes; perhaps a short, eccentric scherzo to follow. But then rhapsodies of failure, a groaning coda and goodnight.
(Russell Davies, review of Melvyn Bragg, *Rich: the life of Richard Burton*, London, 1988, *Observer*, 2 October 1988.)

In 1897 the English musicologist and educationist W.H. Hadow published a remarkable monograph on Haydn entitled *A Croatian Composer*, in which he challenged the currently held assumption that Haydn's music was 'Viennese'. Hadow was intensely interested in the question of nationality in relation to music at a time when Wales was yet again striving to become aware of her national distinctiveness. He contended that 'the composer bears the mark of his race not less surely than the poet or the painter, and there is no music with true blood in its veins and true passion in its heart that has not drawn inspiration from the breast of the mother country.'[1]

In October, 1951, the municipality of Swansea held an exhibition, devoted to 'Music in Wales', as part of the young Swansea Festival which was itself the last official musical event in that Festival of Britain year. The exhibition was opened by the most successful Welsh composer of the immediate post-War era, Daniel Jones, a native of Swansea. Surrounded by ancient crwths, harps, pibgorns and stiff-backed civic dignitaries, he used the occasion to mount an attack on Welsh musical complacency:

All around you you see what might be taken as evidence of the poverty of music in Wales... Wales has not produced an abundance of music, and the organisers have had to scrape for material... The history of music in Wales has had its ups and downs, but I am afraid it has been mostly downs... The tragedy of the Welsh composer is that he has no tradition on which to rely. There is a lot of talk about tradition in

Wales, but if you examine it closely you will find that the vital thread has been broken. There is actually nothing handed down except the folk song...[2]

Poised chronologically between those two statements there flourished in Wales a unique institution, the University (sometimes called the National) Council of Music, founded in 1918, whose activities were an attempt to transform the musical life of the Principality. With financial support from the University of Wales, and generous donations from private sponsors and public trusts, the Council was the vital organism of collaboration between the colleges, the secondary and elementary schools, the chapels, the Church in Wales, the Eisteddfod and various agencies of adult learning.

Its nuclei were the music departments of the university colleges; and its antennae reached the smallest rural communities in the form of lecture-recitals, courses for the training of choral conductors, violin classes for schoolchildren, and non-competitive festivals on a grand scale. The Council promoted hundreds of concerts, not only of the European classics, but of new works by contemporary Welsh composers. It brought to Wales English musicians of great distinction: Elgar, Holst, Vaughan Williams, Frank Bridge, Boult, Sargent and Henry Wood. At the colleges of Aberystwyth, Cardiff and Bangor a tradition of chamber-music and orchestral performance was initiated such as Welsh communities had never before encountered; and in the depths of the Great Depression it provided music-making and musical education of the best quality for the unemployed of the coal-mining valleys. Its lasting influence on the life of ordinary schools was immense; and, in conjunction with the Central Welsh Board – the main external examining body for Wales – it earned for music an honourable place in the secondary schools and, consequently, in the higher work of the colleges.

The main purpose of this study is to describe and analyse the work of the Council of Music, and in particular to assess the influence of its first Director, Walford Davies, during his years in office, from its inception in 1918 until his death in 1941. The stinging attack of Daniel Jones in 1951 would seem to suggest that the Council had achieved little. But the very fact of its creation raises a prior issue: why was it thought necessary, in what was reputedly the 'Land of Song', to have such an official institution at that time? After all, Wales was then thought to possess a long, if somewhat mythical, history of musical accomplishment; and particularly in the late-Victorian era, her choirs had gained for Wales a reputation of being the most 'musical' part of the Empire. What need was there in 1918 for galvanizing the already flexing sinews of Welsh popular musical culture?

CHAPTER ONE

A Land of Singers? Folk-song and Hymnody

The myth of Welsh musicality had been thoroughly established by 1900, and its provenance was substantial, even if there were disputes about the historical evidence among scholars and enthusiasts. The most ancient branch of the musical tradition was sealed in a patriotic hide which made it virtually inviolable. It was almost as if the Welsh had always sought to live according to the description offered by Gerallt Cymro (Giraldus Cambrensis) in the twelfth century:

> When they come together to make music, the Welsh sing their traditional songs, not in unison, as is done elsewhere, but in parts, in many modes and modulations. When a choir gathers to sing, which happens often in this country, you will hear as many different parts and voices as there are performers, all joining together in the end to produce a single organic harmony and melody in the soft sweetness of B-flat.[1]

Such ambiguities became the stuff of belief in a long continuous tradition of vocal music-making. The Welsh were, therefore, reputedly the most musical of the British peoples.

Another kind of myth-making, blended with dubious antiquarianism, grew up in the eighteenth century through, for instance, prefatorial remarks in collections of 'national' airs such as those of the harpers John Parry of Rhiwabon and Edward Jones.[2] For much of the nineteenth century their findings were simply repeated without question. Parry, Jones, and others after them – like another John Parry (Bardd Alaw) – were naturally concerned to stress the central historic role of the harp, which became – conveniently ignoring similar traditions in Ireland and Scotland – a 'Welsh' instrument. The crwth, equally ancient and played with a bow, was practically obsolete by the end of the eighteenth century, as were the pibgorn (or hornpipe), the bagpipe and the tabret (a small drum). Welsh harpists did, however, make a deep mark in fashionable England during the first Georgian era. Edward Jones of Llanderfel played at one of Dr Burney's soirées in 1775, and eight years later became Bard to the Prince of Wales. Burney, impressed by his performances, wrote of

JONES, a Welshman, who is blind, and the best performer on the harp of his time. The old Duchess of Marlborough would have retained him in her service, with a pension, as an inmate; but he could not endure confinement, and was engaged by Evans, the landlord of a well-accustomed home-brewed ale-house...in Fleet-street, where he performed in the great room upstairs during the winter season. He played extempore voluntaries, the fugues in the sonatas and concertos of Corelli, and most of his solos, with many of Handel's opera songs, with uncommon neatness, which were thought great feats, at a time when scarcely any thing but Welsh tunes with variations was ever attempted on that instrument in the hands of other harpers...[3]

Blind John Parry, domestic harper to Sir Watcyn Williams-Wynn of Wynnstay, went even earlier to London, in 1746, and was said to have earned Handel's praise. He is chiefly celebrated in Welsh musicology for having played before Thomas Gray at Cambridge, thus inspiring the writing of 'The Bard', an ode whose significance vibrated through Wales's perception of its musical and poetical self during the Victorian period and into the early twentieth century.

Gray's Pindaric verses (1757) contained an elegant epitome of what the Welsh needed to believe about their cultural history as a true sense of national pride struggled to be born at the end of the eighteenth century. 'The Bard' was founded on the legend of Edward I's having ordered the death of all bards when he annexed Wales: a lamentation and a curse upon the English conqueror, it foretells the resumption of Welsh pride at the rise of the house of Tudor and the flourishing of a new bardic tradition. The modern successors, however, never recovered the nobility and dignity of the medieval poets. Elizabeth I, granddaughter of Henry VII, sent a commission to certain Welsh gentlemen in 1567:

> ...vagrant and idle persons naming themselves Minstrels, Rythmers, and Bards are lately grown into such intolerable multitude within the Principality of North Wales, that not only gentlemen and others by their shameless disorders are often disquieted in their habitations, but also the expert minstrels and musicians in tongue and cunynge thereby much discouraged to travaile in the exercise and practice of their knowledge...[4]

After the sixteenth century, according to Osian Ellis, the great stream of bardic harpers, men of considerable power and status in princely courts, dried up, though royal and noble patronage persisted for a few of the best of them. More than two hundred years after Elizabeth's death, Mendelssohn would probably have had good reason for agreeing with the general tone of her censure. Staying with new English friends near Mold in August 1829, he wrote to his family,

> No national music for me! Ten thousand devils take all nationality! Now I am in Wales, and dear me! a harper sits in the hall of every reputed inn playing incessantly so-called national melodies; that is to say, most infamous, vulgar, out-of-tune trash, with a hurdy-gurdy going at the same time! It is distracting, and has given me the toothache already...[5]

Mendelssohn was a tourist, a not uncommon phenomenon in north Wales by the beginning of the nineteenth century. From a late-twentieth-century 'heritage' aspect, it is easy to appreciate that the incursion of curious foreigners had a long, debilitating effect on the quality and creative energy of singers of Welsh songs to the harp. Not all visitors were as critical as the young Mendelssohn. John Parry (Bardd Alaw), after a prosperous career as conductor and composer in London, spent some of his commercial talent on producing in 1840 one of the many guides which introduced visitors to the delights of north Wales.[6]

Parry, one of the most beloved metropolitan musicians of his day, nevertheless embodied many of the weaknesses attendant upon the re-creation of Welsh music for the entertainment of a middle- and upper-class British public in the first half of the nineteenth century. On the one hand, relying heavily on the earlier 'researches' of Edward Jones, he compiled large collctions of Welsh airs – mainly harp tunes – with English words, most of them by a Liverpool poet, Mrs Hemans (once a juvenile target of Shelley's lust), for genteel adornment. On the other, he cobbled together what can hardly be called an opera: rather, a third-rate play with songs, *A Trip to Wales*, which was performed, once, at Covent Garden in 1826. This 'opera', relying heavily on the models of Goldsmith and Sheridan, seems to have been merely a rather elaborate advertisement for Parry's printed collections of Welsh airs, some of which were incorporated disjointedly in the drama. By the early 1830s serious London musicians were finding Parry's antiquarian eccentricities mildly amusing. Moscheles, briefly Mendelssohn's teacher and the leading pianist of his generation, recalled a solo performance by the Welshman in 1833 before an audience of the Royal Society of Musicians, a charitable body of which Parry was Secretary:

...old Parry, dressed in the costume of a Welsh bard, carrying his harp, sang his national melodies. He is a favourite with us musicians, who gave him a complimentary dinner and a present of silver plate, in recognition of his many years' services as one of our guild, and in token of his efforts on behalf of poor musicians.[7]

Parry was a prominent member also of the Cymmrodorion Society of London; but his musical confectionery began to flavour too pungently their more serious patriotic and literary deliberations.[8] In the 1820s and '30s, travelling to and from Wales, he also controlled the performances of music at the newly revived *eisteddfodau*.[9] The 'Welsh' music included in these meetings (apart from that played by the native harpist-competitors) came mainly from Parry's arrangements. He had at least the advantage of being a Welsh-speaking expatriate.

The adulteration of the folk-song at this stage in musical history is epitomized even more clearly in the hectic collecting and publishing activity of the Scot, George Thomson, who, enlisting the help, at a considerable distance, of Haydn, Beethoven, Kozeluch and eventually Weber as arrangers, gathered – mainly by correspondence with barely reliable natives – scores of tunes from Scotland, Ireland and Wales. Thomson added words which he thought would appeal to middle-class purchasers in the first two decades of the nineteenth century. In order to make the verses fit (he used Boswell and Burns, among others, as his hack-writers), he was quite content to distort the original melodies. His Welsh collections did not prove popular, especially in Wales,[10] and Thomson's general lack of exactitude is exemplified by his including 'Ar hyd y nos' ('All through the night', exquisitely arranged by Haydn – who had never seen the words) in the *Scottish* collection.

That tourists in increasing numbers came to Wales partly to hear the Welsh sing was therefore hardly due to the work of Thomson, a commercial speculator posing as musical antiquarian, or to Parry, a native cunningly drawing a dividend on his debased musical inheritance. In 1848 the author of *A New Tourist Companion through North Wales*, Edward Gray, noted the 'great simplicity' and antiquity of the Welsh melodies. Their 'wildness' caused him to descant on the Union of Britain, initiating a train of thought about constitutional integrity and social control which was to survive in various guises for the next hundred years. Of the Denbigh Eisteddfod in 1828 (for which music was arranged by Bardd Alaw) Gray claimed that

...the thrilling tones of the Welsh harp now heard within the ancient wall of the Denbigh castle, and the presence of a member of the royal family (the Duke of Sussex), were calculated, at once, to revive in the mind of every Welshman the recollection of the ancient glories of Cambria in the days of her Owens, her Llewelyns, and her Tudors; and to contrast her situation then with what it was at present under the mild and constitutional sway of the house of Brunswick.[11]

The properly systematic collecting of authentic Welsh folk melodies was begun by Maria Jane Williams (1793–1873) of Aberpergwm, a noted soprano singer who presented tunes from her native Glamorgan and from Monmouthshire at the Abergavenny Eisteddfod of 1838.[12] None of her songs had previously been published, and some of them have remained popular, for example, 'Y 'Deryn Pur' and 'Bugeilio'r Gwenith Gwyn'. Five years later the Revd John Broadwood of Sussex printed a private collection of English songs which set off a similar folk-revival in England. The Queen's Harper, also a teacher at the Royal Academy of Music, John Thomas (1826-1913, known by his bardic title of Pencerdd Gwalia) of Bridgend, published between 1862 and 1874 a Welsh collection in four volumes. But that was soon superseded in popularity by *The Songs of Wales* of Brinley Richards (1817–1885). The *Athenaeum* commented,

> ...Mr Richards has done the right thing in not writing elaborate pianoforte passages, and in allowing the air itself to predominate. As an expert pianist himself he might well have been tempted to indulge in arpeggios and other showy exhibitions of manipulative skill. There are several airs that have never before been published with English and Welsh words, and the editor has been at great pains to supply the tunes on the best authority, many of them having been taken from Miss Jane Williams's collection of national airs with her permission. That lady has been a careful and conscientious collector of unpublished Welsh music having noted down from the songs of the peasantry their themes, and having corrected the irregularities and variations arising from the singing of traditional tunes.[13]

Without necessarily in each case setting out to be so, the early collectors of the the Victorian era were casual in attributing antiquity to 'Welsh' tunes. Indeed, a number of the most famous melodies were hardly Welsh at all. 'The Ash Grove', first published in 1802, is remarkably similar to 'Cease Your Funning' in the *Beggars' Opera* (1727–8); 'Pen Rhaw', which first appeared as a Welsh air in 1784, had an affinity to 'John, Come Kiss Me Now', popular in England in the sixteenth century; and 'The Hunting of the Hare' seems to be the English 'The Green Gown' printed in *Musick's Recreation on the Viol* (1652). 'The Bells of Aberdovey', published by Maria Jane Williams in 1844, is reputedly a composition of Charles Dibdin who had included it (with pidgin-Welsh words) in an opera in 1785. There had been no recorded Welsh version of the tune before 1844. As for 'Cader Idris', that was an original melody written by Bardd Alaw in 1802, with words later added by his friend the actor Charles Matthews who gave it the title 'Jenny Jones'. Such confusions were inherent in the flexible transmission of folk-song throughout the British Isles.

The English Folk-song Society was established in 1898. Ten years earlier Baring-Gould had set out to collect songs in Devon and Cornwall, discovering unanticipated riches. Frank Kidson brought out his *Traditional Tunes* in 1891; Lucy Broadwood and Fuller Maitland published *English County Songs* in 1893, while Cecil Sharp completed his Somerset collection in 1905.

The English work of collecting tunes and creating a society for their conservation and transmission was accomplished by the spontaneous coming-together of enthusiasts. This was the consequence of an awakening social conscience at the end of the nineteenth century, and of an awareness that certain traditional patterns of rural experience were inexorably passing away. As the example of Maria Jane Williams suggests, the process of collecting in Wales, while also starting spontaneously, had been, certainly in its particulars, separate from and prior to similar impulses in England. In Wales, too, the founding of a society for the study and preservation of folk-songs was a singular event. In one sense it was the indirect result of the recent creation of another national institution, the University of Wales. The first Principal of the University College of North Wales, Harry Reichel, a Protestant Irishman, married a musical lady. As part of his policy of nurturing a close-knit community of students at Bangor, he invited the Lecturer in Botany, J. Lloyd Williams, to take on the unpaid office of Director of Music. Lloyd Williams, in turn, proposed that, on formal occasions, College performances should be limited to singing arrangements of traditional Welsh airs. He quickly discovered that most of the so-called folk-songs – 'The Rising of the Lark', and so on – were, in fact, not-so-old diatonic harp-tunes.

It was in the new University of Wales, then, that Welsh folk-song found its living and breathing, as well as academic, legitimacy. Bangor college garden parties had usually been dominated by the sounds of local brass bands. Now, at Reichel's and Lloyd Williams's insistence, a group of students, Y Canorion, not only sang traditional folk-songs, but contributed 'new' tunes they had collected recently from their native villages and towns. The singing, wrote Lloyd Williams, 'owed its success more to its unpretentious and effortless character than to any vocal excellence.'[14] The direct result of this Bangor activity was a Cymmrodorion meeting during the Caernarfon Eisteddfod of 1906 at which the Welsh Folk-song Society was constituted. On that occasion it was acknowledged that the originators of the idea were the Irish littérateur Alfred Percival Graves (father of Robert), 'who has done so much for Irish, Welsh and other folk-songs', and Principal Reichel. Graves and Reichel read papers, and it was decided to appoint a provisional committee whose members included D. Emlyn Evans, Lloyd George, Reichel and Graves, with J. Lloyd Williams as one of the secretaries.[15]

In his paper Graves drew attention to the interconnection of folk-song conservation in various countries around 1900. He himself had been one of the original founders of the English Society, attending its first meeting in the rooms of the Irish Literary Society of London, of which he was Secretary. Ireland also, 'with its Home Rule tendencies', had felt the need for her own Society. In this other Celtic movement, basing his work on the Petrie Collection, C. V. Stanford had played a leading part. Its work had been stimulated by officials of the *Feis Ceoil* – the Irish equivalent of the Eisteddfod – who were gathering tunes from fiddlers and singers, and by the Gaelic League's encouragement of traditional singing in the Irish tongue. Graves dismissed the idea that all true folk-songs had already been gathered in; and he offered Grainger-like advice to collectors of tunes from the elderly: 'Friendliness, combined with judicious baksheesh in the way of snuff, tobacco, tea and ale, unloosened their tongues and revived their memories.'[16] The reference to ale betokened Graves's apparent lack of sensitivity to one formal aspect of dissimilarity marked by St George's Channel.

The Unionist Reichel's contribution in Wales was less musical and more political in tone. He thought that one consequence of the Society's existence would be the better interpretation, for the other parts of the United Kingdom, of Welsh thought and feeling:

Our Empire is tending more and more to become a confederation of sister nations, kept together partly by external pressure, partly, and we trust increasingly, by internal attraction. Such cohesion can only exist provided the different parts understand and appreciate each other. Through what medium can they better get to know each other's true spirit and ideals than through their folk-songs, which embody, perhaps in a greater degree than any any other artistic product, the finer national instincts of the particular race from which they spring? I doubt if any better means of bringing about closer sympathy between the component parts of our population could be devised than the habitual use in our schools of the best English, Irish, Welsh, and Scottish national songs.[17]

The founding of the Welsh Folk-song Society thus emphasized not only the distinctiveness of the Welsh tradition of people's music but the universality of folk-song in the British Isles. The unique character of Welsh song, it was discovered, lay primarily in the particular lyrical characteristsics of the language; and this was a feature taken up later by those, like David Vaughan Thomas, seeking to re-establish a vital creative impulse in contemporary Welsh music-making. For educational purposes, however, Graves, along with Arthur Somervell, who arranged many Welsh tunes with good translations, promoted the principle which Reichel had enunciated: that a strong *British* tradition in musical performance and composition should be based on mutual understanding of the various strands of British folk music – or 'national song', as it was often called – encouraged by teaching in the elementary schools, using good examples from all four countries. A significant feature of the society, by contrast with its counterpart in England, was that its officers were generally members of the Welsh academic and political establishment, some of whom, however, were immigrants.

There was, in addition to pure folk-song, a truly unique component of the Welsh musical tradition which was, like the Eisteddfod, both ancient and modern, authentic and artificial. *Penillion* had a historic lineage; yet it was also – in the strictness of its rules, at least – a nineteenth-century construct. There had been a long *penillion* tradition of one kind, in which, to the accompaniment of a repeated Welsh air on the harp, each singer in the company had to extemporize words in rhyme. The modern, much more difficult, north-Walian form, where the singer neither begins with the player nor starts on the first beat of the bar, was the nineteenth-century invention of one man, Idris Fychan. A Welsh cobbler, living in Manchester, he created *penillion* in much the same way as Iolo Morganwg had brought the *Gorsedd* into being. Idris's invention can be given a precise date: the Chester Eisteddfod of 1866, for which he wrote a prize essay on *Canu Penillion*, later published by the Cymmrodorion Society, setting out, for the first time, the strict rules to be followed by later singers and players. As Osian Ellis has recently written,

> Idris Vychan's accomplishment was to extend the scope and scale of *canu penillion* to accommodate the complex metrical poetry, and at the same time placing the onus of melodic improvisation on the singer instead of the harpist.[18]

In pointing out this and other anomalies in the history of Welsh music, Ellis has explained that his intention was 'only to clarify, unemotionally, some aspects of our musical history before musicologists from Texas and Timbuktu fall upon us and confound us even further.'[19]

The Germans in the nineteenth century stigmatized England (and Scotland might legitimately have been included) as 'The Land without Music'. It would appear that the Welsh, with no reason to fear such scurrility, wove a defensive skein of antiquarian deceit in order to protect the uneasy legend of their musicality. When Welshmen working professionally outside Wales – like the London-based Brinley Richards – attacked complacent acceptance of a spuriously continuous musical heritage, the Welsh at home bellowed in wounded pride. Next to the language, music – not simply the love of music, but skill in its creation and performance – was their chief claim to a distinctive national identity; and criticism from ignorant *Saeson* and from London Welshmen who had lost their faith, had to be resisted with virulent irony.

The Welsh surely were musical; and by comparison with their English neighbours they were a singing people. The English vocal tradition was based largely in the cathedral churches and to some extent in the theatres of London and the greater provincial towns: it was, therefore, by definition, narrow and élitist. By the middle of the nineteenth century, on the other hand, Welsh hymnody was a possession of the people, of a Nonconformist people for whom it was the chief democratic expression of deeply emotional participation in the act of worship. D. E. Parry Williams, writing in 1947, admitted that there were good and bad elements in the Welsh tradition of congregational singing. But it can be argued that world-wide acknowledgement of Wales as a musical nation in the first half of this century was based almost solely on evidence of the Welsh as singers of hymns and other religious music, along with the impure shreds of a few folk-songs and a powerfully sung national anthem.

It is unlikely that Gerallt heard his twelfth-century 'singers-in-parts' performing in churches. But there was a strong pre-Reformation devotion to liturgical music in Wales. Even in late-medieval times, Welsh singers were swooping upon England as musical pedagogues. The chief Victorian historian of schools, A. F. Leach, commented, 'it is remarkable that even (in the sixteenth century) two of the song school masters in London whose names are mentioned are Welshmen.'[20] However, between the Reformation and the Nonconformist Revival of the eighteenth century little, if any, liturgical music was published in or for Wales. Initially the Baptists foreswore the pleasures of congregational singing; but John and Charles Wesley and George Whitefield encouraged hymns as the final scene of their services. The floodgates of harmony opened in Wales with the publication of *Llyfr Gweddi Gyffredin* in 1755. William Williams Pantycelyn was the first Welshman to respond to the Wesleys' appeal for new hymns. From the beginning congregational singing was self-sustaining: it was of some significance for the whole future of music in Wales that the early hymn-singers were unaccompanied. This plain mode of proceeding suited William Williams, who wrote in 1762,

> When the blessed gift of the Holy Spirit came upon the people the 'spirit within' was of itself sufficient to the whole man, body and soul, to praise the Lord without any musical instruments other than the media of graces ordained by the Lord, namely, preaching, praying and singing.[21]

What began in the puritan plainness of practical necessity developed into a philosophical principle underpinning a spartan approach to fervent music which lasted for over a hundred years after William Williams's time. David Lloyd George, in a speech at the dedication of an expensive pipe-organ to the memory of his musical daughter at the Clapham Junction Welsh Presbyterian Chapel in 1926, remembered the days of his childhood in a less richly furnished place of worship on the Llŷn peninsula: in Criccieth even a tuning-fork was considered too prominent; an adjustable pitch-pipe was tolerated, if sounded faintly, and much later, horror of horrors, a harmonium was purchased. He added,

> You are going to have a harp in Heaven, but it was difficult to get a harmonium on earth. Why it should be a sort of desecration of the Temple to have an instrument down here with the saints on earth when you could have a *full orchestra* up in Heaven, they never condescended to explain, and to me that is one of the mysteries of the theology I was

taught as a child... The Bishop of Chester would gladly surrender any harp, golden or otherwise, if he might be allowed to play a note or two on the oboe in the heavenly orchestra. Instrumental music, the Sleeping Beauty, ought to be awakened in the villages, even with a caress. I wish that music was more at home in our villages, and our villages more at home with music.[22]

Lloyd George said he had recently asked three great musicians what they considered were the five greatest hymn-tunes. Presumably by consensus they had chosen 'Mannheim', 'The Old Hundredth', the German 'Hallelujah' – 'the great Luther hymn', and the Welsh 'Moab'. 'Just think: "Moab" one of the five greatest hymn-tunes on earth!' There may be some dissenting now from that judgement. But the greatest mover of audiences and congregations of his day was on very sure ground when he judiciously directed their consideration towards hymn-tasting. Welsh musicologists may have been inefficient in collating folk-song in the nineteenth century; but the national heritage of hymn-tunes was of indisputable quality and provenance.

Early-Victorian compilers of hymn anthologies, like John Ambrose Lloyd in the 1840s, were generally parochial in their criteria of selection. The second half of the century, however, saw a flourishing of intense creativity and the raising of standards of taste in the writing and collecting of hymns. Strictly speaking, the leaders of this movement were musical amateurs; and most of them were Nonconformist clergy. Between them, in north and south Wales, they developed a firm framework within which the tentative aspirations of congregational singing could blossom to the point where Welshmen claimed a thoroughly justified pre-eminence in a popular field of musical accomplishment. What happened, between the 1850s and the end of the century, was a Welsh equivalent of the great improvement in the quality of the performance of Anglican church music, led by Gore-Ousely and John Stainer.

The acknowledged leader of the movement in Wales was John Roberts (Ieuan Gwyllt, 1822-77) of Tanrhiwfelen, whose parents had been notable chapel singers. After spells as a pharmacist and schoolmaster – trained at Borough Road College – then as solicitor's clerk, he became assistant editor of a Liverpool-Welsh newspaper, *Yr Amserau*. He preached the first of his many Welsh sermons at Runcorn in 1856. But the burden of the remainder of his life lay in the work of composing and compiling anthologies of hymn-tunes, and of initiating a process of popular education in choral singing all over the Principality. In 1852 he published *Blodau Cerdd* which contained specimen hymn-tunes as well as a programme of elementary music lessons. But it was his *Llyfr Tonau* (1859) which initiated the great age of Welsh congregational singing. Twenty-four of his own tunes have survived, including the celebrated 'Moab'. Like his pupil, D. Emlyn Evans of Newcastle Emlyn (1843–1913), Ieuan Gwyllt stressed above all the need for the highest standards of discrimination in the choice of music for chapel services, whether it was of Welsh origin or not. He was also a practical man, devising the institution of *cymanfaoedd canu*, spiritually orgiastic local singing festivals held frequently in the larger chapels, which provided opportunities for musical education on a grand scale. In 1863 he began to study tonic sol-fa, producing a sol-fa edition of his hymns a year later, and founding Cerddor y Tonic Solffa (an offshoot of the English Tonic Sol-fa College) in 1869.

The extraordinary achievement of Edward Stephen, or Jones (1822–85), of Maentwrog, universally known as Tanymarian, was that he wrote the first Welsh oratorio, *Ystorm Tiberias* (1851–2), later orchestrated by S. S. Wesley. That work's influence on musical sensibility throughout Wales was immense, to the extent that its Handelian and Mendelssohnian qualities froze the models for Welsh composition in a mould from which they did not escape until after 1900. A composer and editor of hymn-tunes, like Ieuan Gwyllt and D. Emlyn Evans, Tanymarian wrote and lectured copiously on music, and was, above all, a delightful singer of his own songs. Together those three men set the tone for one hundred years of Welsh music-making.[23]

CHAPTER TWO

The Making of the Eisteddfod

What the Welsh, in great numbers, accomplished as a result of the work of Tanymarian, Ieuan Gwyllt, and D. Emlyn Evans was undeniably impressive. The achievement would have been less considerable without the help of a process for learning musical notation which had begun at just the right moment in England. Ieuan Gwyllt's enthusiastic espousal of tonic sol-fa in 1863 was not accidental: in the same year John Curwen had founded the Tonic Sol-fa College. Its method was based on a centuries-old principle; but his innovation was to use visible symbols – in essence, the Modulator – as the vehicle for efficient teaching. Curwen's was a course of elementary instruction rather than of musical education. He included in the propaganda for his work educational aphorisms from Herbert Spencer, among others. But his chief importance lay in the creation of a wide pattern of transmission emanating from the College's headquarters at Plaistow, with lines of communication extending into thousands of Sunday schools, day schools and places of worship. In Wales the unslakeable thirst for draughts of simple musical experience caused tens of thousands in the late-Victorian era to drink avidly of Curwen's plain elixir. His *Teacher's Manual* became a Welsh best-seller.[1] In Curwen's system the Welsh discovered the short-cut to becoming musically grammatical, if not poetical. By 1910, of the 500 licentiates of the Tonic Sol-fa College, 300 were Welsh.[2]

An epitome of the effect of tonic sol-fa on communal singing in Wales was provided by a distinguished guest at the Ammanford National Eisteddfod in 1922. In his address, the Rt. Hon. T. J. Macnamara MP recalled a holiday at Clarach Bay, Aberystwyth, before the Great War, when he had encountered a group of young working men and women:

When they came near me they formed a circle and pulled from their pockets copies of the *Tonic Sol-Fa Reporter*. One stood in the middle and conducted with his index finger as a baton. It was a four-part song... The attack, the precision, the phrasing, the light and shade, the charm of the tenor lead, the gusto of the bass reply, remain with me to this day...[3]

The inspiration of Wales's leading musicians and the encouragement offered by Curwen's principles of mass musical training found a precise focus in reviving the institution of the Eisteddfod during the second half of the nineteenth century. There the good and bad among Welsh musical impulses had regular means of expression. Annually a moment occurred when the main strands of musical life and inheritance – *penillion*, national airs, the performance of hymns, anthems and oratorios – could be woven into a colourful fabric. The finished tapestry may have been primitive, but its public effect was universally powerful, providing entertainment, competition, conviviality in an otherwise harsh society, informal education, and, perhaps most important of all, a sense of identity for a largely lower-class population which was split between countryside and industrial communities, and in the latter case was increasingly non-Welsh in origin.

At least four distinct threads were interwoven in the creation of the late nineteenth-century eisteddfod: historical (or mythical), musical, religious and social. First, from a romantically opaque past came the memory of aristocratic contests among bards at the courts of native princes – Gray's 'Bard', in very truth; and also a growing, potent realization of the subtlety of ancient Welsh poetry, particularly the soaring lyrical and witty achievement of Dafydd ap Gwilym. These were embodied in antiquarian recollections of the *eisteddfodau* at Carmarthen in 1451 and Caerwys in 1523 and 1568, and the prizes anciently offered to the poet (*prydydd*), the family bard (*teulwr*) and the wandering minstrel (*clerwr*), with categories for music on stringed instruments (*cerdd dant*). By the eighteenth century that superior bardic tradition had declined into the inns of Wales and also the London ale-houses patronized by the well-read, and often well-heeled, exiles and visitors to the capital. Some London Welshmen professed literary learning of an elevated kind; and their two leading societies promoted the first formal revival of the late-medieval eisteddfod tradition at Corwen in 1789, from which event its subsequent nearly continuous development can be traced. The influence of wealthy or otherwise powerful Londoners – often members of Cymmrodorion – is a leading theme in the evolution of modern Welsh musicality. The Corwen Eisteddfod initiated a new series of competitive public festivals which was crowned by the institution of the National Eisteddfod of Wales in 1880.[4]

Among the grandest of these early-modern festivals was the Carmarthen meeting of 1819. It set a number of precedents, the first of which was the predominant interest of the public, not in the serious, scholarly work of the literary competitions, but rather in the singing for prizes. The second precedent was the importing of more sophisticated choral and instrumental talent than the native Welsh were thought capable of mustering, to supply artistes for the evening concerts. At Carmarthen, for instance, a choral society was brought all the way from still fashionable Bath to entertain, in St Peter's Church, audiences which were an odd combination of curious members of the local middle class, neighbouring gentry, and a handful of sympathetic noble patrons.[5]

In the 1820s and 1830s the eisteddfod concerts assumed an even more central position, and were mainly under the direction of the London-based Denbigh musician John Parry (Bardd Alaw), who also employed leading English singers and instrumentalists: like the soprano Miss Catherine Stephens who was to achieve another kind of fame by marrying the aged Earl of Essex a year before he died and outliving him by forty years; Braham the Jewish tenor and British patriot (composer of 'The Death of Nelson'), and Puzzi, the Dennis Brain of his time. Parry made concessions to national pride by including his own travesties of Welsh airs; but his programmes eventually occasioned the complaint that the Welsh should not have to listen to 'Italian concerts' of operatic arias at their native *eisteddfodau*. During the 1830s gradual changes took place, which are epitomized by the discovery of young Brinley Richards, son of the organist of St Peter's, Carmarthen, as pianist and composer at the Cardiff Eisteddfod of 1834;[6] also by Lady Llanover's economically judicious invention of the standard Welsh costume, and by the more authentic collecting work of Maria Jane Williams at Abergavenny in 1838. These early events tended to be deferential presentations before prominent guests like the Earl of Powis, the Marquess of Bute and Sir Watcyn Williams-Wynn. (This could have advantages: after his success at Cardiff, Brinley Richards's training at the new Royal Academy of Music in London, and later in Paris as a reputed pupil of Chopin, was sponsored by the Duke of Newcastle.) The peak of John Parry's career in its eisteddfodic phase was his arrangement of music for the visit of Princess Victoria and her mother to the Beaumaris meeting in 1835, where the royal guests were greeted by an orgy of bardic forelock-pulling.[7] Such assemblies were opportunities for the littérateurs to meet and exchange englynion, and for the majority of the audience to hear bland music or observe sentimentally the customary performances of blind, impoverished harpers.

The second strand in the modern eisteddfodic tradition was formed by the convergence of several forces, around 1880. During the preceeding thirty years the drive towards creating a successful annual festival had faltered financially because of those petty local jealousies – and a complementary failure to organize a continuous general administrative committee – which have constantly beset a variety of Welsh endeavours. The randomly chosen locations of the mid-nineteenth century led to fluctuations even in the quality and quantity of musical participation. In 1864 Matthew Arnold – while questioning the wisdom of inciting competitors, chiefly from the labouring classes, 'to make doggerel' which in some cases had 'more of Billingsgate than Parnassus' in its diction – devoted his attention to the music at the Llandudno Eisteddfod:

> ...It is well known that the people of Wales are musical, and that nearly every village has its choral meetings or its band. Yet for the choral competitions at Llandudno no candidates appeared; only one brass band; only one set of glee singers, who were rejected as unworthy of the prize...[8]

Arnold noticed, however, that a few promising Welsh musicians were already being promoted by their eisteddfodic success to scholarships and exhibitions at the Royal Academy of Music in London, and elsewhere outside the Principality:

> ...In matters musical the operations of the Eisteddfod thus bear fruit, because *music is the language of all time and all nations*. This, or any other society, may find out a deserving subject and remove him or her beyond the reach of *local prejudice and narrow provincial views* to some seat of learning, where the best uses will be made of the talent thus discovered and assisted. The results of such study and training away from Wales appeared in the concerts which were given during the meeting, the principal performers at which...were natives of the Principality.

The most general of the consolidating and improving forces in the period which followed Arnold's philippic was the resurgence of national feeling, mingled with political Radicalism and muscular Non-

831 END OF JAN 8

SARAH RAINSWORTH

PONY POWER

MR MONMOUTH

PAULA - PAIN

KAREN - super. cracker

PAULA - CHEESE

or Kiss me
0800 066 990
24.2.98

Ragstorme
Ragstorme

KAMCHARKA
RUSSIA.

WRITERS

your personal reference library of news and views, tips and ideas, facts and figures.

To claim your FREE binder just fill in the slip below and send it to Writers' Monthly together with your completed credit card or banker's order subscription form.

I claim my free Writers' Monthly binder. Please send it to me once my subscription payments begin.

Name _____

Address _____

_____

_____ Post Code _____

Signature _____

_____ Date _____

conformity; and *eisteddfodau* provided theatres for their formal interplay. The creation of a more secure financial and constitutional framework in 1880 coincided with the initiation of systems of secondary schooling and higher education in Wales.[9] By the early 1890s Wales possessed three growing university colleges and a system of intermediate schools which were the pride and, to a large extent, the creatures of the people. The economic texture of Wales was rapidly changing, and a new cultural dimension was emerging, located in the vortex of the burgeoning industrial south-east and the fitful vitality of the slate region of the north-west. The Eisteddfod formed a powerful link between the old traditions of rural Wales and the new, dynamic 'frontier society' of the industrial areas. People were able to meet and find a sort of identification with one another through the medium of the most ancient language in Europe, but chiefly, it would appear, through the joy of singing.

Gladstone, a sponsor of the new Welsh National University and, concurrently, of Irish Home Rule, visited the Wrexham Eisteddfod in 1888 from his castle-home in nearby Hawarden. His speech there blended effusions from springs of current concerns. Acknowledging the great antiquity of the Eisteddfod, he said (in a reputedly Liverpudlian accent),

> ...it was customary on the part of many...to deplore, as an economical error, the maintenance of the Welsh language. They would like us to be all alike – one tongue, one speech, one communication, one market of labour... I wish to say that in my opinion the principle of...local patriotism is not only an ennobling thing in itself, but it has great economical value...
>
> It is a matter of familiar observation, even in the extremest eastern parts of Europe, wherever free institutions have supplanted a despotic government, the invariable effect has been to administer an economic stimulus to the industry and wealth of the country... I wish prosperity, ladies and gentlemen, to Wales and prosperity to the Eisteddfod as a great means of promoting the welfare of Wales.[10]

As musical amateur and social engineer Gladstone might well have appreciated that one considerable consequence of Welsh industrial prosperity in the second half of the century had been the proliferating phenomenon of choral singing, and its attachment, in a most competitive form, to the renascent Eisteddfod. Local communities, in the period immediately before the emergence of organized Association and Rugby Football, poured out supporters in excited train-loads towards the gladiatorial choral contests which took place each summer. Almost all of the preceding twelve months had been spent in preparing two or three test-pieces for the eisteddfod, and the prizes gained in competition – £100 or £200 – added greed to local ambition and pride. It might be that the President of the day at the eisteddfod was Lord Aberdare or Lord Tredegar, accompanied perhaps – as was Aberdare in one instance – by a sympathetic English exotic like Matthew Arnold. The occasion was magnified by such presences. In 1889, at Brecon, a remarkable conjunction occurred: the President was Mabon, the great labour personality from the Rhondda, who led the community singing in a fine tenor voice. One of his formal tasks was to introduce Adelina Patti – the most celebrated coloratura soprano of the age – who had just alighted from the winged chariot (more prosaically the Brecon and Merthyr railway carriage) which had borne the *diva* from her home, an extraordinary sham *castello* in the Swansea Valley – Craig-y-nos. Patti's publicly expressed appreciation of Mabon's voice, after her own brief performance, was a piece of consummate flattery which nourished the roots of pride in an audience drawn largely from the coalfield towns. She even led the singing of 'Hen Wlad fy Nhadau' (the Welsh national anthem): the Queen of Song celebrating the Land of Song in its most sacred place.[11]

The choirs which challenged for titles each year were re-grouping almost as rapidly as Nonconformist chapels divided and multiplied in the valley communities. Yet, alongside the experience of the *cymanfa ganu*, the new competitive tradition within Wales produced a collective pride in the accomplishment of combined Welsh vocalizing. When opportunities for display outside the Principality arose, they were theatrically grasped, and the resulting victories, particularly on English soil, helped to construct a myth of choral superiority. Among the strong personalities who created large choirs, the most popular hero was Griffith Rhys Jones of Trecynon, whose first group, Côr Caradog, lent him the name by which he has remained known in south Wales. In 1872 he trained and led the great collective choir which competed at the Crystal Palace for a massive Challenge cup and a prize of £100. In the following year Caradog's five hundred voices defeated a London ensemble, the Paris Sol-fa Choir, before a panel of adjudicators which included the ancient Sir Julius Benedict, Weber's favourite pupil, and Joseph Barnby, later to become first director of the Cardiff Musical Festival.[12] More musically influential conductors were to take up

Caradog's baton; but the brief, brilliant achievement of Y Côr Mawr in the 1870s apparently justified a pride in the supremacy of Welsh choral singing which has lasted in national mythology until nearly the end of the twentieth century. The telling of Caradog's achievement – truly a tale of Celtic triumph at the Saxon imperial court – enlivened many a Welsh fireside evening. Thomas Jones of Rhymney whose magnificent choir was to be successful on five occasions at the National Eisteddfod before the Great War, told a story of public recitations in his native village:

> ...And there was the Twyncarno tailor who recited in Welsh with an Oxford accent, so to say. His favourite was *Y Côr Mawr* (pronounced *Mewr*)... This was a detailed description, down to the whistle of the steam-engine, of the visit of Caradog's choir...to compete at the Crystal Palace, and its triumphant return with the prize.[13]

The reciter even included word-portraits of the adjudicators and of all six choral set-pieces. The petty differences which usually separated men (and women) of the mining valleys became submerged in the glory of recollecting collective victory over the heathen on their own territory. The new late-nineteenth-century coal port of Barry soon had a statue of its entrepreneur-founder, David Davies of Llandinam (grandfather of the Misses Davies of Gregynog, later patronesses of Walford Davies) at the entrance to the new docks; the fast-growing capital, Cardiff, collected a mausoleum of statuary of Great Welshmen in Gorsedd Park at the middle of the city. But at Aberdare, in the heart of the singing south Wales coalfield, the iconic focal point of the community became a grand statue of a hero who had united local people in their greatest common endeavour – Caradog.

As well as helping to establish a choral tradition, *eisteddfodau* discovered outstanding solo voices, as Matthew Arnold had implied.[14] Some, like Eos Morlais, chose to confine their musical careers almost exclusively to performances in Wales. Others, celebrated at the end of the nineteenth century – Ben Davies, David Ffrangcon-Davies, Maggie Davies, Mary Davies (later to become wife of the Registrar of Bangor University College and a founder-member of the Welsh Folk-song Society) and John Henry – made reputations throughout Britain. Ben Davies, from the Swansea Valley, was an oratorio-singer and operatic tenor of international renown; and Frangcon-Davies, of Friars' School, Bangor, and Jesus College, Oxford, developed a baritone voice which deeply impressed Sullivan, Parry, Stanford and Elgar.

It was, however, the competitive element in choral, rather than solo, singing which drew the vast crowds increasingly year by year as the end of the century approached. And here a further feature of the Eisteddfod became fused with the myth of Welsh musicality. There had been another Welsh 'rite' in the eighteenth century which, since it had almost always occurred at harvest time, coincided roughly with the annual moment appointed for the National Eisteddfod in late-Victorian years. This was the local *gwylmabsant*, which commonly consisted of competitions of various kinds, after which the victors were supplied with ale by the vanquished. Some writers, like Sir T. Gwynn Jones, attempted to trace the Welsh love of musical and literary contests back to this primitive saint's-day festival. But since it was primarily an occasion for lively recreation, and drinking, 'it succumbed to the attacks of puritanism'.[15] Intoxication and fighting were widespread features of *gwylmabsant*. With its decline, some of the former clientele translated such crude jollifications into local fairs, whose necessary economic purpose protected them from too much censure. W. R. Lambert has recently pointed out the clear connection between early local eisteddfodau and public houses: the first recorded Aberdare Eisteddfod was held at the Swan Inn in the late 1820s;[16] Merthyr literary societies of that time generally held their early nineteenth-century meetings in public houses, which were then also the settings for radical political activity and the visits of miniature circus troupes.[17] Such effusions were staunched by the bandage of Nonconformity as the century progressed; but *gwylmabsant* and ritual intoxication were replaced as social safety-valves by the contest hysteria occasioned through *eisteddfodau*. Even Nonconformity itself, which directed vulgar energy into the disciplined enthusiasm of the *cymanfa ganu*, added its own competitive savour to the gruel of diurnal existence. There was a strong element of the contest in the ostensibly theological rivalry between chapels, as Thomas Jones again noted in Rhymney. 'The serpent of dissension', he said, 'was a frequent visitor in the garden of religious life.' The inhabitants of Rhymney remembered a most famous public battle which had occurred over two days in November, 1841, in the open air on ground between two chapels: 'Fighting there certainly was...'[18] And violence and mayhem were never very far beneath the usually genial social surface of *eisteddfodau*.

English musical gentlemen frequently officiated as adjudicators at *eisteddfodau*. Almost all of them were impressed in varying degrees by the fervour of Welsh singing; some were undisguisedly terrified at having to offer their judgements in the face of passionately involved, partisan audiences.[19] The mood of the vast throng of listeners could oscillate between rapt attention, as if in chapel, and misbehaviour which would now be considered gross in a football crowd. There was also a high degree of quaintness in the presentation of the competitions which appalled dignified outsiders, but which, for volatile Welsh audiences, contributed to the high pleasure of the occasion. In 1883 the London *Musical Times* commented on the attempt of an adjudicator at the Cardiff Eisteddfod – Sir George Macfarren, Principal of the Royal Academy of Music, and by then completely blind – to restore order to what he considered irregular proceedings before an audience numbering some 15,000. During the Chief Choral competition, the Mayor of Cardiff, Mr Clark, intervened to propose a vote of thanks to Dean Charles Vaughan of Llandaf, Chairman for the day.

> This proved too much for the patience of Sir George Macfarren. Lifting up his voice (he) announced the number of the next competing choir. 'No 5', demanded Sir George, 'go on with the competition! This interruption is most indecent.' All eyes were turned upon him in astonishment for the majority present were born to the Eisteddfod manner and saw nothing unusual in the proceedings. As for Mr Clark, carried by the stream of his eloquence, he halted not. Sir George, however, was not to be beaten, and, raising his voice to its highest pitch, he exclaimed, 'Unless the competition goes on the adjudicators will retire in a body.' This was enough. Mr Clark subsided, looking daggers and bottling up his rhetoric for another occasion...[20]

The Times reporter at the same meeting noted that 20,000 had assembled to hear the combined singing of the leading choirs. The police did their best to keep order; 'but the barriers were overleaped and the rear portions of the higher seats were freely occupied by the crowd.' Also, a slight delay in the giving of Macfarren's adjudication had led to 'furious signs of disapprobation.'[21]

In a remarkable paragraph, W. G. McNaught, an English adjudicator, recorded an incident at the very successful Llanelli Eisteddfod of 1903:

> One of the striking features of the gathering was the methods adopted to manage the excited and sometimes threateningly turbulent crowds, who were interested only in the greater events, and whose patience was sorely tried under circumstances of personal discomfort. Now and then it seemed that the competitions would be wrecked... Then someone would start a well-known hymn-tune or national air and in a few

moments the angry muttering cloud disappeared, and as the sun of glorious four-part harmony poured forth from all corners of the building, the audience forgot its angry strife and became a magnificent resonant choir. Some of us were thrilled to tears and we were all better men in a new and exalted mood. Where else than in Wales could such an incident happen?[22]

Such English musical visitors were hypnotized by the Welsh ability to sing in a disciplined, passionate manner; but the effect occurred across a chasm of misunderstanding. In England choral meetings were usually staid, orderly affairs – even those of the East End working class noted in the 1880s by George Bernard Shaw.[23] There was a turbulence in the atmosphere of *eisteddfodau* which sometimes disturbed the objectivity of English adjudicators. Annual reports in journals like the *Musical Times* were often devoted as much to the extraordinary atmosphere of the Eisteddfod as to evidence of musical accomplishment.

CHAPTER THREE

Doubts and Criticisms

The National Eisteddfod was annually providing a domestic 'Great Exhibition' for Welsh choral singing, and a meeting-point for thousands of devotees. With the founding of the first University College at Aberystwyth in 1872, the possibility for initiating a new line of serious development emerged. But when Brinley Richards spoke at its opening ceremony he chose to remind his audience of the essential peg on which Wales's musical reputation hung:

> ...I am bound to acknowledge, although I am a churchman, that if we want to hear hearty and earnest congregational singing we must still go to the chapels of our Nonconformist brethren. But surely the country which could produce the choir which sang at the Crystal Palace last season, ought to be the country above all others where we would naturally expect congregational singing.[1]

The most recent historian of the College has noted that, from the beginning, despite considerable financial difficulties, the governors had argued that 'an intense love of music was an important ingredient of the Welsh genius', and that any such institution 'ought naturally to foster its study.'[2] In the first month of the College's existence it was suggested by a leading London-Welsh journalist, writing under the nom-de-plume *Gohebydd*, that a professor of music be appointed and, further, that the appointee should be his own man, Joseph Parry. Originally from Georgetown, Merthyr Tydfil, Parry had been prize student at the Royal Academy in London, a protégé of Brinley Richards, and was currently making a reputation as teacher and composer in the Welsh industrial parts of North America. Without demur, Parry was duly inducted in July 1873, being given the task of 'lifting the standard of music in the nation generally', and of acting as 'a stepping-stone' for musical Welshmen 'from the village choir to the Royal Academy of Music.'[3]

This splash of inspiration for inaugurating higher musical education in Wales soon dried on the cold rocks of doubt. The College's first ten years were difficult: funds were meagre, and without the fuel of grant-aid its early strong principles weakened. Musical education, as has so often been the case, was jettisoned from a leaking ship. Parry had begun to make the College choir a much-needed binding medium in the new student society at Aberystwyth, even persuading the authorities to accept female students so that he would have women's voices for choral concerts. However, in America he had learnt the skills of the money-maker, and he used his new academic status to fashion a profitable simultaneous second career for himself as composer, adjudicator and conductor at *cymanfaoedd canu* all over Wales, in term-time as well as out. Also, as Walford Davies was to find – initially – after the Great War, the College concerts offered the rowdier students opportunities for letting off steam in a most unacceptable manner. As a teaching body the Music Department effectively came to an end in 1878; Parry, not for the last time, sought to supplement his diminished income by running a private local academy. But eventually in 1880, the townspeople turned out to bid him farewell.[4]

Ironically, it was not merely his great hymn-tune, 'Aberystwyth', which enabled him to promote the reputation of the faltering College: his work as a teacher had also attracted widespread attention. When Aberystwyth was about to receive its first Government grant in 1885, he wrote to the College authorities trying to revive their former assocation, but in vain. In the end, he took his status as a national musical figure to another new University College at Cardiff. He was undoubtedly an inspiring and gifted teacher. Flustered by short-term money problems, the men of Aberystwyth had certainly missed the chance of of using his gifts as the basis for creating a network of musical education in Wales. A generation was to elapse before a similar opportunity arose again, also at Aberystwyth. Meanwhile the academically martyred Parry wrote music at a rate which in itself ensured that the quality of his utterance declined. No longer was he in a position to set new standards: his task henceforward was to satisfy the appetite of a public hungry for dead tin-types of Handel and Mendelssohn. Yet his myth grew; and 'Y Doctor Mawr', as he was universally known in the Principality, became involved in two novel experiments which, once again, though promising, proved ultimately fruitless as means for regenerating musical Wales.

Apart from old John Parry's macaronic effort for Covent Garden in the 1820s – *A Trip to Wales* – there had been no Welsh 'opera'. In the absence of suitable halls, and in the face of puritan zeal, this was not surprising. Joseph Parry, reviving memories of his namesake's pastoral piece – perhaps also remembering the Irishman Michael Balfe's simple successes of the 1830s and 1840s, and certainly ignoring the religiose musical preoccupations of many contemporary Welshmen – struck out in the last quarter of the century with not one but five offerings in the genre. He wrote *Blodwen* at the end of his Aberystwyth sojourn. First produced at Aberdare in 1878, and later at Alexandra Palace, it enjoyed a fitful popularity for a number of years, and was to be revived occasionally in the twentieth century. The others, *Virginia* (1883), *Arianwen* (also a pastoral piece), *Sylvia* (1895), and *King Arthur* (1897), quickly fell into decent obscurity. The completion of *Arianwen* in 1890 did produce a *frisson* of hope that Parry might be indicating a new direction for musical development. Welsh singers who enjoyed British renown, like the tenor Ben Davies, appeared frequently in London operatic performances. It may then have seemed a sensible proposition, as it did to the founders of the Welsh National Opera during the Second World War, to employ the dramatic potential of Welsh voices on the operatic stage in Wales. In addition, of course, the greatest international operatic star of her generation, Adelina Patti, had deigned to live in Wales (when she was not scouring metropolitan coffers), and occasionally (as at the Brecon Eisteddfod mentioned earlier) impeccably trilled Italian arias and English ballads on Welsh concert platforms.

In the summer of 1890, amid a labour crisis which was threatening strikes by dockers and railwaymen, 'Truthful James', the 'Society' correspondent of the *Western Mail*, wrote a series of mincing articles as he toured Wales with Parry's new Welsh Opera Company performing *Arianwen*. The tour began in an unpromising spot: 'Rhymney does not possess many natural beauties, its chief characteristic being smoke.' The company included the Misses Miles and Morris, Louis Batten (Louis Battenberg?), and Digri Gwyn.[6] The flippant reporter, commenting on the surprising cleanliness of the Rhondda (and the total absence of public houses in Ferndale), said that at Pentre 'the clergy were well represented (in the audience)...they seemed to enjoy the performance thoroughly.' At Dowlais, 'the capital of music in Wales', the opera 'went with a capital swing.'[7] In Tenby, 'the birthplace of our most brilliant Welsh comedian, poor George Stone', the audience were 'screaming with laughter', and 'the clergy turned up in strong force.' The same correspondent, dipping into a threadbare philosophical bag, commented,

...It is a peculiar fact...that in this most Conservative town in Wales, the receipts have been greater than in any other except Cardiff, another proof that, socially and politically, the Conservatives are more patriotic, and encourage national matters more than their loud-mouthed opponents...[8]

But despite the evidence of popular and financial success offered in the scribblings of 'Truthful James', that short tour was the end of the matter: opera, Welsh or not, was in Wales simply a momentarily satisfying change of diet. It may seem odd that Welsh failure to promote opera in 1890 was not subjected later to Walford Davies's critical survey of music in the Principality: one of the effects of his broadcast influence on the progress of British music generally in the 1920s and 1930s was to guide his countless BBC listeners, and thousands in his lecture audiences, away from opera, which he considered a coarse, hybrid art-form.

Parry's operatic ventures collapsed. The plots and libretti he chose were awful, but hardly more risible than those of some popular Italian pieces. He maintained the allegiance of his Welsh public by continuing to write oratorios and cantatas, mainly on religious subjects. It was therefore natural that he should also associate himself with the attempt to foster a Festival movement in late nineteenth-century Wales.

The Three Choirs Festival, rooted in the English cathedral tradition, provided a model for imitation by industrial towns and cities wishing to establish their identities as culturally significant places. Leeds and Birmingham in particular set the nineteenth-century tone. In 1890 a small cohort of Cardiff singers went to the Worcester Three Choirs meeting to help the local chorus. Parry's opera experiment had begun and ended in the same year with a week of performances in Cardiff. In a long series of letters to the press he urged Welshmen 'to desist from dissipating their strength in countless minor *eisteddfodau*' and to 'combine together for the creation of some gigantic musical gathering which should be of purely Celtic character', and would lead to the formation of a distinctively Welsh school of composition.[9] Cardiff was then passing through the most dynamic phase of its nineteenth-century development. At the city's 1883 National Eisteddfod, audiences had been surprised by the local committee's employment of sixty London instrumentalists, at a cost of £600, and the provision of 'high-class concerts'. The *Musical Times*, in October 1892, commented, 'For some years, in fact, ever since the National Eisteddfod visited Cardiff in 1883...the musical public of the great Welsh port have had the question of a Festival before them.'

In 1892 the first Cardiff Festival was the creation of a few hopeful locals, mostly of English origin, and the model they set up was also based upon the bedrock, not only of temporarily imported London instrumentalists, but of an English Director, Joseph Barnby, the leading British choir-trainer. This was hardly a propitious beginning for Parry's proposed Welsh musical renaissance. Sonely-Johnstone told the story of the first Festival with wit and irony, and in a chapter resonantly entitled 'A Storm in a Teacup' he pointed up an event which, though it seems peripheral to the new venture, illustrates clearly the cross-currents which were dragging promising elements in Welsh musical life off course. Joseph Parry was at the centre of a controversy which bordered upon scandal.

His talented son, Haydn (one of the first Welsh scions to be named after a foreign composer deified by classical distance), was in 1892 a professor at the Guildhall School of Music. But, like his father, Haydn Parry had an eye to the main commercial chance. Having written an operetta with the then louchely attractive title *Cigarette*, he arranged to have it performed at Cardiff in 1892 with, as its leading singer, the great Ben Davies. This was unfortunate: young Parry's operetta was to be performed a mere five weeks before the opening of the new Festival; more importantly, one of the vocal luminaries of the Festival concerts was to be the same Ben Davies, singing in one of Joseph's oratorios. The *Western Mail*, in any case sceptical of the Festival's success, seized on this collision of interests with glee, and its sarcasm was further fired by the knowledge that one of the chief works to be performed at the Festival was Parry Senior's *Saul of Tarsus*. The motives of the Festival Committee in preventing Ben Davies's appearance in the comic opera were, the writer thought, both mixed and hypocritical:

> ...I will not suggest that it was a Puritanical spirit that resulted in the action... It may have been the commercial spirit which taught this clever Committee that, as most of its receipts would come from Nonconform-ist sources, it would be well not to have any artiste engaged who was distinguished by a local theatre taint. Grand opera in London, or even comic opera or burlesque – amusements our local saints are always ready to patronise when abroad on their travels – might be all very well, but to allow to tread the boards of the Cardiff Festival an artiste who five weeks previously had been creating the role in a comic opera at the Cardiff Theatre – well, well, it may not have been that after all. It may

have been a fear that Mr Ben Davies would have exhausted his popularity by a week's appearance in the Wood-street Temple of the Drama... There, the murder is out. A Welsh musician and Welsh music snubbed in the capital of Wales by a hybrid Festival Committee. Oh, the pity of it!...[10]

As it turned out, the quality of the Festival Choir's singing ought to have been a greater cause for concern; and, given the fire and brimstone of the Ben Davies–Haydn Parry controversy, even the question of whether Cardiff really needed to import London players for the Festival orchestra was forgotten. Barnby uttered the opinion that it was right that Davies should not appear in *Cigarette*, and so a conflagration was narrowly avoided. But he went further and adopted that heavily patronizing tone, when criticizing Welsh musical taste and skill, which other English interlopers were to use when they came to Wales nearly thirty years later. Sir Joseph recalled his last visit to Cardiff for the 1883 National Eisteddfod when a classical concert had been interrupted by hearty renderings of 'Men of Harlech':

> ...He was so irritated by this lack of success that he left Cardiff with the greatest dissatisfaction, and vowed that he would never be induced under any consideration to return to the Principality. Latterly, however, he began to think that Cardiff would follow the order of nature, and he was fully prepared to believe that there had been progress in the musical art no less than in the more practical and commercial aspects – (hear, hear)...

And Barnby, unprompted, appealed to the susceptibilities of the commercial men he spoke to – in the midst of a trade-union crisis – and anticipated the socio-political concerns of Welsh business later, in the inter-war years:

> ...there was no greater element in civilisation... than the art of music. He has spoken to his friend, Mr Arthur J. Balfour, and he would take care to suggest it to Lord Salisbury [the Tory Prime Minister] that it would be a wise thing in all towns of a certain population to establish choral societies, believing that it would tend more than anything else to the promulgation of a feeling very much averse from 'treasons, stratagems, and spoils.' (Laughter, and applause.) [11]

However, the musical programme of that first Festival mingled the radically new with the currently fashionable. The Committee had failed by the radius of a baton to get the ailing Sullivan to conduct his *Golden Legend* (his appearance would have reverberantly counterpoised Haydn Parry's light opera); Berlioz's *Faust* was an almost revolutionary choice, balanced by the conventionality of Mackenzie's *Dream of Jubal*. A greater, English Parry was represented by what was surely the first performance in Wales of *Blest Pair of Sirens*, and it is equally certain that Dvořák's *Stabat Mater* was a real novelty, as was Stanford's *Revenge*. Patriotic feelings – mainly outside Cardiff – were partly satisfied by the performance of *Saul of Tarsus*. Parry's intention that what became the Cardiff Triennial Festival should mount new Welsh works was partially fulfilled in the years up to its discontinuance in 1914: in 1895 David Jenkins's *A Psalm of Life*, and the first performance of Stanford's *The Bard* (at least he could claim Irish ancestry); Harry Evans's *Victory of Garmon* in 1904; David Evans's *Coming of Arthur* three years later, and in 1910 another setting of *The Bard* by the young David Vaughan Thomas.[12] These works stood alongside other first Welsh performances: of Verdi's *Requiem*, Beethoven's *Choral* Symphony, *The Dream of Gerontius*, Wagner excerpts (from *Parsifal* and *The Ring*), and even Franck's *Beatitudes*, Berlioz's *Romeo et Juliette* and Saint-Säens's *Samson et Delilah*. Some of these would cause unusual excitement were they to be included in St David's Hall concerts in present-day Cardiff; in late-Victorian and Edwardian Cardiff they must have seemed like emissions from a cultural spacecraft.

Those elements of musical 'revolution', however, have to be viewed in perspective. Festival attendances were usually disappointing, and, in any case, the Cardiff concerts were hardly reliable indicators of changes in the general musical life and taste of Wales: the chief function of of the recently created city in those days was simply to suck in, and then to disgorge world-wide, the material product of the coalfield. To the hard-headed coal plutocrats of Cardiff, a musical festival was perhaps a somewhat tiresome, but necessary, form of displaying civic opulence and pride, and the city's superiority over neighbours like Merthyr, Newport, and Swansea. The triennial concerts, with their expensive tickets, probably meant more to the readers of London musical papers than to the choralists even in nearby Glamorgan mining towns and villages. No integral link was established between the Cardiff events and the National Eisteddfod, though, as far as a handful of Welsh composers were concerned, the Festival did offer limited, intermittent opportunities for precious hearings of their works, played by efficient bands and large choirs.

There was another Welsh musical festival which, excepting intervals when it temporaily vanished, was more typically Welsh in flavour and character. Harlech, initially a gathering of Temperance choirs, began in 1867, and was held under open skies within the English conqueror's famous castle. It was non-competitive long before such a principle was uttered seriously throughout Wales, and the programme of the day reflected a conviviality absent from *eisteddfodau*. It flourished until 1890, and was revived in 1910. W. G. McNaught in 1913 thought that Harlech represented 'the unquestionable love of the Welsh folk for music.'[13] Like English cricket crowds the festival adherents were also masochists, for almost invariably the singers were drenched in mist and rain blown across the Irish Sea.

CHAPTER FOUR

Pressure for Change from Within

More significant than the festival in the progress of Welsh music was
the emergence of a generation of thoughtful musicians who not only
produced works in new styles, but, with others, began to polemicize
about standards from within the Principality, also taking into account
the disinterested comments of English observers. In the 1890s the view
began to prevail that the confidence of Welshmen in their musical
prowess rested on decaying foundations. At the same time the three
university colleges gained a Royal Charter and took their place at the
top of an educational edifice above a middle stratum of intermediate
schools for boys and girls, newly created throughout the rural counties
and industrial areas. In advance of England, therefore, Wales now had
the publicly funded educational means for achieving social, economic
and cultural ends. Music in particular, it was widely acknowledged,
should be one of the leading beneficiaries by this new apparatus.

Addressing the Liverpool Welsh Nationalist Society in 1893, on 'The
Present State of Music in Wales', Francis Lloyd, Mus. B., a frequent
eisteddfod adjudicator, diagnosed a degree of sickness in Welsh music
which made the Principality less healthy even than England, where a
renaissance had begun. The Welsh were undeniably musical, but their
experience of the variety of music – of chamber and orchestral music,
for instance – was limited: '...it is impossible for a nation to become
musical in the modern acceptance of that term, unless its people are
constantly brought into contact with, and are taught to appreciate,
good music, and have opportunities of becoming accustomed to new
effects and new combinations of sound.' In recent years those conditions had started to prevail in England, but not yet in Wales. Just as
in a paper he had given at the Swansea Eisteddfod in 1891, Lloyd
argued for the encouragement of a more general cultivation of orchestral music in Wales, a view which was to become a continuous theme
in the evolution of Welsh musical experience over the next fifty years.
He advocated dividing the country into districts under the supervision
of a central society, each district having its own committee and a
thoroughly qualified professional musician who might act as head of

a local school of music. Under that leader there should be perhaps half-a-dozen instrumentalists 'who could themselves form the nucleus of a band, and who might, in addition to teaching...give concerts in various parts of the district.' These players could also form the core of a complete local orchestra. The scheme would be accompanied by a system of local examinations. In broad outline, though it omitted consideration of the University's possible role, this part of Lloyd's scheme was a clear anticipation of the kind of organization which was to be created by Walford Davies after 1918.[1]

Lloyd wanted the Eisteddfod to become more efficient in its promotion of the work of Welsh composers. At present the music chosen by its local committees was mediocre. A well qualified permanent musical board ought to be appointed to choose works for competitions. 'In this way the best interests of the art would be served, and the Eisteddfod would have much greater educational value', providing the kinds of opportunities for Welshmen already enjoyed by the English at their great festivals. 'I don't mean to exclude standard works of the great masters from the Eisteddfod programmes – that would be suicidal of course...' In his opinion, Welsh musical insularity was due to the persistence of the native language, and the relative geographical isolation of many parts of Wales.

In his *Notable Welsh Musicians of Today* (1896), Frederick Griffiths, principal flautist at Covent Garden, devoted a long preface to the condition of Welsh music. Like Lloyd, he assumed that, even in the most advanced Welsh communities, 'the great classical masterpieces are practically unknown; in fact classical music is seldom performed at all.' In oratorio performances the orchestra was still regarded as 'a necessary evil.' There was instrumental talent; but it was not encouraged and had to find professional opportunities outside Wales. Some of the exorbitant fees paid to vocalists could be spared for the training of skilful players. But even in choirs, said Griffiths, weaknesses had been revealed: at the recent Cardiff Festival few choralists could be found locally who were capable of learning eight or nine unfamiliar pieces in a short period of rehearsal, so inured were they to spending long months memorizing a single work for eisteddfod competition. The Welsh were still too insular, shrouded in their pride: 'The true artist transcends all national lines. He is a cosmopolitan who shakes hands with his colleague whether he be English, Welsh, Ashantee, or Matabele.'[2]

Joseph Bennett, a much respected London critic who hailed from just across the Severn, had often visited Wales as adjudicator. In 1896 he was invited to address the Cymmrodorion Society on 'Music in Wales'. He frankly pronounced that wide-ranging reforms were necessary, under five main heads: an authoritative advisory board for the Eisteddfod; the substitution of honourable rewards for the huge money-prizes, 'sums large enough to arouse cupidity' and bad behaviour; the choice of test-pieces which were whole works rather than fragments; encouragement for choristers to read Old Notation; and a widening of the scope of general musical study among the people. Bennett wanted to rescue the Welsh – and particularly the eisteddfodic Welsh – from a cave of Adullam. Since his early days he had been an adherent and teacher of tonic sol-fa: 'Music-lovers in this country owe more to Tonic Sol-fa, as an agent of artistic progress among the people at large, than they can ever pay.' But the benefits of the system were largely confined to vocal music, and it was in any case simply 'a first stage towards the higher knowledge and culture, towards full participation in the universal musical life.' In practice, music which had not been translated into tonic sol-fa was inaccessible to the vast majority of Welsh people.[3]

Lloyd, Griffiths and Bennett were not dispassionate commentators, though they spoke variously from outside. The Welsh had their progressive spokesmen who from within were acutely critical of musical stagnation. In a number of cases these significant figures were grouped around the influential native journal *Y Cerddor*. Its editors, David Jenkins (1848–1915) and D. Emlyn Evans (1843–1913), were men of their age in that they worked in the Welsh vocal tradition. Essentially self-educated – both had started upon careers as apprentice tailors – they lived in the shadow of Joseph Parry's more brilliant reputation, but probably exerted a much more profound educational influence upon the progress of music in Wales. Jenkins, a student of Parry at Aberystwyth in the 1870s – gaining a meritorious Cambridge Mus. B. – ended his days as Professor at his old college (and therefore as Walford Davies's immediate predecessor). Both Jenkins and Evans were ardent critics of what they identified as weaknesses in Welsh musical life, providing substantial support for occasional commentators like Lloyd and Griffiths. Evans and Jenkins set the agenda for reform in Welsh music: liberation of choral accomplishment by opening out the repertoire; educational effort, primarily through better practical training and encouraging an awareness of the riches of

European music; promotion of instrumental teaching, and elimination of large money-prizes at choral competitions.

D. Emlyn Evans was a regular Welsh correspondent for the *Musical Times*. He told its readers in July 1907, that Wales had travelled along a downward path. Intelligent Welshmen looked back regretfully to the time when the best choirs were content 'to enter the arena of song solely for art's sake, and to be proud, not of the performance of certain announced test-pieces alone', but of submitting themselves also to a greater technical ordeal, 'reading at sight.' He also raised the issue of Eisteddfod test-pieces. A comparison between the works set for the Blackpool Festival and the Eisteddfod in 1908 revealed that in the former there were works by Scarlatti, Arensky, Cornelius, Brahms, Tschaikovsky and Bantock; whereas, of the nine pieces at Llangollen, seven were by Welsh composers. The *Musical Times* editorially resisted making a cheap comment and merely said that 'composers who can boast of Welsh extraction succeed best when they merge themselves into cosmopolitan art.' And it was subtly noted that Bantock had withdrawn his services as adjudicator from the Llangollen Eisteddfod 'on the ground of the inadequacy of the programme to the importance of the event.'[4]

At the 1903 Llanelli Eisteddfod the Chief Choral was won by the Choir of Dowlais and Merthyr. Its remarkable conductor, son of a local plate-roller, was Harry Evans, thirty years younger than D. Emlyn Evans and Jenkins and, in the period up to his premature death in 1914, the chief bearer of the standard of musical reform. He was of the first generation to benefit by having been entered for the new Associated Board Examinations. His only formal musical training consisted in piano lessons (though the family never owned a piano) and practical advice from his father, an avid choral conductor. Having trained as an elementary-school teacher, he decided to risk making music his profession. Eventually he became FRCO and achieved unrivalled status as a choir trainer. 'What I earned by music I spent in going about to hear good music, and in purchasing organ, pianoforte and theoretical works.' His choir won a surfeit of prizes, and then in 1897 he decided to withdraw from competitive work. At the Merthyr Eisteddfod he conducted an orchestral concert which included the *Tannhäuser* Overture and Beethoven's Fifth Symphony, 'an orchestral concert being a novelty at this important national meeting.'

Harry Evans became conductor of the Undeb Corawl Cymreig Lerpwl in 1902 – there were 100,000 expatriate Welshmen in Liverpool

– and over the next few years they gave electrifying performances of *Hiawatha*, *Dream of Gerontius*, and even the *St Matthew Passion*. The commissioning of his own work, *The Victory of St Garmon*, for the Cardiff Festival of 1904 has been noted already. Giving advice to aspiring Welsh musicians in 1907, he said that his musical education had been obtained largely through experience: '...coming into contact with and learning much from singers, composers, and conductors; spending my savings in going about for many years, to London in particular' – Covent Garden Opera, Queen's Hall symphony concerts, Albert Hall oratorios – as well as the Birmingham, Leeds and Three Choirs Festivals. 'I never came away without having picked up some-thing fresh, and I have always made it a point...of hearing something new, whatever it might cost.' Welsh choirs, on the other hand, had become drugged by money-prizes: '...their thoughts are centred on winning the prize and beating the neighbouring choirs, rather than on the music they are performing.' As a choir-trainer in Liverpool he always got choristers 'to understand the significance of what they perform, and the exact position of everything they sing in a work, with the result that they sink individuality into one common whole.'[5] The *Musical Times* in 1907 noted that 'discontent was coming to a crisis in Wales', but that 'the healthy ferment...will lead to great results.'

In 1909 Harry Evans contributed a paper to a meeting of the Association of Musical Competition Festivals in London, entitled 'The Eisteddfod and the Competition Festival Movement', in which he reinforced his earlier criticisms. He also took part in a discussion on Walford Davies's paper, 'The Spirit and Letter in Competition Festivals'; Walford agreed with him over 'the great educational advan-tages of competitions amongst church choirs.'[6] At the Colwyn Bay Eisteddfod in the following year, however, evidence of reform in the choice of pieces – Elgar's *O! wild west wind*, among others – seems to have produced a barren result: only one Welsh choir entered the Chief Choral.

Harry Evans's appeal in Wales lay perhaps in his carrying the native choral tradition in his knapsack along with a programme of reform and regeneration. His influence was at its height during the Edwardian era. The first decade of the new century was reputedly an unbroken summer in English society. Economically and politically, however, it was an age of turmoil. In A. P. Graves's Ireland Home-Rule strife was boiling up, while in England the Fabian supporters of the new Folk-song Society had their counterparts in the first Labour representatives at the Imperial Parliament. Militant feminists were ripping the conservative gender agenda apart, and Syndicalists in south Wales threatening to rend Welsh economic life in tatters. The contrapuntal reverberations of these greater discontents lay beneath the dissonances in Welsh musical life, the substance of which was intrinsically bound into the society of the south Wales coalfield and its industries. The political and economic instability of Wales – with the use of troops to stamp out demonstrations in Llanelli and Tonypandy – caused anxieties which were aggravated by detailed reporting in English newspapers. It was at this point that a bulky leader of leftist cultural activity in England began to involve himself in the musical life of Wales and its transformation.

Granville Bantock had already expressed his low opinion of the repertoire of Welsh choirs by refusing to adjudicate in the 1905 National Eisteddfod. At the beginning of the Wrexham meeting in 1912 the sudden death of the half-caste Coleridge-Taylor necessitated asking Bantock to take over much of the adjudicating work at short notice. The Wrexham week was to prove a turning-point in Welsh musical life. It was dominated by two events.

The chief guests on Thursday were the Chancellor of the Exchequer, David Lloyd George, his wife, and two of their daughters, Olwen and Megan. (Perhaps it was not fortuitous that another platform guest was Major-General Sir Francis Lloyd.) The entry of the Liberal hero occasioned the most violent Suffragette demonstration so far to occur in Britain. The Tory *Western Mail* had an eisteddfod field-day:

> ...A well-known Nonconformist minister near the platform was seen to hit off the hat of one of the women... Blood flowed from the face of one of the women, the scalps of all of them bled owing to the uprooting of the hair, and it was recorded by a credible eye-witness that a knife was used against one of the women... One of them was seen almost stripped of her upper garments, and she presented a most sorry spectacle...

Above the pandemonium (presumably *not* divided into four parts this time) Lloyd George – whose interest in women usually descended to another level – continued to descant in his most windy style:

> ...I was saying that this was the Festival of the Democracy... Not only is the Eisteddfod representative of the Nation, and popular amongst the people, but it shows an improved culture among the people, and if you look at the history of the Eisteddfod you see how education has improved among the masses... The tide is rising...all over Wales, like a

flood of light, bringing green to the vales and driving away the mists from the hill-tops... At next year's Eisteddfod prizes are to be offered for translations from the Latin, and the boys [sic] who go through the democratic schools of Wales will win them...[7]

What the feminist Bantock thought of those events is not recorded. But he was able to provide the second most exciting episode of the week. The *Western Mail*, under the heading 'Advice to Welsh Musicians', reported the following:

> Taking advantage of a fine opportunity, Mr Granville Bantock delivered a message of sound advice to Welsh musicians. He sugared his medicine cleverly, and the disagreeableness of the dose was completely disguised in the sweetness of the admixture. His one remedy against the risk of Welsh music being overwhelmed by the more modern methods of English choirs was the establishment of a school of music for Wales, and in this advice he paid an unqualified compliment to Mr Harry Evans...[8]

Bantock was not only Elgar's successor as Professor at Birmingham, but also Principal of the Music Department – in effect a provincial music college with over 1,000 students – attached to the Birmingham and Midland Institute; so he spoke as a practical man rather than a Utopian rhetorician. And the words which he had prepared for the Wrexham audience were transformed into a more permanent record in the form of an article written for the *English Review* in the following year. He noted that the Denbighshire Society had already met to discuss the idea, in the knowledge that, beyond having private lessons, Welsh musical aspirants had to travel to Manchester, Birmingham or London for sound advanced tuition. Wales needed a centre of musical excellence. He was careful to stress that a new college should be 'national' only in the widest sense:

> Why should not this musical Welsh nation have its own music school which shall help to keep alive its own national flavour in music, not by an unhealthy inbreeding, so to speak, not by studying Welsh music only... Culture, as someone says, is the knowing and absorbing the highest and best thought in the world; and it is essential in the present day for a musician to know what is being done in England and Germany, France and Russia, etc., and to be abreast of the age.

He acknowledged that two of the university colleges already had music departments, but much of their purely instrumental and elementary teaching, as in Birmingham, could be taken over by two affiliated specialist music colleges, in north and south locations depending on accessibility to the population. He reckoned that if every Welshman gave a shilling, £125,000 could be raised.[9]

At Cardiff, in January, 1912, a meeting was convened by one of the city's more far-sighted fathers, Alderman Lewis Morgan, for considering the notion of establishing a National College of Music. Harry Evans, the main speaker, argued that such an institution 'would enable Wales to keep pace with other nations in modern musical progress', while its existence would not interfere with the work of the university colleges. Another participant, W. T. Price, deprecated the use of an examining board as a means of raising the necessary funds and advocated 'the extension of the sphere of influence of the University Colleges.'[10]

Cyril Jenkins of Pontypridd had won a composition prize – for a violin-and-piano reverie – at the Wrexham Eisteddfod. Born in Swansea, he had received most of his musical training in the organ lofts of English cathedrals where he had absorbed some of the cosmopolitan elements in English musical culture. He did not lack talent as a composer (his *Coriolanus* was to become one of the staples of the twentieth-century brass-band repertoire), but his chief gift to Wales, in the decade straddling the Great War, was as a publicist for the orchestral concerts of contemporary music he organized, including the compositions of young Welshmen. He opened his campaign with an article published early in 1913:

> Musical England is living in the year 1913, but musical Wales is lagging behind in the early Victorian days of of 1845 to 1860. She possesses no composer of the first, or even of the second rank; she has no orchestra, no opera, no National School of Music, and no chamber music... Wales, indeed, is no longer musical in the real sense of the term; she is a country of organists and doctors of music.

Jenkins attributed the Welsh malaise to the absence of reputable composers: unless composers posed difficulties for performers to overcome, then the general level of performance was sure to fall. Bach and Beethoven had not possessed academic degrees in music; nor indeed did Professor Bantock and Sir Edward Elgar: 'Learning was never yet a good substitute for inspiration... If a young Welsh composer cannot boast of being a doctor of music, his compositions are treated with contempt in many quarters of Wales.' Even in England that was not so. The current state of retrogression was to be seen in every aspect of

Welsh life, he claimed – in the chapel, in the choral society, in the home, and among such amateur orchestral societies as existed.

> Wales must wake up. She must free herself from tradition... We have temperament, imagination, feeling; but through ignorance and through lack of leadership, we put them to poor uses... I, for my part, look to one or two of our younger men to step forward and show Wales how she may use her material to the best advantage.[11]

His wish came near to being granted almost immediately. In December, 1912, it was reported that delegates from Mountain Ash, Swansea and Neath had met in Neath Town Hall to consider holding what was called 'a musical entente' in south Wales in the following April. 'The idea is to show that Wales is progressing in music on modern lines' and that 'the opinion held in certain quarters that Welsh choirs cannot cope with modern works has no basis in fact.'[12] With Jenkins's help an enterprising series of concerts was arranged, involving Henry Wood's Queen's Hall Orchestra. Works to be played included Bantock's *Omar Khayyám*, and Elgar's *King Olaf* and *Gerontius*. This was the beginning of the expensive endeavour which Jenkins sustained intermittently in south Wales towns – an itinerant Welsh musical festival – until 1920.[13]

It is hardly surprising that many musical English critics should have remained unaware of such progressive enterprise in the Principality, whose proven backwardness some might have wished to retain as a lowly mark against which to measure English sophistication. In 1913 the *Daily Telegraph* published an interview with Sir Frederick Cowen, who had succeeded Barnby as director of the Cardiff Festival. He uttered the usual platitudes about Welsh failure to develop musical talent, and attributed her backwardness to an unusual cause: 'My own theory is that the retention and use of its language has served to isolate Wales from this great world of Art. Devotion to language does not, as a rule, make for progress... I was at an Eisteddfod twenty years ago, and from that time to this I have seen no progress in the love of music for itself.'[14] W. G. McNaught, who had been so electrified by his experience as an adjudicator ten years earlier at the Llanelli Eisteddfod, hastened to reply next day. While remembering 'a remarkable performance' of the *St Matthew Passion* in Cardiff, he referred chiefly to Jenkins's 'South Wales Musical Festival', held in four towns between 21 and 24 April, with Elgar conducting *King Olaf* and a performance of Edward German's *Welsh Rhapsody*. 'There was no competition, and, therefore, no prospect of monetary reward, and all the singers paid their own expenses.'[15]

At the beginning of 1914, then, there was increasing evidence to support the opinion that musical Wales was about to be transformed on two interdependent levels of activity. In the lower stratum efforts were being made to match the intensity and enthusiasm of singing with a new choral and orchestral repertoire which was beginning to include British contemporary works and European masterpieces by Bach, Rossini, Verdi and Brahms. On a higher plain it seemed that the young Turks of Welsh music were aspiring to write pieces which took account of recent developments in England and on the Continent, while seeking a 'Welsh' voice in composition. It also appeared that the Eisteddfod might truly become an educational force in the transmutation of popular taste, setting before choirs, instrumentalists and the public works which would test flexibility and expressiveness in new ways. There was a growing consciousness of a vacuum in the experience of music-making: the need to encourage higher and more commonly accepted standards of instrumental performance.

Current developments, formal and informal, at the increasingly confident university colleges were pointing other ways forward. Just as the Welsh Folk-song Society had grown out of the initiative taken by a handful of enthusiasts gathered in Bangor, so appreciation of the alien art of chamber music was being nurtured at Aberystwyth. The leader of this movement was not a member of Professor David Jenkins's Music Department, but Lucie, wife of André Barbier, who had been appointed from Manchester to the Chair of French at the University College of Wales in 1909. Trained as singer and pianist at the Paris Conservatoire, she used her links with leading French musicians of her generation to promote a remarkable series of concerts at Aberystwyth. Already, in Manchester, she had devised concerts in which Gabriel Fauré, among others, had participated. She also knew Debussy, Ravel, Hahn, Saint-Saëns, d'Indy and the pianist Jacques Février. Her new Welsh home became the scene of musical experiences which were certainly novel in Wales. She established a College Musical Club and, with missionary zeal, took music into neighbouring schools in the form of lecture-recitals. During the years 1910 to 1915 she organized twenty-three Musical Club meetings at which over three hundred different works were performed. The repertoire was not simply French: Aberystwyth audiences in those days heard Elizabethan madrigals, French trouvère songs, German *Lieder*, Schumann piano pieces, the compositions of Arthur Somervell, Elgar and Stanford, and, in recitals by the now legendary Ricardo Vines, the works of Albeniz, Granados and de Falla.

She organized a Welsh vocal quartet which in 1911 travelled to Paris to perform arrangements of Welsh folk-songs. Reporting a concert given by artistes grouped around Alfred Cortot, the *Cambrian News* noted that, though the works were long and complicated, and the concert had lasted two hours, 'the audience, like Oliver Twist, asked for more and rewarded the distinguished artists from acrosss the Channel with sustained applause and the College yell.' The same paper reported in 1912,

> Monsieur Vines...revealed a wonderful attainment of technique. Debussy's advanced music was played with consummate skill in its forcible expression and richness of harmony... As the meetings are intended for the furtherance of music education and wider musical thought, they are likely to produce results of permanent benefit.

The College Students' Handbook in 1913 suggested that the people of Aberystwyth – not simply the students – then had more opportunities for hearing French music than did the rest of Britain, with the exception of London.[16] Among the 'British' performers at Mme Barbier's extraordinary concerts were Gervase Elwes, the leading English tenor; Arthur Somervell, composer, HMI, and leader of the Schools Music movement at the Board of Education; and, playing her 'Parke' Stradivarius, Gwendoline Davies of Llandinam, one of the heirs of the Davies industrial fortune.

Although there was another chamber music society in Wales, founded in Cardiff by a group of local ladies based in the Girls' Intermediate School in 1895,[17] Mme Barbier was an exotic flourishing alone. Yet her energetic enthusiasm presaged, and justified, a much wider encouragement of musical development after 1918 which was also to issue from Aberystwyth. Walford Davies built extensively on foundations laid by Lucie Barbier.

Her work was informal. An opening of a more formal, academic kind occurred in the summer of 1914. The *Musical Times* noticed that

> The sum of £75,000 has been given to University College, Aberystwyth, as an endowment for the establishment of a School of Music. It is understood that the donors are Mr David Davies, MP, and his family.[18]

CHAPTER FIVE

A New Beginning

In 1916 a Royal Commission under Lord Haldane was appointed to investigate the condition of the University of Wales and to make recommendations for its future development. Although their final suggestions were by no means as disturbing as many interested Welshmen had anticipated, they remarked particularly upon the poverty of the University's contribution to the musical life of Wales. The Final Report stated, in 1917,

> From the time of their earliest records the Welsh have been conspicuous for their love of music, and at the present day there is no people in Europe with whom song is a more intimate means of expression. It may, indeed, be said without exaggeration that Wales is a land of singers, and that she has the power of making, in music, a contribution to the art of the world which is comparable to the highest achievements of painting or poetry or sculpture. The beauty and variety of her folk-songs, the strength and dignity of her traditional hymn-tunes, her gift of spontaneous part-singing and of ready improvisation all combine into an endowment of natural resources which, if fully utilised, will place her among the first musical countries.[1]

The musical suggestions of the Haldane Commission were expressed just as powerfully as its remarks on the work of the University in connection with, for example, applied science and technology, and Celtic studies. The Commissioners had been made aware that only Cardiff among the Welsh colleges then had a thriving Music Department; the Chair at Aberystwyth had been vacant since the death of David Jenkins in 1914; and it was recommended that, in addition to college choral societies, there should be opportunities for making chamber and orchestral music, for all students in all three colleges: 'Some of the English Secondary Schools have already got very promising school orchestras. It ought not to be difficult for the Welsh Colleges to follow their example.'[2]

The Commissioners wished to see greater co-operation in musical matters between the University and other agencies like, for instance, the Central Welsh Board, and especially the National Eisteddfod, which they saw as being in urgent need of reform. But their chief proposal in 1917 was that the musical life of Wales should be given greater cohesion and a sense of unified purpose by the appointment of a Musical Director for the University – the incumbent having professorial status – who would preside over a Council of Music for Wales located in the University. 'This Council', the Report said, 'should act as the supreme consultative body on all matters with which the musical education of Wales is concerned.' They went further, and set out a detailed strategy for what was to become a mission to make Wales truly musical, a campaign which, unlike some of the more materialistic proposals made in 1917, was to be enacted with energy and vision over the next twenty years.

The Council should (and eventually it did) consist of representatives of the University Court, of the National Eisteddfod, the Welsh Folksong Society, the Associations of Headmasters and Headmistresses in the Secondary and Elementary Schools, and of the Central Welsh Board. It might well undertake the task of compiling collections of national songs and hymn-tunes for daily use in schools; it would make annual reports on the progress of musical developments in Wales, and outline future policy.

> Most of all, perhaps, the value of the Council would be to serve as an organised embodiment and expression of Welsh nationalism in music, not by excluding or discouraging the practice of the greatest masterpieces of other countries – on the contrary, in any sound system of musical education these should be cordially welcomed – but in so using them as to educate the national genius and to train it to deliver the national message.

The model which the Haldane Commission took for this striking suggestion was not English but Russian. Such a Council in Wales would do what a group of Russian enthusiasts – the 'mighty handful' – had achieved half a century before: 'The material which Mussorgsky and his friends set to work was certainly not richer than that which is at the disposal of the Welsh musicians today... Wales can do at least as well...if she will set herself to the task.'[3]

As a quotation from an otherwise staid Report, those words seem remarkable, and display a feeling for the recent history of Western music which cannot have been common among British academics. But their author was a very uncommon figure in contemporary intellectual and artistic life. W. H. Hadow wrote that section of the Welsh University Report; and it was he who, from within, had directed the discussions of the Haldane Commission firmly towards music as a possible keystone for the edifice which was to unite more closely the work of the University and the lives of the people of Wales. Of course Hadow was not making particularly original proposals: it should have been noticed already that what he was suggesting had some of its roots in the kind of debate about Welsh music proceeding before the War. But as a leading member of the Commission he made it his business to consult figures who mattered in Welsh life. In the absence of hard evidence, it may be presumed that, apart from Reichel and J. Lloyd Williams of Bangor College, another of Hadow's informants was a ubiquitous member of the Welsh 'Establishment' who gave evidence on a number of occasions.

Daniel Lleufer Thomas, son of a west-Wales farmer, an Oxford graduate and a founder-member of the Dafydd ap Gwilym Society, was a stipendiary magistrate (at Pontypridd during the great Cambrian strike), and a member of the Council of the University of Wales. In the 1890s he had served as Secretary to the Welsh Land Commission whose task had been to reveal the iniquities of land tenure for native farmers. In 1915 he addressed a Cymmrodorion meeting at the Bangor Eisteddfod on the subject of 'University Tutorial Classes for Working People'. While acknowledging the splendid effect of the new intermediate-school system on the life of the nation, he said that Wales lagged behind her neighbours in the provision of adult education. He thought that much excellent work was waiting to be done by the university in sociology and economics, in language and literature, on the history of Wales, 'and probably also in Music... No scheme for the higher education of the workers of Wales could be deemed at all complete, if it made no provision for bringing within their reach instruction of a University standard in Music.' He noted that a committee under Harry Reichel of Bangor had recently been considering the possible place of Music in such a tutorial-class system; and that they had received a paper from the Principal of Armstrong College, Newcastle-upon-Tyne, Dr Hadow, outlining a scheme for a three years' course in the history and appreciation of music with the aim of producing 'intelligent and cultivated listeners who should take the same sort of interest in Music as intelligent readers take in Literature.'[4]

The North of England Scheme was published complete as an Appendix to Lleufer Thomas's paper. Hadow had stressed that it might include elements of practical music-making; their main aim was to teach 'the history, the general aesthetics, and, above all, the principles of appreciation of Music.' The Board of Education, in July, 1914, under Hadow's influence, had expressed broad approval of experiments with adult musical studies; and already, in the following October, the temporarily headless Music Department at Aberystwyth had inaugurated a programme which foreshadowed what was to happen in Wales after the Great War:

> Concerts will be conducted in all centres in Wales where there is an earnest desire for a better musical culture. These concerts will be arranged with a view to encourage in each centre the formation of Musical Clubs and Orchestral Classes. The works on the programme will be performed, as far as possible, in chronological order, and whenever found possible, the concerts will be preceded by a lecture on the works on the programme. Works by composers of all nationalities will be given...[5]

It is possible to detect the hand of Lucie Barbier in this Aberystwyth plan.[6]

What was the intellectual power-base from which Hadow was able to deploy such a strong influence upon the progress of music on the Welsh tuft of the colonial fringe? His reputation as an administrator in higher education and as Chairman of the Board of Education Consultative Committee now tends to obscure the breadth and depth of his scholarly interests. It can be argued that, with help from colleagues of the calibre of Arthur Somervell HMI, he created the agenda for aesthetic, and particularly musical, education in Britain at the turn of the century.

In the 1880s, as a Fellow of Worcester College, Oxford, he had been an inspirer of the movement to transform the musical life of the University. He was a founder-member of the Oxford Musical Union, an alliance between dons and undergraduates which encouraged the highest standards in frequent performances of chamber and orchestral music within an institution hitherto notorious for its Philistinism in those fields.[7] A juvenile member of the Union, as pianist and accompanist, in the 1890s, was the Old Llandoverian David Vaughan Thomas. Through the Union Hadow became a friend of Joseph Joachim – Brahms' amanuensis in creating the Violin Concerto – and also of his nephew, Henry Joachim, who was to become an Oxford Professor of Philosophy. So when, with his meticulous approach to research, he started to write a biography of Brahms in the early 1890s, Hadow went to meet the composer in Vienna armed with an enthusiastic testimonial from the elder Joachim; and it is perhaps typical of Hadow's style that the letter he sent ahead to Brahms's secretary, Mandyzchevski, was written in Latin. The composer greeted the young Englishman, on his arrival, with a gruff 'Sie schreiben Lateinisch, nicht war!'[8] Hadow's interest in Haydn, noted earlier,[9] and his work on Dvořák and Brahms kindled in him a genuine feeling for the aesthetic value of folk-music and helped to counteract any tendency to adopt an élitist approach to musical study. He strove to make the very best kinds of music accessible to the 'common man'. On the other hand, his *Studies in Modern Music* (1892) was a trenchant indictment of of the spineless type of British musical criticism of that time, and marks a watershed in the development of scholarly writing about music on this island. The fundamental principle of all that he worked for is summed up in his own words: '...the laws of music are few and simple; and able to be mastered by any well-instructed intelligence.'[10]

Hadow was also a composer, an accomplishment about which he was, perhaps, in the long perspective of history, suitably modest. Yet his E-flat String Quartet was granted four performances in Oxford between 1888 and 1914, and was even heard in Germany;[11] and he possessed a gift which ought to have appealed to his Welsh acquaintances – for creating singable melodies matched immaculately with verse. With his sister, also an Oxford don, he built a reputation as a literary scholar. But his main concern was not to expand his own range as a composer; rather he wished to extend to the masses the boon of musical appreciation and to develop in them basic skills such as sight-reading and melody-writing; and also to make sure that they were 'well-instructed'. In 1911 he wrote to Macmillans, the publishers of *Grove's Dictionary of Music and Musicians*,

> ...There is an institution in the North called 'The Home Music Study Union', which has its centre at Leeds. It is a *bona fide* concern: I happen to be its President...and it is doing a great deal to spread knowledge of music and musical literature among working people. The difficulty is with regard to books. Comparatively few libraries have much of a musical department and the students, who are mostly poor, cannot buy many books for themselves. Sir Hubert Parry gave permission that his 'Studies of the Great Composers' should be re-printed in cheap form, his publishers agreed, and the book I believe has had a considerable circulation. Do you think it would be possible to re-print in pamphlet form

some of the larger articles in Grove...? They could be sold very cheaply at a profit...[12]

In the years immediately before the Great War the Home Music Study Union became a force in the land, to the extent of organizing the first musical 'Summer Schools' (known then as 'The Musicians' Holiday'). The Secretary, J. E. Lawrence of Leeds, convened the 1912 School at Bideford, where lectures were given by M. D. Calvocoressi on Liszt, modern French music and Russian music, and by Stewart Macpherson ('Musical Appreciation Study – a Coming Force?')[13]

In June, 1918, just after his appointment as Director of Education for the YMCA in France, Hadow delivered the third of the Barnett House Lectures in Oxford, entitled 'The Needs of Popular Musical Education'. On that occasion his Chairman, who also wrote the preface for the subsequently printed paper, was H. A. L. Fisher, Lloyd George's President of the Board of Education, magisterial historian, draughtsman of the 1918 Education Act, and Vaughan Williams's brother-in-law. Fisher, who was currently piloting through Parliament his epoch-making act with its revolutionary day-continuation clause, remarked that 'Sir Henry Hadow speaks upon musical education with an authority which no wise man will challenge. In no way can the general refinement of life in this country be more effectually fostered than by the restoration of music to its proper place in the scheme of our common education'.[14]

In his paper Hadow argued for the central place of music in the schools' curricula and upwards into the universities. Teachers had to rid themselves 'absolutely and altogether' of the belief that music was something apart from the rest of intellectual life; on the contrary, it had a grammar which could be learnt and a literature capable of being appreciated. Its inclusion in school work 'does not mean adding further burdens to an already overcrowded curriculum. It means teaching subjects in a different way from that in which they have been taught hitherto.' He made an analogy between the barren manner in which music was then being offered to children, and the teaching he remembered at public school in Malvern of another maligned subject thirty years earlier:

I do not think I learnt any History at school – any History of England. What passed under that name was an account of the disputes in which the people of England were from time to time engaged, and the blood-thirsty way in which those disputes were usually settled. When I was

W. H. Hadow (by permission of the University of Sheffield)

fifteen...I certainly could not have told you of any single invention during that period which had done anything to ameliorate the lot of men.

He poured scorn on a lady who had recently said to him, "'I adore Bach... He is so far above the common herd". I remarked that most of my friends seemed to enjoy his music.' Hadow wished to return to the age of the Elizabethans and particularly to their feeling that musicality ought to be a common possession, leading to an appreciation of the principle that in music 'the beauty of form is identical with the beauty of meaning: the rise and fall of the phrase and its rhythm is the meaning of melody...'[15]

Hadow was undoubtedly in the vanguard of 'progressive' musical education, but he was also part of a long-established tradition in England and Wales which had emphasized music as a *useful* subject. In the late 1830s James Phillips Kay (later Sir James Kay-Shuttleworth) had been so impressed by what he had seen on the Continent of Mainzer's and Wilhem's musical teaching among workers and artisans that, on taking up his duties as the first Secretary for the new Committee of Council on Education, he immediately appointed Charles Dickens's friend, John Hullah, to manage the progress of musical studies at the Battersea Teacher-training College, and later encouraged the tonic sol-fa movement of John Curwen, which so influenced the common development of Welsh musical achievement. There was a simple reason for Kay's promotion of music in the elementary curriculum: a nation without innocent amusements, he claimed in 1840, was generally demoralized. He conceived of popular song as 'an important means of forming an industrious, brave, loyal, and religious people.'[16] He anticipated Hadow's stress on popular melody by asking Hullah to insert traditional English airs into his *Manual* for schoolteachers.[17]

In December, 1864, at a Swansea choral meeting, Henry Austin Bruce, amateur flautist of some distinction, MP, friend of the musical Gladstone, and currently in charge of the Liberal government's educational programme, gave a brief lecture on 'Music'. He referred to the musical proclivities of warlike men – particularly Frederick the Great (a fellow flautist) and the Duke of Wellington, whose father had been Professor of Music at Trinity College, Dublin. But he chose as his chief advocate Alexander Pope, who had coolly written,

By music minds an equal temper know,
Nor swell to high, nor sink too low...

Warriors she fires with animated sounds;
Pours balm into the bleeding lover's wounds;...
Intestine War no more our passions wage,
And giddy factions hear away their rage...

Bruce (later Lord Aberdare) was speaking in Swansea 'especially for the purpose of promoting and cultivating the practice of music among the working classes.' As far as he could determine, the practice of music by working men had persuaded them 'to desert the public house' and to seek 'some higher and better occupation.' Of all pursuits, none could be purer, or freer from dangerous influences, than 'the choral cultivation of music.' Music had charms, of a socially and politically soporific kind.[18] But, apparently, Bruce was being too optimistic.

In 1878 the *Contemporary Review* published a paper by the political economist Stanley Jevons entitled 'Amusements of the People'. He complained that, though day schools had been built, penny readings started, penny banks and libraries established, yet 'crime and ignorance and drunkenness show no apparent diminution...' Traditional popular pastimes had necessarily been suppressed by the magistrates, and there had lately been a progressive degradation of the amusements of the people. The 'most efficacious mode' of raising the quality of common life, thought Jevons, was by 'the cultivation of pure music... Music is the best means of popular recreation... It is greatly to the low state of musical education among the masses...that I attribute their helpless state when seeking recreation.' And he added that in most continental towns, as a general rule, one found 'a fair orchestra' at daily open-air concerts. He pointed to the influence of Charles Hallé in Manchester, aided by 'a large, resident, well-cultured German middle-class population.' In the Free Trade Hall the bourgeoisie had the means of receiving an education in musical taste 'as they are educated in no other province of the United Kingdom.'[19]

For the Revd H. R. Haweis, writing on 'Music and Morals' in 1871, 'the music of the people is still ballads. Our national music vibrates between "When other lips" and "Champagne Charlie".' He remembered a visit to the Paris Exhibition of 1867:

...In the German refreshment rooms...there were rough bands working steadily through the symphonies of Mozart and Haydn, while the public were never found so intent on *sauer kraut* and sausages as not to applaud vociferously at the end, and sometimes even encore an *adagio*. Fancy the frequenters of Cremorne encoring a symphony by Mozart!...

Haweis noted the progress of musical taste in England, even in the music halls of the poor with their travesties of genuine Negro music:

> The negro is more really musical than the Englishman. If he has a nation emerging into civilisation, his music is national... If we could divest ourselves of prejudice, the songs that float down the Ohio river are one in feeling and character with the songs of the Hebrew captives by the waters of Babylon...[20]

To the concern of Kay and Jevons for the moral and social condition of the poor (and gentling the dissatisfied masses), and to Haweis's ambivalence about the 'music of the people', Hadow, after 1890, added his enthusiasm for the development of aesthetic sensibility. Yet in the years immediately preceding the Great War there was a powerful undertow of anxiety about the possible shattering of society, a feeling based substantially upon evidence of political violence in the south Wales coalfield. As was noted earlier, the Tonypandy 'Riots' engendered the most widely disseminated reports of economic and social disruption in Wales; and the seismic recording continued throughout the War. In 1917 the Prime Minister, Lloyd George, commissioned an inquiry, led by Daniel Lleufer Thomas, into the causes of political unrest – that is, the high incidence of strikes and violent demonstrations – in Wales during the War. Its Report remains one of the most intriguing documents of Welsh social history. A chief conclusion of the inquiry – conducted simultaneously with the work of the Haldane Commission, to which Lleufer Thomas gave extensive evidence – was that the University of Wales had to re-assert itself and wrest the initiative in providing adult education from the trade unions, who had already established their own structure of political and economic 'tutorial classes' in south Wales, as well as an outpost at the Central Labour College in London.[21] The social undercurrents still flowing in the year of the Bolshevik Revolution, allied with the political instability of industrial communities in Wales, help partly to explain the ready acceptance, by some Welsh-people-who-mattered, of Hadow's visionary proposals for shaping the future of musical education in the whole community of the Principality.

Despite his desire to create a public for the performance and appreciation good music, and his liberal tastes, Hadow was never more than an ironic commentator on cultural developments in the Soviet Union. In the Romanes Lecture he gave at Oxford in 1933, while accepting recent dodecaphonic developments, he poked fun at a performance in

1922 at Baku when the concept of 'proletarian music' was realized in a work which included 'the foghorns of the whole Caspian fleet, all the factory sirens, two batteries of artillery, several infantry regiments, a machine-gun section, real hydroplanes, and finally choirs in which all the spectators joined.' This kind of spurious musical populism was, for Hadow, 'beyond the reach of burlesque.'[22]

In the summer of 1918 Hadow took up his temporary appointment in France; and a year or two later he seems to have been assisting Lloyd George's government in organizing the publication of anti-Soviet propaganda.[23] In the same year, 1919, he moved from Newcastle to become Vice-Chancellor of Sheffield University. Henceforward his administrative tasks allowed him few opportunities for pursuing musicological researches; and during the 1920s his responsibilities on the Board of Education Consultative Committee further limited the range of his academic activity. It seemed unlikely, therefore, that he would be any more than indirectly involved in the prosecution of his earlier proposals for the future of Welsh musical education. The crucial work of ensuring that his ideas were implemented was left to another unofficial statesman of education whose commitment to the social, economic and cultural interests of the Welsh people formed the core of a long public career.

Though it can be claimed that Dr Thomas Jones was in a number of ways the most influential engineer of reform in Wales between 1911 and 1939, by his own typically honest estimate he was not a musical man. Yet he became the motivator and organizer of considerable change and upheaval in Welsh musical life. The love he bore his first college, Aberystwyth, and his informal role as the chief agent for the philanthropy of the Davies family, of Llandinam and later of Gregynog, caused him to stage-manage operations in the train of consequences which ran from within the Haldane Commission.

Speculation about change in musical education at Aberystwyth started before the Great War.[24] In 1914 the *Musical Times* noticed that

> ...the Committee appointed by the College of Wales at Aberystwyth, to report on the offer of £3,000 a year that has been made for the purpose of founding a school of instrumental and vocal music at the College, has recommended that the offer be accepted.

But the offer seemed conditional upon the engagement of teachers from the Schola Cantorum in Paris, and specific French and Belgian names had been mentioned. 'Some reasoned justification for this clean cut of all British influence is surely called for'.[25] Even though the French were our brave allies in war, at this stage chauvinism was rife, and local pride at Aberystwyth was hurt by such speculations. All of Mme Barbier's considerable pioneering work could not justify this proposed extension of political entente into the delicate national realm of music. Amid the flutter of subsequent activity, despite her former close association with the Davies sisters, she, and others from within Wales, were to be overlooked in the process of planning the regeneration of Welsh music.

Thomas Jones's role was played on a stage which might almost have been set intentionally for his kind of subtle performance; though in a Stoppard-like way, most of his best lines were delivered from behind the scenes. During the War he was Lloyd George's left hand in the Cabinet Room; the Prime Minister appointed the historian H. A. L. Fisher, deeply sympathetic to musical idealism in schooling, to fashion a new Education Act; the future of all educational activity in Britain seemed rosy. The Davies family, led by Major David Davies, future promoter of the League of Nations in Britain, was encouraged by the strongly felt desire for international co-operation to endow new chairs at Aberystwyth in Geography and International Politics. The offer of large funds for the reconstruction of the Music Department at the College came from his sisters, Gwendoline and Margaret Davies. Thomas Jones was the conduit which ensured that the Davies money flowed toward Aberystwyth and was not dissipated throughout the whole University.

When possible candidates for the newly constituted Chair of Music at Aberystwyth were first considered, the general feeling in that place was that a Welshman ought to be appointed. The Registrar, J. H. Davies, very much a local man, received from L. J. Roberts at the Board of Education in Whitehall, the recommendation that the best person for job was David Vaughan Thomas, former pupil of Joseph Parry and a sound representative of new impulses in Welsh cultural life.[26] But in the event, Vaughan Thomas's peculiarly appropriate qualities were ignored, with far-reaching consequences for both the work of the National Council of Music and musical culture in Wales.[27]

It seems, from what 'T. J.' himself recalled, that it was Hadow who first suggested Dr Walford Davies as the only serious candidate for the post of Director of Music for the Welsh University. Born in Oswestry on the wrong side of the border in 1869, Walford had received his musical education in the heartland of English music-making as a royal chorister at Windsor and later as Scholar under Parry and Stanford at the Royal College of Music. From 1898 until 1918, at the Temple Church in London, he built a reputation as the leading choir-trainer of his day, simultaneously establishing himself as a composer, mainly of oratorio and songs. He had taken some of his early works in his luggage on a pilgrimage to meet Brahms in Vienna. His mature compositions, performed frequently at the Three Choirs and Leeds Festivals, brought him to the notice of Elgar, who was thereafter an influential musical friend and adviser.[28] In 1918 Walford, like Hadow, was in France, as organiser of musical activity within the newly formed RAF – he was, of course, the author of the RAF 'March Past'. 'T. J.' remembered the impression made on their first meeting, at the Air Ministry in the Strand, of 'a big burly figure in Air Force blue.' In the same year Walford had produced a pamphlet, *Part Songs for the Use of Male Voice Choirs and Glee Clubs in the RAF*, the first of many such publications for the 'ordinary musician',[29] which was sponsored personally by Lloyd George at a critical point for wartime morale.

The trick which Thomas Jones had to perform was to persuade Walford Davies into the fastnesses of Wales and away from his nest at the Temple Church in the centre of metropolitan musical activity. By his own account he arranged a meeting at 3 Buckingham Gate, where Walford met Hadow and Professor Henry Jones, the Welsh shoemaker's son who had become the 'philosopher-king' of university scholarship in Scotland where he had been T. J.'s teacher. But his real persuasiveness consisted in inviting two other guests whose influence was probably of a more powerful kind. These were the gentle, wealthy sisters, Gwendoline and Margaret Davies of Llandinam in mid Wales whose money was being offered to energize a Welsh musical renaissance at Aberystwyth. Hadow supported the sisters' intention that their offer should be devoted to funding and founding not only what became the Gregynog Chair at Aberystwyth, but also the associated post of Director of a Council of Music for the whole University. In the paper he published soon after Walford's death in 1941, Thomas Jones chose not to provide a broad context for these negotiations. The context and the consequences together throw penetrating light upon tensions in Welsh society during the War and in the early post-War years, and particularly upon the continuing parochialism of Welsh academic and religious politics. Those tensions inhibited the exfoliation of the work of the University of Wales in patterns suggested by the Haldane Commission.

It is clear from the private papers of Dr Thomas Jones that the matter of Walford's appointment was more complicated than his elegant résumé in 1941 suggested. In the first place the earliest contact between Walford and T. J. had been by letter early in 1916. There was a tragic irony in the subject of that correspondence. Walford wrote that his friend, Gervase Elwes – one of Mme Barbier's performers at Aberystwyth concerts before the War – had brought her plight to his notice. It seemed her work was about to be curtailed; but, Walford wrote, 'if she only has substantial support from someone in authority – who is able to see the real significance of musical work at the moment, and in Wales especially – she will yet bring a work well begun to a fruitful issue...'[30] Soon after Walford innocently wrote that letter, Mme Barbier's fate was to be sealed by plans hatching, aided by Hadow's incubatory zeal, within the Haldane Commission.

Hadow and T. J. were in conversation about musical matters in April, 1917. The Englishman described Wales as 'an unworked gold-mine.' Nowhere was 'so much musical talent undeveloped.' Hadow's first thoughts might have been best, for, at this point, he offered the admonition - unheeded later, as far as many sensitive Welsh people were concerned – that 'this widespread gift' should be cultivated 'from within, rather than from without.' Across a broad front he wanted 'greatly increased teaching of music' at the colleges, with professors in Bangor, Aberystwyth and Cardiff, each at £500 per annum. The primary aim would be to encourage instrumental music; Cardiff ought to get 'a small orchestra', which should travel about Wales from time to time: local orchestras, he thought, were hardly possible in the other two colleges. University tutors would 'visit the villages' to hold classes, 'stimulating and guiding local effort.' Following Somervell's example at the Board of Education (which he had assisted) he further suggested the production of a cheap book of National Songs in sol-fa and old notation for use in Welsh elementary and secondary schools. In this task Dr Lloyd Williams of the Welsh Folk-song Society and Bangor College, he thought, 'could render valuable assistance.'[31]

A few weeks later, in June, Gwen Davies of Gregynog was enquiring whether the matter of 'Walford' had moved forward. T. J. replied that he was writing to 'Haddow' (sic) about approaching 'Walter (sic) Davies'. He was also rounding up Sir Henry Jones and the Davies family's adviser, Mr Owens, who was handling the bequest to Aberystwyth.[32] On the same day Thomas Jones was asking Hadow to sound out 'Waldorf' (sic) Davies 'in ever so tentative a way' to see whether

Walford Davies (by permission of the Welsh Music Archive)

a situation in Aberystwyth appealed to him. Several days later Hadow reported that Walford was 'torn in two' by the offer: 'the most unselfish of men', he wondered whether his real work would not still be in London, where his organ recitals were drawing huge crowds. More promisingly, he had begun to make stipulations about a Welsh post: it had to be 'not only influential but authoritative', and involve 'the hearty co-operation of the schools...as well as of the Eisteddfod and of the local eistedfodau.' Hadow, playing Satan to Walford's Saviour, outlined a choice: did he prefer (a) a supreme directorship of Music for the whole of Wales, carrying with it primacy over all the other Music chairs at the colleges; or (b) a division of Wales into districts with each professor supreme in his area, while the director would join with them in a 'general musical council' representative of musical education, of all institutions in which music played a prominent part? After huffing and puffing, Walford plumped for the latter. Hadow thought he had judged well: 'The former is a little too autocratic for Wales; and the latter gives all the safeguards for democracy, and allows the best man still to be the most influential.' And he took it that the best man would always be the Davies Professor.[33]

At this stage, with Walford already hooked, the University Commission's formal deliberations were still proceeding. Hadow wanted local advice from T. J.: there had to be a 'Standing Committee' for Welsh Music; but how could the Eisteddfod be best involved? The co-operation of the schools was 'absolutely essential'; but how would school music be properly organized and inspected – through the Board of Education, the Central Welsh Board, 'through Sir Owen Edwards', or how else? He apologized for all the questions, but the matter was 'most absorbingly interesting.' Percy Watkins, the leading Welsh civil servant of the day, told T. J. from Cardiff, 'This music thing is amazingly good. What a wizard you are!' He was specially interested – given the current report on political unrest being offered by Lleufer Thomas – to link the Workers' Educational Association to the work of the proposed new Council of Music.[34] Watkins's advice was fed into the machinery of the University Commission by Hadow, and passed on to Sir Henry Jones, prior to a dining appointment with Walford at the Athenaeum some time early in July, 1917.[35]

As an inducement to final acceptance, Thomas Jones sent Walford a copy of the newly issued Haldane Report; in reply, in March 1918, he called it 'an inspiring document' which presaged great things.[36] By mid-April T. J. could tell Gwen Davies (who was on nursing service in France),

> In the midst of the gloom of War, and of Ireland, I have a piece of good news which will rejoice your heart! Sir Henry Hadow called here yesterday. He had a walk on Hampstead Heath on Sunday with Walford Davies, and he came to tell me that Walford Davies has now definitely made up his mind to accept the posts at Aberystwyth, and in the University of Wales, if they are offered to him.[37]

All that remained was to square a London meeting of University of Wales bigwigs the following week. In advance of that he wrote to Principal T. J. Roberts of Aberystwyth telling him of Walford's frame of mind and remainding him of the details of the Davies sisters' bequest. Walford's salary was to be £1,000 a year, divided equally between Chair and Directorship; the Chair money would come from the £100,000 gift to Aberystwyth, and that of the Directorship from the £10,000 donated to the University of Wales.[38] The matter seems to have been informally settled during a meeting of the Adult Higher Education Committee at the GWR Hotel, Paddington, late in April, comprising Principal Roberts, Major David Davies of Llandinam, Lleufer Thomas and Professor Bryner Jones, among others.[39] A more official stamp was pressed downwards at a meeting of the University Music Committee on 23 July, attended by Hadow – who spoke at length – Thomas Jones and the Davies's representative, Mr Owens. Hadow explained that the function of the Director would be 'to stimulate and co-ordinate the national musical effort.' Dr Mary Davies of Bangor, formerly a soprano of distinction and now of the Folk-song Society, also argued winningly on Walford's behalf.[40]

After this combination of private and official interchanges, Walford accepted the Aberystwyth Chair and, more importantly, the Directorship of Music not just for the University but for the Principality as a whole. Above all people in the current music world he revered his old teacher, Sir Hubert Parry – another Englishman from just over the border, in Gloucestershire – who was anxious that Walford should find his true métier in 1918, after pouring his enthusiasm so fervently into RAF work. Of the Welsh opportunity Parry wrote in 1917, 'It ought to be a scheme of huge possibilities to justify your leaving the Temple and London... Of course you would serve the Welsh University magnificently.' A year later, in July, 1918, he said, 'So it's to be Aberystwyth when the war ceases its roarings! No doubt you will inspire the Welsh with great ardour; and I hope induce them to look beyond the borders for some things they can't provide inside them!'[41]

Later in the same month Walford was writing to T. J. confirming that the creation of a Welsh Academy of Music, on Bantock's pattern, was neither required nor appropriate: Wales's musical future was to be plotted from within the university colleges. He was going that very day to Reichel in Bangor 'to help them with certain points on which they ask advice, and still more to try to learn my job'.[42] There he also met Dr Mary Davies and the formidable Miss Rathbone. It is difficult to over-estimate the power of the hand of Dr Thomas Jones in all these proceedings of conception and fulfilment: once he had been convinced by Hadow of the liberalizing and binding qualities offered by the systematic development of Welsh musical potential, he had used his gifts of persuasion to ensure that the Davies's money was not simply expended but attached to the specific appointment of an imposing figure in British musical life.

Two matters remained to be resolved, one consitutional, the other political, and in both of these Thomas Jones played prominent parts, in the former as instrument, in the latter as object. The constituting of the Welsh National Council of Music, under Walford as Director, began at the George Hotel, Shrewsbury, in January 1919. As Vice-Chancellor of the University, Reichel formally presided over this important passage of events. T. J. advised from the sidelines, as and when his involvement in preparations for the Paris Peace Conference permitted.[43] Reichel undertook the task of liaising with Mr Owens; the legal process of constituting the Council according to the Davies sisters' deed of gift lasted for nearly two years after the moment of Walford's appointment.[44]

By 1924 the Council's composition had settled to an unwieldy committee of twenty-three members. In addition to Walford Davies, these included the University Vice-Chancellor (in 1924 A. H. Trow of Cardiff); E. T. Davies and Professor David Evans (representatives, respectively, of the Music Departments of Bangor and Cardiff); three members of the University Court (one of whom was Percy Watkins); Professor J. Lloyd Williams (squeezed in on behalf of the Guild of Graduates); Tom John from the central Welsh Board; Dr Mary Davies (for the Welsh Folk-song Society); Gwendoline Davies (officially the representative of the National Library); two county-school heads, one of whom was the remarkable and influential Arthur Lyon of Hawarden; two elementary-school headteachers; a delegate of the

Students' Representative Council; D. W. Evans of the National Eisteddfod Association and the Gorsedd; the Revd G. Parry Williams of the National Eisteddfod Local Committee for that year; and three co-opted members, Hadow, Reichel and Mortimer Angus. As will become apparent later, however, this leviathan was steered chiefly by Walford, and was kept afloat by his personal charm. Some rather sharp rocks lay ahead in the immediate post-War years.

The second, political, matter, though it seems indirectly linked to musical events, nevertheless affected adversely what was to happen in Welsh academic life in the 1920s and 1930s, and reflected the continuing parochialism of thought and action in Wales.

The new Director-Professor set to work immediately. In the autumn of 1919 he wrote with his customary ebullience to Thomas Jones describing a 'delirious' audience for one of his early Beethoven concerts at Aberystwyth. In the same letter he congratulated T. J. on the quality of his testimonials for the vacant post of Principal at Aberystwyth.[45] A year earlier, wind of Jones's possible candidature had reached Walford who wrote, suggestively, how glad he was that 'I may work in close co-operation some day with you and under your guidance. May it be so...'[46] Walford, like many native Welshmen who mattered at that time, hoped to see Jones appointed to succeed T. J. Roberts. For him as a new Professor it would have meant the secure freedom of working under a sympathetic Principal in the turbulent aftermath of the Haldane Report; for others it appeared to present an opportunity for transforming the life of the premier Welsh college by bringing in a cosmopolitan Welshman (and sometime Aberystwyth student) to manage its future.

Walford's pleasure in the quality of Thomas Jones's testimonials was wholly justified. Their general tenor was reflected in the letter which accompanied Hadow's formal offering:

> ...I am delighted for the sake of University Education in Wales that you have consented to stand for Aberystwyth. I enclose a testimonial which I hope will be of service – I could not have made it stronger without swearing... Henry Jones is, I suppose, working for you already...[47]

Lord Haldane, declaring his support, emphasized Thomas Jones's 'large endowment...of idealism... The spirit of Edward Caird... inherited by Professor Henry Jones, and passed on to Mr Thomas Jones, is the kind of endowment I have in mind'.[48] Sidney Webb, perhaps remembering his own experience in London University nego-

Thomas Jones (by permission of the National Library of Wales)

tiations, spoke of 'his eminent qualifications from the standpoint of...what I may call the statesmanship of University management...'[49] R. H. Tawney wrote, 'He has the indefinable quality, insight, prevision, sympathy, genius – call it what you like, which makes a man a natural leader... I can't imagine anyone better suited both by experience and natural capacity to bridge the divisions of the future, which may, if they are not bridged, swallow a good deal that is valuable in our present way of existence.'[50]

The interviews for the Aberystwyth position took place on 7 November 1919. Walford – who by this time had told friends that he thought Thomas Jones 'the most wonderful man in the world' (with the possible exception of another Welshman who was Prime Minister)[51] – wrote to his idol on the night before in the foyer of Jones's Aberystwyth hotel,

> My dear Friend,
>   I came along to your room, but you were settled in and asleep. Only just to express my hope and prayer that the Council will lay the burden on your shoulders tomorrow and Heaven give you a stout heart to shoulder it...[52]

Due to a combination of religious animosity (caused by Jones's declared agnosticism) and parochial antagonism (he had spent most of his mature professional years outside Wales, in Glasgow, Belfast and the Cabinet Office in Whitehall) the Cardiganshire-dominated Council appointed instead 'their' man, the acting Principal and Registrar of the College, J. H. Davies, who had a year earlier been involved by T. J. in guaranteeing Walford's appointment. A few days after this disaster, H. A. L. Fisher, another of Jones's referees, wrote to him, 'You can hardly be more disappointed than I am for one of my chief hopes for the realisation of the high aims of the Welsh University Commission depended on your election, and this hope is now shattered. I am really very despondent as to the educational future of the University...'[53]

The fact was that Jones's supporters, led by Lleufer Thomas, had prepared his way too well. In the turbulent wake of the Haldane Report – which was seen as outside interference by many – not only had the Misses Davies created the new Chair and Directorship for Walford, but their brother – a passionate League of Nations man – had used his largesse to found two other chairs, most notably that in International Politics. These bequests stirred feelings of defensive nationalism. Professor Sir Henry Jones's son wrote to T. J., 'I fear the

Welsh horizon is still as narrow as in the days when they drove my father out...'[54] A local newspaper commented, 'Major David Davies's idea of the future mission of the College is international rather than national; cosmopolitan rather than provincial... The chair of music, too, with Dr Walford Davies to occupy it – even this action...has an international touch to it...'[55]

Hankey, Thomas Jones's boss in the Cabinet Secretariat, commiserated, but added, with perhaps innocent perceptiveness, 'there is a brighter side. The University's loss is the State's gain... So, I beg you to bear up, and to give your country your best service in the much wider sphere which lies open to you...'[56] Hankey already appreciated Jones's consummate skills in dealing with industrial action, particularly by the miners; and the Welshman's subtlety was to be crucial in the Government's negotiations with the Irish over the next two years. In a less formal way – and most appositely, given the declining social and economic condition of industrial Wales – Thomas Jones was released to devote his efforts to establishing Coleg Harlech and to organizing the funding of collective support for a wide range of ameliorating schemes in Wales throughout the 1920s and 1930s; and these were to include the continuing work of Walford Davies and the National Council of Music.[57]

Thomas Jones, for all his powerful allies, was forced to retreat before the opposition of entrenched conservatism in November, 1919. Walford Davies was already having to parry the jealous thrusts being directed at him by members of the internal musical and cultural establishment.

CHAPTER SIX

A *Pied Piper's Campaign*

How jovial was his laughter,
How great his gift to share
The things he loved so simply
With thousands everywhere.
Wide-hearted, wise and gentle,
A good man all his days,
He went his way rejoicing,
His life a song of praise.
Wherever he may travel,
This is the certain thing:
The people there will love him,
And he will make them sing.
     (Joyce Grenfell)

That kind of response to the memory of Walford Davies, quoted by
Thomas Jones soon after the musician's death in 1941 (Joyce Grenfell
had been an observer at close quarters in Gregynog and at the Malvern
Festival), probably seems far too fulsome now.[1] The official biography
did reveal one or two hairline cracks in the human edifice;[2] but despite
Colles's failure – quite justifiable, given the constraints of a task
undertaken only three years after its subject's death – to indulge in
superficial Freudian scratching, the bulk of the available evidence then
suggested that Walford had indeed been as good, honest, energetic,
winning, charming and convincing as his friends and colleagues remembered. To a certain extent his personal qualities, as described by
close companions, are beside the point. The fact is that, soon after he
came into Wales in 1918 to take up his large new appointments, he
encountered criticism of a kind which had never before been directed
against him; and by no means all of it was motivated by jealousy, envy
or malice. His Welsh critics were not collectively petty-minded or
parochial, and their arguments not always *ad hominem*.

    He was surely a larger-than-life character. Colles, Thomas Jones
and others all commented on his physical size. He loomed, but in a

most benign way. His legendary verbal fluency and spontaneity remain on record in a few preserved excerpts from the celebrated BBC broadcasts; much of that work – it is difficult to credit it in a very different 'media' age – was completely unscripted yet thoroughly convincing. Such inventiveness was a natural part of the man, but was also necessitated by the variety of activities he chose to undertake simultaneously after 1918. He did not have time to worry over writing and refining a mere script, whether for a broadcast or an important speech. His books – *The Pursuit of Music*, for instance[3] (that title serves as a suitable metaphor for his physical restlessness) – give the impression of having been dictated hastily during the railway journeys which were an almost daily feature of his life.

Colles made it clear that Walford had been riven by psychological doubts of various kinds; for a considerable early period, as boy and young man, separated by long distance from his family in Oswestry, he had depended on strong emotional relationships with older people. Though he seems always to have been confident of his general musical vocation, his original qualities as a composer were not deeply marked, except in the successful oratorio *Everyman* and in some of the songs; and after his Welsh work began in earnest he functioned only fitfully in the field of original composition. In this he was unlike his closest models and mentors, Hubert Parry and C. V. Stanford, who had seemed able to combine much official teaching and administration with frequent bouts of musical creativity.

Hadow and Walford were very different in training and attitude, though somewhat similar in their intentions. Both were musical evangelists; but while Hadow was, by inclination and education, objectively cerebral and scholarly – an eccentric Oxford man – Walford remained addicted to the English cathedral tradition, with a leavening of aspiration added by his studies in London. Both men met Brahms; but whereas Hadow absorbed that experience and moved on, Walford never quite managed to escape the effects of their encounter and remained frozen in the stylistic modes of Brahms's (rather than Wolf's or Mahler's) Vienna. A visit to the Oxford University Music Department Library reveals that, until his death in 1937, Hadow was still avidly tasting, if not necessarily relishing, the very latest effusions of European music: the catalogue of scores he bequeathed to the library includes the very latest of Schoenberg, Stravinsky, Hindemith, Walton and, at last, even Constant Lambert and Britten. His roots were no less baroque and classical than Walford's; but, despite his deserting the composer's role, until the end his fertile mind remained open to new experiences.

Hadow was not a passionate Wagnerite, but he came to accept that the innovations of Wagner, Strauss and even Schoenberg were inevitable consequences of the search for new modes of aesthetic and tonal expression. And, as has been said earlier,[4] even Hadow's classical preoccupations suggested to him that Haydn offered insights, through the mysteries of east-European folk music, which might induce British acknowledgement of native well-springs of melody. Walford accepted the folk-song heritage but abhorred most of what had happened in the name of musical innovation after 1900. He also had one particular detestation: 'Grand Opera, as it stands today, seems still an astonishing and phenomenal enormity.'[5] For him, the terms which mattered in the description of music were the ancient *Kinde* ('Humanity'), 'love', 'holy', 'fitness', 'grace from heaven', and so on. Such high-mindedness, for some of his critics, came close to being sanctimonious.

Even before his appointments in Aberystwyth he had become the butt of public sarcasm. Like Philip Heseltine in the same generation, 'Gerald Cumberland' (Charles Frederick Kenyon) hid behind a pseudonym when indulging in waspish criticism of contemporary musicians. Writing just before the Great War, he attacked Walford witheringly. They met in Liverpool at a diocesan conference on ecclesiastical music. All went well until Cumberland praised Wagner. Then:

> ...Davies spoke: earnestly, like St Francis, frenziedly, like Savonarola, passionately, like Venus...no! no! no!...passionately like St Paul. Eschew Wagner! That's what it all came to... Wagner, it appeared, was one of the devils. Absolutely pernicious... Have you ever noticed how accurately you can estimate a man by his adjectives? Dr Walford Davies used 'pernicious' eleven times, 'poisonous' twice, 'very-much-to-be-distrusted' once, 'naughty' once ('this naughty man' was the phrase), 'unlicensed' thrice, and 'immoral' fifteen times...

By Cumberland's account Walford spent the rest of the evening 'shooting little pointed darts at me from his eyes.' But in partial mitigation he remembered Davies's setting of the Grace, with 'its Blake-like simplicity, its Aerial freshness.'[6]

He noticed that, when 'preaching' of Brahms, Walford 'poises a white hand in the air.'

> How exasperating it must be to possess a temperament that can only accept part of what is admirable! It seems to me that Walford Davies

distrusts his intellect: in estimating the worth of music, he seems to say, intellectual standards, artistic standards, are of no value. To him the only sure test is temperamental affinity. And he wishes all temperaments to conform to his own limitations.

Cumberland conjured with a memory of having seen Walford near the Temple, 'with choirboys hanging on his arm, with choirboys prancing before him...a shepherd with his sheep.' He was sure that such a scene represented a 'good influence.' But in musical matters, 'how bad that good influence may be! Did ever a worshipper of Wagner walk the rooms of the YWCA?'[7] That was rather silly, even smutty comment. But the words Cumberland used to describe 'poor virginal Walford Davies' – 'asceticism, fine-fingeredism, religiosity, "mutual improvement", narrowness of intellect, physical coldness' – suggest that there was something in the public manner which seemed, to some, too good to be true. On the other hand, amid the genteel aspirations of the respectable middle classes between the Wars, those were among the very qualities which had wide appeal, and secured his pre-eminence as musical pedagogue and missionary to the bourgeosie in search of salvation through sanctified knowledge.

The undergraduates Walford met at Aberystwyth immediately after the War were, according to one student, 'a difficult crowd.' Frank Phillips remembered his first meeting with 'a man of imposing stature dressed in the uniform of a Major in the RAF.' He and all those first music students were treated as equals, and soon, with Walford in charge, they were discussing 'a new Students' Song-Book, arrangements for weekly concerts, plans for the college choral, open lectures to all students and a hundred and one other schemes.' At one of the first college concerts there was an undignified clamour for the new Professor to accompany a comic song; 'he did so, and his extemporising on a tawdry little effort captured the "gods".' This gave Walford space to deliver a talk on Beethoven. 'A memorable occasion was capped when the "gods" carried him shoulder-high around the quadrangle after the concert.'[8]

Straightaway Walford identified precisely his long-term tasks in Wales. The first was to revitalize the teaching and performing work of the colleges; the second to diffuse the effects of musical education through all available agencies, from the lowliest schools to adult groups, in every town and village; the third was to shift Welsh choralists, with their proven primitive talent, away from the narrow competitive ethic into a wider appreciation of 'good' repertoire drawn from the whole treasury of European music. Finally he wished to implant a true feeling for the riches of instrumental music, from which the development of local talent might follow. His first mistake in Wales, however, was to utter these aims unequivocally, since a positive statement of intent would certainly be interpreted as negative criticism of what had already been achieved.

It has been shown earlier that leading Welsh musicians and academics had themselves begun to take matters in hand before the Great War. At Aberystwyth a scheme had been proposed for the dissemination of higher musical values among rural communities; and Mme Barbier had organized her impressive Musical Union with its array of distinguished visiting artists. Harry Evans, from an outpost in Liverpool, and D. Emlyn Evans from within had been trying to undermine the competitive side of the choral tradition. And there was considerable evidence, albeit limited to a few localities, of a strong desire to improve instrumental and orchestral performance. Cyril Jenkins, in his acerbic way, had started to provide professional models of orchestral playing with his mobile festival in the south Wales coalfield towns. Walford was to benefit from all these earlier developments; but, in his first official statement of intent, he did not acknowledge sufficiently the work of his predecessors. It was as if, in order to ensure appreciation of the magnitude of his proposed achievement, he had constantly to deplore all that had preceded his advent. He did not identify a John the Baptist. Instead he placed all his faith in a Trinity: Lloyd George as political God the Father; Hadow as musical Holy Ghost, and Thomas Jones as instrumental Son on earth. Walford would have found the role of St Paul quite congenial – with some added touches of conviviality.

The work of annihilating false Welsh gods had been started by others. For instance, Walford had no need to attack the reputation of Dr Joseph Parry. In 1921, as part of a book intended to commemorate Y Doctor Mawr with some reverence, Cyril Jenkins offered an essay which tore Parry's memory asunder. He uttered what should have been said gently in a manner calculated to affront anyone who still innocently enjoyed humming 'Aberystwyth' or a melody from *Blodwen*:

> I believe it to be my duty to take this chance...to destroy the tradition and influence created by Parry, so that no young Welsh composer who

finds himself in the situation I was in twelve years ago should have to suffer the disadvantages that I did or be stifled by the muggy atmosphere of his music.

For all his gifts, Parry never had the ability to differentiate between his good compositions and 'the ones which are inescapably bad.' *Blodwen* was in the latter category. Parry was what he had to be, a man of his time. But Jenkins blamed him for not having taken advantage of a privileged musical training in London, a Cambridge doctorate and the experience of living and working in the airier climate of North America. His remaining followers were Welsh people who possessed 'an unfailing love for music' while lacking 'enough musical culture to be able to tell the difference between good and bad.' Public taste, not Parry, was to blame for the enduring popularity of his work. In thus seeking to destroy a deity – the only candidate thus far for the accolade 'genius' in the pantheon of Welsh composers and musicians – Jenkins sealed his own fate in Wales, as Caradoc Evans was simultaneously managing to do in literature, even more mordantly.[9]

Late in 1921 Walford Davies read a paper to the Cymmrodorion Society, 'Our Mother-Tongue: A Musical Policy for Wales'. The occasion was remarkable for two connected reasons: the meeting was held in 10 Downing Street, and Walford's chairman was the Prime Minister, David Lloyd George, a Vice-President of the Society. The new Director of Music began by saying that Wales was a trilingual country: '...she speaks Welsh, English and Music – and the greatest of these is Music.' Like Jevons forty years earlier, he inveighed against the vulgarization of popular musical taste. He thought that Wales was in need of a 'restoration to freedom, naturalness, and vision.' Like Hadow he considered the folk-song movement 'a God-send, in bringing us back to simple melodic meanings.' Above all he believed the remedy for Welsh musical ills lay in the schools, and particularly in making and appreciating good melody:

> Perhaps Wales, by reason of her singing habits, her manageable size, and her educational system, has special aptitudes for training this practical ideal more easily and quickly than other nations. If it be so, she can make a valuable, educational contribution to the world.

He concluded by suggesting – in the presence of the Prime Minister who had appointed H. A. L. Fisher, the only true educationist to become President of the Board of Education – that every school in the land should possess a good gramophone and library of records; should enjoy a minimum of ten minutes' daily singing, and a weekly concert of forty minutes 'given *by* the school *for* the school' at which pupils' compositions should be heard alongside the great works of musical literature; should encourage the writing of melody by pupils; and should have a good supply of suitable song-books in melody editions.[10]

As with so much that has been written in the name of educational progress, what Walford said, though it sounded flashingly original, was already becoming common coin in the exchange of ideas about the schools' curricula in England and Wales. These were basically the same draughts as Hadow had dispensed more philosophically in his 1918 Oxford paper.[11] Since 1905 the Board of Education had included in its volume of *Suggestions for the Consideration of Teachers in Elementary Schools* a weighty chapter on the significance of school music and its teaching. That contribution was the work of the composer-HMI Arthur Somervell, another pupil of Hubert Parry, who was also responsible in the same year for the Board's publishing a list of recommended 'National or Folk Songs' for school use, to be followed in 1906 by his *National Song Book*.[12]

Somervell, a true follower of Matthew Arnold in defining what popular culture ought to be, was also in the tradition of James Phillips Kay sixty years before and of Pestalozzi even earlier, being convinced of the social as well as aesthetic value of school musical training. He shared with Walford a concept of 'self-expression subservient to the general good' which seems paradoxical when viewed from outside the perspective of social and political turmoil in the decades before and after the Great War.[13]

At the same time, the headmaster of Eton, Edward Lyttelton, admittedly a pacificist, wrote, of singing in schools: 'As an unconscious training in the sense of social service and in combined harmonious unselfish effort, there is nothing to compare.'[14] And even within the English public-school system this attitude was part of a recently established tradition, reaching back to the pioneering work of Edward Thring, headmaster of Uppingham School, where the musical activity had combined aesthetic aims with notions of loyalty and obedience, and gestures of social service (which, in Uppingham's case had involved sending its choirs to sing in East End settlements in the 1880s).[15]

In the light of these widely publicized theories about the possible purposes of musical education, it might not be too fanciful to detect resonances of social control in the paper which Walford read in 1921 to a Welsh Prime Minister in Downing Street in the presence of a considerable Welsh social engineer, Thomas Jones, at a time when strikes and industrial dissension were threatening to tear society apart. By his regular visits to the National Eisteddfod, at least, Lloyd George would have recognized that music demonstrably had more than simple aesthetic charms. In a turbulent, economically unsettled age it could still be a 'useful' subject.

In concentrating upon school music in his Downing Street paper Walford might legitimately have claimed that he was about to repair a real, rather than an apparent, Welsh weakness. Just as the founding of the University had not led to significant advances in higher musical training, so the Intermediate Education Act of 1889 had failed to produce a widespread unfolding of school music-teaching in the Principality. Official reports had recently contained evidence of how little purposeful musical activity went on in the secondary schools of Wales. David Jenkins's report for the Central Welsh Board in 1908, for instance, had been perfunctory to the point of insolence. Near the end of the Great War, however, the Central Welsh Board, with an eye to the general educational plans which would have to be submitted by Welsh local authorities under the terms of the 1918 Education Act, commissioned a much more detailed inquiry.

The investigation was to be carried out by David Vaughan Thomas of Swansea in his role as temporary Specialist Inspector in Music. This appointment embodied a great irony. At the very time, in the summer of 1918, when Vaughan Thomas was struggling through his inspection of music in more than half of the number of Welsh secondary schools, Walford was accepting the posts of Director and Gregynog Professor, precisely the kind of appointments to which the Swansea man had aspired since the beginning of the century, and for which, perhaps unbeknown to him, he had been recommended in the first instance. He had probably taken on the temporary inspectorship as a stepping-stone to greater things, and the views he expressed in his report were confident (with a touch of pomposity), wide-ranging and, given the usual constraints imposed upon official publications, surprisingly subjective in tone. He mingled his observations on specific schools with remarks about the general musical condition of Wales which he consciously related to the suggestions very recently made by the Haldane University Commission. And, by a twist of chronological fate, his CWB words may have been absorbed by the eclectic, forward-planning Walford Davies.

Vaughan Thomas, too, saw the better future of Welsh music in 1918 springing from the work to be done in the schools, as a counterpoise to the continuing indifference about standards among the general public, who attached too much importance to their children gaining 'cheap diplomas and certificates.' He wished the Welsh to rid themselves of 'the frequently expressed antagonism towards so called secular music... A Music-Hall tune wedded to sacred words will be welcomed, while a spiritual utterance in a symphony will be ignored.' The new local education authorities, set up under the 1902 Act, had not yet 'begun to encourage music as part of the school curriculum.' Neither had the public conscience been awakened to the dignity of true artistic endeavour: dross was still turned into the ordinary coin of Welsh music. 'The motto is "Write down to the level of the people". This, I am told, is the principle of "business"...'[16]

The schools should have been promoting a better understanding of the real connection between the great tradition of Welsh lyric poetry and living modern music, through imitating contemporary settings of the best English verse by Bantock, Parry, Elgar and Somervell. Vaughan Thomas wanted more opportunities for orchestral playing, and more instrumental teaching, perhaps provided at first by players from existing orchestras in Llandudno, Colwyn Bay, Cardiff, Swansea and the Rhondda throughout their surrounding districts. Referring to his own experience as a teacher, he stressed the necessity for more numerous illustrated lectures: 'This is one of the greatest needs of the country at large' – talks, rather than 'academic discourses.'[17] Such things were already happening under enlightened teachers: at Hawarden especially; at Howell's (Llandaf) where standards of instrumental performance were admirable; and at Towyn, Tregaron, Rhyl, Bangor (Girls') and Merthyr Tydfil. If further progress were to be assured, however, appropriate printed material would have to be made available for use in every school.[18]

For all its self-advertisement – Vaughan Thomas's reference, for example, to his own work 'for the past twelve or fifteen [sic] years in public lectures and adjudications at the National and provincial Eisteddfodau' – this was a well-judged prescription for improvement. More emphatically than Walford, of course, he identified the specifically Welsh paths which progress might take; but he ended by advising that, alongside a deeper concern for the characteristics of 'our own National music', there should be 'a proper conception of the canons of all true art.' A genuine hope for the future development of Welsh music would emerge only by establishing a balance between the native and the universal. Vaughan Thomas may have felt, even as he prepared his CWB text, that the authority from which he spoke might be taken as a reason for his appointment to the offices recently proposed by the Haldane Commission. The root of such optimism lay perhaps in the printed programmes he had proudly preserved from Hadow's Oxford Musical Union concerts in the 1890s, in which he had frequently participated as chamber-music pianist and accompanist[19]. The disappointment he suffered on hearing of Walford's double preferment in 1918 ran palpably through the remainder of his career.

Walford opened his public campaign in Wales, a month before his inaugural lecture at Aberystwyth, with a lecture at Pengam, one of the leading county schools of south-east Wales, on 'Post-War Music' in June, 1919. He saw his new task as 'a lovable responsibility': to promote, through music, 'a spirit of manliness and a host of homely qualities' in what was 'a veritable land of song.'[20]

The sting of the Haldane proposals, however, ensured that he was not alone in the work of musical reform. At the 1919 National Eisteddfod in Corwen Lord Howard de Walden came from his temporary residence at Chirk Castle[21] to preside over a performance of *Blodwen*. Opera, that gentleman thought, was peculiarly suited to the Welsh genius. But de Walden also announced his interest in the plan of the Neath musician, T. Hopkin Evans, to found a Welsh National Orchestra in order to dismiss the taunt that Welsh choralists had to import London orchestras for their performances.[22] Within a year the burgesses of Cardiff, led by the Mayor, G. F. Fosdyke, had offered support, backed practically by experienced local orchestral conductors, like Arthur Angle of Cardiff and Arthur E. Sims of Newport, both of whom were sustaining adventurous amateur experiments with choral and orchestral concerts. Through the mists of the recent past the Cardiff Festival offered precedents; and the new venture had the support of Dr David Evans of the University Music Department in the city. 'Orpheus' of the *Western Mail* pronounced the subsequent series of concerts throughout south-east Wales 'an artistic success', and particularly praised the inclusion of contemporary Welsh works, like T. Hopkin Evans's *Brythonic* Overture and the *Solemn Melody* of Walford Davies, 'another Welsh composer' (sic), alongside Debussy's *L'Après-midi* and Bantock's Ballade in A minor. As with later experiments, the orchestra relied heavily upon players from local theatres and on good amateurs and teachers, in this case mainly from the Angle Orchestra.[23]

Alongside this ephemeral achievement, Cyril Jenkins was to persist for one more season with his series of 'educational' concerts in south Wales, using the London Symphony Orchestra. In 1920 his project went down in a blaze of distinction: among his conductors that season for concerts in Cardiff, Newport and the Valleys were Elgar, directing his own Second Symphony, and Vaughan Williams in the first performance of his *Four Hymns* for tenor and orchestra. Except in the massive Pavilion at Mountain Ash, audiences were disastrously small.[24] It is interesting that in the same year Cardiff recitals by 'lions' like de Pachmann and Albert Sammons attracted reasonable houses.[25] In the 'capital' of Wales the 'celebrity' recital, so closely akin to the Victorian 'miscellaneous' concert, could be guaranteed to transcend financially an opulent orchestral performance directed by the greatest living British composer.

At the Corwen Eisteddfod Alfred Kalisch, critic of the *Musical Times* (and contemporary of Hadow and Vaughan Thomas at Oxford), who always strove to write favourably about Welsh music, was welcomed into the Gorsedd, as 'Dafydd o'r dwerain'. On this occasion he reported that the best of the singing had been 'beautiful in tone and blend', and this caused him to wonder whether the discipline of the singers, 'many of them from South Wales collieries', could not be harnessed to another purpose: he asked 'why our not too economical Government does not spend a few thousand pounds on male-voice choralism as an antidote to Bolshevism.' At Corwen the choralists were obedient to every gesture of their conductor, 'never stopping to reflect that, after all, he was an autocrat... Nobody stopped to demand a soviet, and there was no talk of downing voices'. This reflection may have been prompted by two current features: the restiveness of the Corwen audiences (again quietened with a hymn), and the great Dock Strike which caused the government to despatch a destroyer and two companies of the King's Own Yorkshire Light Infantry to the port of Cardiff.[26] Reverting to mere musical matters Kalisch urged that Wales's chief needs were local orchestras and chamber-music groups; it was therefore disappointing that at the next year's Eisteddfod in Barry, despite the prospect of an enterprising programme of test-pieces, the committee, having invented the splendid idea of providing an orchestral accompaniment for the Chief Choral competition, should have complacently engaged the LSO, rather than forming a special Welsh band.[27]

For the time being Walford chose to ignore the proceedings in and around the stodgy city of Cardiff and even in turbulent Corwen, though the idea of the de Walden 'National' orchestra gave him pause for reflection. His base of operations, for the time being, was Aberystwyth: in his inaugural lecture, on 5 June 1919, he chose to say, 'What Aberystwyth dreams and does today may become the vision and experience of Wales tomorrow'.[28] The first Festival there opened modestly in late spring, 1920, an essential model for other such annual meetings away from the greater centres of population – at Harlech, Newtown and Gregynog – over the next twenty years.

Another seaside event of great significance for change in Welsh music occurred in August, 1920. The new wealthy port of Barry, created by David Davies, grandfather of the Misses Davies of Llandinam and Gregynog, was host to the National Eisteddfod. Walford Davies was too much of a newcomer to take over the planning of the Barry week, but he was a member of the local committee, along with Lord Howard de Walden. This Eisteddfod's energy and novelty may have had something to do with the new Director's declarations of intent; but it seems more likely that its distinctive qualities were the products of a heterogeneous community which, since the 1880s, had been rapidly swelled by incomers from rural and industrial Wales and also from the west of England.[29] Leslie Tusler, a renowned Barry amateur musician of the town's second generation, explained the dynamism of the place as resulting partly from the influx of a cohort of energetic imaginative teachers – lured by higher-than-average wages – when the town's first schools opened at the end of the century. These talented professionals then led the process of creating from scratch the social institutions – golf clubs, dramatic and musical societies – of a lively, rumbustious town. Within a generation Barry had made its own new patterns of leisure behaviour.[30] One of the earliest of the musician-teachers, D. J. Thomas, of High Street Boys' School, became first conductor of the Barry Male Choir, and also of the Barry Harmonic Society which, according to the *Musical Times*, boasted 'a fine orchestra'.[31]

From among Barry teachers, however, came a musician who was to be one of the chief props of Walford's campaign to raise standards. W. M. Williams, a north Walian, after working briefly under D. J. Thomas, took a post at the new Romilly Boys' School in 1909. There he created one of the most remarkable school choirs in Europe. In 1912 it won the Gold Crown at the Paris International Musical Festival; in 1914 (returning just before hostilities began) it toured North America, performing for President Wilson at the White House; in 1921 it won first prize at a festival in Liège. Williams's Romilly Choir was the jewel in Barry's musical crown. In 1924 it was to become the star attraction of Walford's Welsh Week at the Wembley Imperial Exhibition. In 1923 Leslie Tusler, accompanist to the Romilly Choir, was also pianist in the Barry Boys' County School Orchestra. This was created by its great headmaster, Edgar Jones (close friend of Thomas Jones, briefly a Barry resident), who, with Hadow and Henry Jones, had met in London to persuade Walford towards Wales in 1918. Tusler's predecessor as choir accompanist had been Williams's daughter, Grace, who in 1918 had left for Cardiff University to read music.[32] Subsequently, after a period of study with Vaughan Williams, the same Grace Williams was to become one of Wales's leading composers, taking on the mantle of Morfudd Llwyn Owen whose tragic early death in 1918 had deprived British music of a brilliant creative career. Men of the calibre of W. J. Williams and D. J. Thomas, supported by Edgar Jones, powered the epoch-making Barry Eisteddfod in 1920.

Walford, with Vaughan Williams and David Evans, participated at Barry as adjudicator. There were two chief novelties. First, in addition to conventional competitions for glees and anthems, and following the precedent set by Cyril Jenkins's Festivals, prizes were offered for an orchestral tone-poem and for settings for chorus and orchestra of Newbolt's 'He fell among thieves'; the winning pieces were published beforehand and performed during the Eisteddfod. Second, the LSO was to play the new compositions and also accompany the main competing choirs in complete performances of Stanford's *Revenge*.[33] Reviewing the Eisteddfod as a whole, Kalisch drew particular attention to the comments of Walford and Vaughan Williams on the choirs. The former said that, though the quality of sound was often magnificent, there was 'unnaturalness' in the singing, which spoiled the outlines of beautiful phrases; the latter warned that choral performance was 'not an affair of stunts and monkey tricks.' Kalisch reported Walford's belief that the only remedy in the long run was to develop a greater natural appreciation of the subtleties of orchestral music, which would result in an ability to understand 'purity of melodic outline and the structure of great works.' The LSO concert performances, conducted by Walford, were marred by the drumming of rain on the corrugated-iron roof; and the audience received 'Infernal Dance' from Stravinsky's *Firebird* with 'an air of bewilderment.' Walford did not like the work in any case. The innovative competitions for writing large-scale works produced little in the way of originality, but proved that young Welsh musicians were escaping 'mere slavish imitation of mid-Victorian models', and were now taking their lead from Elgar, Walford himself and Vaughan Williams. A further key to unlocking the future was embodied in the very popular Children's Concert, for which W. M. Williams had trained a local schools' choir of 700 voices.[34]

Walford used Barry as a convenient platform for disseminating his Welsh ideas. At a Cymmrodorion meeting there, in a talk entitled 'The Council of Music for Wales: Its Objects and Aspirations', he told a large audience that it aimed primarily at 'inculcating a love of music, and fostering and directing special talent in the rising generation', very much the appropriate words to utter in Barry. He stressed the central importance of folk-song; but in the subsequent discussion Cyril Jenkins deprecated too much folk music, and Samuel Langford, the respected *Manchester Guardian* critic, seemed to reflect some of Walford's imminent problems when he advised that unity was essential to success in the endeavour to bring about Welsh musical progress.[35]

While beginning to spread the gospel, the Director had also to select disciples, or, at least, a team of paid assistants who would undertake the continuous tasks of administration, correspondence, teaching, lecturing and performing during his necessary absences from Wales while he was engaged on other duties. First, in August 1919, he advertised for an executive secretary. The short list of applicants was impressive. W. M. Williams of Barry must have come near to getting the appointment: in addition to his Romilly successes, he had lately been appointed Music Secretary of the 1920 Eisteddfod and since 1917 had been Music Lecturer at Barry Training College. Among his referees were Edgar Jones and Silyn Roberts. There was strong competition from T. Hopkin Evans who, with Cyril Jenkins, was initiating the South Wales Orchestral Festival. He had just been appointed Harry Evans's successor as conductor of the Liverpool Choral Union, and brandished glowing testimonials from Bantock. Both were Welsh-speaking Welshmen, a qualification essential in Walford's deputy. Hugh David Jones of London, an original member of J. Lloyd Williams's *Canorion* in Bangor and a folk-music researcher, offered testimonials from Reichel himself, and the interesting experience of having trained 75,000 American troops in 'gas defence' (potentially useful, perhaps, in dealing with Walford's eloquence). W. J. Phillips of Kidwelly had studied music under Mme Barbier; and W. T. Price masqueraded otherwise as 'Orpheus', the well-informed music critic of the *Western Mail*. A Welsh-speaking American, Dr T. D. Edwards (his doctorate was 'honorary') probably disqualified himself through his former involvement in Grand Opera across the Atlantic.

The post went to a Welsh-speaking north Walian of Scots descent, J. Charles MacLean, FRCO, aged forty-three, then music master at Aberystwyth County School and organist of Tabernacle Chapel, a recitalist of some renown throughout Wales, an oboist, and sometime Secretary of the Harlech Festival. Walford chose well, as he was ultimately to do in all his key Council appointments. MacLean, later to become father-in-law of Leslie Tusler, was a Secretary of great energy and loyalty and, after a career in Walford's shadow during the 1920s and 1930s, succeeded to the Directorship in 1941. The burden of administrative work in the new post, however, meant that his days as a performer and conductor were virtually over.[36] The admiration which 'The Doctor' engendered is probably represented by the fact that even W. M. Williams's 'failure' in the matter of the Secretaryship seems only to have drawn him closer to Walford, in interest, collaboration and mutual respect.

Quite soon after Walford's coming in 1918, Reichel, Hadow and Thomas Jones had begun to press upon him the urgent need to establish an out-station of the Council at Bangor University College, with a new post of Director of Music there. The natural candidate would seem to have been David Vaughan Thomas, but he even withdrew at a very early stage from his seat on the the Council of Music, apparently viewing Walford's executive manner as an affront which he could not publicly overlook. Walford, perhaps confident of Vaughan Thomas's intransigence, wrote to him in April, 1920, pleading that he remain, but the Swansea man remained adamant.[37] Vaughan Thomas became a reluctant commander of another army, and his personal and professional frustration grew with almost every year which followed Walford's advent.

Thomas Jones advised choosing a Welsh-speaker for the Bangor post, if only as a gesture towards national pride; but for some time Walford clung to the idea of securing 'the best' man. In April, 1919, he wrote to T. J., 'Look at this! It is the best way if they can secure him. What a boom (sic) we may have!'.[38] Enclosed was a letter from Mary Davies in Bangor suggesting the possibility of persuading Ralph Vaughan Williams to take the post. In a later, undated letter Walford was plumping for Herbert Howells; but he must have known already that Howells's doctor had ordered him to rest for a year. Through all this he appeared euphorically optimistic about getting exactly the man he wanted for Bangor; and, more than that, his definition of 'Welshman' was exceedingly elastic, since Howells had been born in Lydney and was very much a 'Three Choirs' man, while Vaughan Williams merely claimed a Welsh surname and a barrister-grandparent born at Johnstown, Carmarthenshire, in the early nineteenth century.

In the end an inspired compromise was reached. E. T. Davies, a Dowlais man possessed of genuine lyric compositional gifts, and a widely respected conductor, teacher and adjudicator, had perhaps most lately drawn himself to the notice of people who mattered by organizing in 1920 a chamber-music concert by the London String Quartet in Merthyr Tydfil – the *Musical Times* had congratulated the town on possessing 'an energetic enthusiast...in the cause of instrumental music'.[39] Earlier in the year Walford had written to T. J.,

> ...I saw ETD for two hours and was well impressed. He is full of zeal still; and seemed to take to the notion of a complete uprootal of himself. Of course, my talk was non-commital. But I cannot think that we could possibly do better than offer him the new post at £600...[40]

In November the *Musical Times* noted E. T. Davies's appointment as director at Bangor.[41] More than any other Welsh musician of this transitional period, he bridged the gap between old and new. His early schooling had been in sol-fa; achieving honours in the Associated Board examinations, he was advised by Stanford to take up music as a career, but had to be content with work as an office-clerk until 1898, when he was nineteen. He accompanied Harry Evans's great choirs, and travelled in America with another choral party for eight months. He became FRCO; conducted 'G and S' and many orchestral performances in Dowlais. Gradually building up a career as a superb teacher, E. T. Davies achieved his early apotheosis as adjudicator at the Corwen Eisteddfod. The first historian of Merthyr musical life wrote in 1921, 'He has opened upwards of a *hundred* new organs in Wales alone'.[42] At the London Eisteddfod of 1909 he was awarded by Stanford the prize for a setting of Elfed's 'Ynys y Plant'. Walford must have used all his juiciest wiles to entice him to north Wales; but after he had been there only a year, David Morgans wrote, E. T. Davies had already established regular chamber-music concerts and a college orchestra. In the next twenty years, under his guidance, Bangor became musically the liveliest of the three university colleges. The great unfairness must be that E. T. Davies was never offered a Chair.

The most strident criticism had been made of Welsh instrumental playing, or the relative lack of it; Walford surely needed to make an appointment under the Council in that field. Complaints of the poverty of orchestral resources had arisen since the 1880s, but, as with other facets of Welsh weakness, there had recently been growing evidence of improvement. Indeed, even as far back as the 1883 Cardiff Eisteddfod, Sir George Macfarren, awarding a prize of £25 in the orchestral competition, had to admit, 'It is one of the things of which this part of the country is to be congratulated, that, although not quite complete, there is so large a proportion of orchestral completeness brought before us today, and such merit in the performance...' But it must also be said that the winning band had come from Cardiff, and the second from Merthyr: in other words, the pit-orchestra and brass-band experience in both places hardly made them representative of the whole condition of Welsh orchestral effort.[43] In a remarkable article, devoted primarily to the Côr Mawr phenomenon in Aberdare, Gwilym T. Ambrose has presented a detailed picture of the diversity of musical activity in that place during the second half of the nineteenth century.[44]

Aberdare and Mountain Ash, at the centre of the district from which Y Côr Mawr emerged in the 1870s, were, it might have been thought, almost exclusively choral communities of the Cynon Valley. Yet Ambrose has shown that Caradog himself was the local provider of 'bread-and-butter' string-band entertainment, 'welcomed warmly in churches and inns.' Combined with the local brass bands – there were five in 1873 – those string players could offer accompaniments for the extraordinary performances of Mozart's *Twelfth Mass*, and of similar settings by Weber and Haydn, at the local *Catholic* church around 1870. Such players may even have attended concerts in Aberdare like that given by Pezzi, principal cellist at La Scala, Milan, when he played a Beethoven sonata; or have been members of the Aberdare Musical Association which in 1861 gave a performance of the Beethoven sextet, with local artists playing piano, violin, viola, cornet, cello and flute. They might even have participated in the exercises in Gregorian chant which the Revd Evan Lewis introduced into St Elvan's church, along with Tallis Responses, in the 1860s. In the chapels, which seem to have proliferated by a process akin to cell-division, the gallery orchestra was often the most attracting feature: good instrumental players were poached by rival sects, as Gethin Jones, an Aberdare amateur musician of the 1920s still remembers.[45] The brass bands of Wales – tracing their genealogy to the Crystal Palace prize-winning Cyfarthfa Band of 1852 – continuously provided accompaniments for local celebrations: for the triumphant return of the Caradog choir in 1873; as in north Wales, much later, for the home-coming of young W. J. Gruffydd to Bethel in Caernarfonshire after his Crowning at the 1911 London Eisteddfod.[46] The artistic ferment of a community like Aberdare, with neighbouring Mountain Ash, was something which Walford Davies could not have anticipated when formulating his altruistic plans.

Elgar's amanuensis in writing the Violin Concerto was W. H. Reed, now chiefly remembered as a notable leader of the London Symphony Orchestra. Reed's first encounter with Aberdare music-making occurred at the Ammanford Eisteddfod of 1922. There, as adjudicator, he heard a remarkable series of performances in the orchestral band competition, of a quality which can have had little to do with Walford's very recent injunction about the need to improve Welsh instrumental performance, and may have had more to do with the inheritance of musical experience in the Cynon Valley. Gethin Jones of Aberdare still remembers cavorting as a schoolboy around the Ammanford field after the competition, with other string players from Aberdare, and being congratulated informally by Reed on their performance.[48]

The writer and dramatist J. O. Francis said that Ammanford in 1922 was 'the Mecca of the Welsh', despite recent attacks upon the Eisteddfod's provenance to the sound of 'trumpets of the higher criticism...by the heretics of Bangor'.[49] The chief adjudicator at Ammanford was Sir Hugh Allen, then Professor of Music at Oxford, reforming Principal of the Royal College of Music, and director of a revolutionary Oxford Music Festival in 1922 which had embraced folk-song, dance, symphonic concerts and ballet. At Ammanford he had to judge an orchestral competition in which there were thirteen competitors. Six became finalists. His remarks 'moved the audience deeply.' He began,

> I said yesterday that you ought to have a Welsh Symphony Orchestra. You have already got it (cheers). If you put two of the orchestras you have heard together, you would have as fine a band as anybody could wish to hear (applause).

Allen said that he had come to Ammanford assuming that Welsh orchestral music-making was poor. 'It is humbug.' He continued – as if he wished to become Prince of Wales –

> ...you have got in generous terms what we in England would very often
> give great deal to have... I do not think that as regards wind players I
> have heard anything better.

Those wind players, in all probability, had come out of the brass-band
tradition in Welsh industrial communities, where bandsmanship was
ambivalently placed at the service of economic 'masters', while also at
other moments celebrating the achievements of popular heroes. So
convinced was Allen of the general level of accomplishment that he
persuaded the other adjudicators to award a second prize of £25. He
thought the players they had heard would have an effect, not only in
Wales, 'but in the whole of the British Isles'.[50] His co-judges were
E. T. Davies, who considered this a 'red-letter day in the history of the
National Eisteddfod', and W. H. Reed, who said the standard had
been 'beyond anything he had ever imagined.' Second prize went to
Herbert Ware's Cardiff Orchestra; third to the Mid-Rhondda Orchestral Society; the Aberdare Philharmonic Society came fourth.

The first prize was awarded to the Aberpennar Orchestra (Mountain
Ash). In its conductor, J. Bumford Griffiths, a local barber and self-
taught musician, Walford discovered another of his essential co-
helpers. In later days the Director of Music was to claim that he went
to Mountain Ash for a haircut and found a musical genius wielding the
scissors. Partly at Walford's own expense, and with the assistance of
the Davies sisters, Bumford was spirited away to Aberystwyth for
formal musical study. In 1927, aged thirty-five, he was appointed
Assistant Musical Organizer for Wales, with a salary guaranteed by
Miss Gwendoline Davies. His subsequent influence on the growth of
music in schools, and on the childrens' festival movement throughout
the Principality, was immense.[51]

For the time being Bumford completed the skeleton staff at headquarters. There were, of course, others in the field, based at the three
colleges, whose work was a continuously important and indispensable
part of Walford's campaign. His strategy in relation to those who were
to help him had been touched upon in his inaugural lecture:

> ...Almost all who listen tonight can help. There are three kinds of
> helpers in this room: 1. Those who know what can be done. They are
> potential leaders. 2. Those who will do what is to be done when told.
> They are potential workers awaiting a lead. 3. Those who will welcome
> new efforts even at the cost of some of their personal comfort. They are
> appreciators, essential to the bargain. And then these classes of music-

The Aberpennar Orchestra (Mountain Ash), winners of the National Eisteddfod, 1922 (by permission of Cynon Valley Public Libraries)

lovers are not in water-tight compartments. An appreciator can, sometimes, become a worker, and occasionally a worker can help to lead with brilliant suggestions...[52]

That statement communicates the flavour of Walford as inspirer; but it was also an accurate declaration of intent. Among his essential workers in the colleges were the instrumentalists in the trios – violinists, viola-players, cellists and pianists. And those workers were craftsmen and craftswomen of remarkable skill. Professor Ian Parrott has pronounced elegantly on the wide range of their accomplishments deployed on Walford's behalf in the years between the Wars: Charles Clements, extraordinary organist and pianist, who refused to leave Aberystwyth for what would surely have become a much more celebrated public career; Kenneth Harding, viola-player, remembered now mainly as a composer; his brother Ronald, an outstanding cellist who had been interned in Germany during the War; the violinists Beatrice Langley, Evelyn Cooke and Esme Silver; the singers Tom Pickering, a tenor who also taught adult appreciation classes, and W. R. Allen, a bass who doubled as choir-trainer and conductor in mid Wales. At Bangor and Cardiff there were similar, though smaller, groups under E. T. Davies and David Evans, who likewise went on musical missions taking the gospel of chamber music to curious thousands in out-of-the-way places. It was through the work of these people that the lecture-recital became a relatively well known feature of Welsh cultural life at all levels after 1919.

All these men and women worked unremittingly for the achievement of Walford's ends. Their professional lives had to be almost as hectic as his: instrumental and vocal teaching in university term-time, combined with railway journeys to often remote places where they usually played two concerts in one day. But their loyalty to the Director was never in question; and he probably needed their commitment and adoration, for, as has been suggested already, from the moment he stepped into Wales Walford was under attack.

Up to the Great War the old *Y Cerddor* had stimulated new thinking about Welsh music. Under the young W. S. Gwynn Williams it was re-launched in 1920 under the title *Y Cerddor Newydd* as the flagship of musical nationalism. That was its avowed aim: to promote and emphasize Welshness in music.

W. S. Gwynn Williams set out the new journal's prevailing attitude in his first editorial:

We firmly believe that if Wales is to contribute something through music to the civilised world, that something must be something Welsh said in a Welsh way... We must never forget that Welsh music, to be of any intrinsic value, must be definitely nationalistic in character, and not merely a copy of some foreign school, however wonderful that school may be.[53]

For him, and for similar adherents, Welsh music was inextricably part of 'our national culture'.

In almost every subsequent issue of *Y Cerddor Newydd* Walford was the obvious or disguised butt of stinging comment. In the eyes of the 'nationalists' he was Teutonism in music personified; and this was a quite handy personification for his critics to use in the years immediately after the Great War. Williams, in a later editorial, asked, for instance, why, if a Welshman aspiring to write did not have to learn the German language, did a Welsh musician, wishing to learn 'the most intimate language of all, the language of sound', have to become acquainted with 'German Classical Music'?[54] A month later another hobby-horse emerged from the stable:

The New 'Stunt' – We are hearing a tremendous amount nowadays about the great need in Wales for courses in 'musical appreciation'. One might really think that 'musical appreciation' was quite a new thing for the Welsh! Anyway, progressive London directors, we are told, are falling over one another in the efforts to provide musical missionaries for the Welsh 'Stations'. English publishing houses are being asked, we understand, to supply the necessary Teutonic texts. We have even heard it suggested that certain firms of Gramophone makers are being induced to enter into contracts for the sale of some hundreds of instruments for 'educational purposes' with specially selected non-Cymric records.

The next 'stunt', thought Williams, might be that English pianola-makers were asked to supply 'a large number of Welsh harps with handles... Never was there such a time of Welsh musical development!' He ended with the mordant point that Wales should not be made English simply for the purpose of supporting English commercial enterprises by buying their products. As a Welsh music-publisher himself (and publisher of his own music), he was grinding a favourite barrel-organ.[55]

Y Cerddor Newydd contained weightier and less waspish comments than these in its more extended pieces and quickly became the platform for the expression of positive ideas about the possible future of

Welsh music. Some of its early issues coincided neatly with preparations for the discussion of that topic at the Ammanford Eisteddfod of
1922. The Cymmrodorion Society chose as the subject for its Wednesday meeting at the YMCA in Eisteddfod week 'Musical and Literary
Criticism in Wales'. Sir John Morris-Jones presided, and a number of
prominent English music critics were present. In his leading paper
David Vaughan Thomas chose to attack English commentators on
Welsh music. Their remarks, he said, were often determined by
'superficial cleverness' and 'impudent smartness'. Englishmen were
notorious for mocking the noble language and literature of Welsh-
speaking Wales; but 'the Cockney and provincial lingual atrocities' of
visitors to Snowdonia also provoked 'intense amusement and often
corrosive satire' among the Welsh. His chief conclusion was that the
most suitable key for unlocking Welsh musical potential was a sound
knowledge and appreciation of the characteristics and quality of
Welsh poetry, coupled with 'a wide outlook' in the art of music. He
held the view that the Eisteddfod was primarily a literary festival, and
that it should be organized 'on purely Welsh lines, where every item
sung and every speech and adjudication would be delivered in
Welsh...'[56]

A gentle rejoinder was offered by Samuel Langford. He felt that
English critics were mainly sympathetic. Wales, particularly in its
smaller, isolated communities, did need something like the local
institutions of education which had encouraged the growth of musical
accomplishment throughout Germany in the previous century. Parts of
provincial England suffered equally in that respect. Langford's was
followed by the contribution of an extraordinary figure whose
sometimes witty and often scurrilous comments on Walford Davies's
Welsh mission were frequently published in the *Western Mail*, *Y
Cerddor Newydd*, and wherever else, as a journeyman writer, he could
find space.

Leigh Henry was a rogue. The son of a celebrated Liverpool-Welsh
singer, teacher and composer, John Henry, he had travelled in Italy
and Germany where he had been incarcerated as an alien for the
duration of the War. His wildness as a critic was tempered only by his
real appreciation of contemporary music of all kinds; but even this gift
was flawed by emotional and subjective fads. An aspiring, though
never successful, composer himself, he had become an uncritical worshipper of David Vaughan Thomas's music and artistic principles ever
since hearing a performance of 'The Bard' at a Liverpool concert in

1911.[57] The 1920s were his hey-day, when he gulped in the heady air of nascent Nationalism which had begun to permeate Welsh literary and musical life. His brand of nationalistic fervour was to become even more extreme, eventually tipping over into Fascism in the 1930s, when he reputedly corresponded with Ezra Pound. For the time being, however, he was content to ride into battle against English musical Teutons on the gentlemanly coat-tails of David Vaughan Thomas.

At Ammanford Leigh Henry questioned Langford's and Walford's confidence in 'musical organisation' which, he thought, if carried to a highly finished point, lost its spirituality and became 'as sterile as German music is today.' English music itself was only just beginning to emerge from a German servitude, and Welshmen ought to remind themselves that the greatest period of British musical accomplishment had been when Welsh Tudor monarchs were on the English throne. The Welsh ought to ignore foreign interlopers: like the Russians, the Welsh 'would become more international by being more national'.[58] Henry had earlier used Bartók as a talisman: just as that young composer was, with Kodaly, rescuing their native music from the grip of Austrian imperialism, so the youth of Wales should take advantage of the defeat of Germany to escape 'the Teutonic dominion of the Victorian era' and resist 'the misguided alien efforts for our musical regeneration'.[59] The speakers at Ammanford were surrounded by all the trappings of Henry's hated Teutonism, in the form of a chorus from the *St John Passion* as set-piece, and a complete B-minor Mass at an evening concert. German influence was, however, counteracted by means of large-scale performances of Cyril Jenkins's *Freedom*, *Magic Cauldron* and *Two Welsh Landscapes*.

Walford's continuing attempt at musical reformation caused fewer tremors at Ammanford than another set of theses. The 'heretics of Bangor', led by W. J. Gruffydd, had recently attacked the ghost of Iolo Morganwg (the modern Eisteddfod's creator), denouncing all his works as forgeries. The trumpet of this higher criticism, far from causing the pavilion walls to collapse, only served to inspire positive attempts to preserve a beloved institution in peril. The Gorsedd subsequently took several measures to defend its standing, in particular constituting a new music committee of the Eisteddfod, *Y Bwrdd Cerdd*, at Mold in 1923, which, as Leigh Henry gleefully imagined, would deal once and for all with 'alien influences and propaganda' and especially with 'the Germanized ideal of Aberystwyth'. Mold also witnessed the inauguration of the Society of Welsh Musicians, which was one in the eye for those who claimed that 'the small egotism' of the Welsh hindered their acting in a united way. The Welsh Nationalist composers were not chauvinists; but, even if they were, Henry claimed, 'first-hand Chauvinism is surely more natural and healthy than second-hand Chauvinism'.[60]

Mold marked a watershed in Walford's campaign. After the experience of the B-minor Mass at Ammanford, in 1923 the climax of the Eisteddfod was to be a performance of the *St Matthew Passion*, with a primed audience joining in the chorales. This was the public epitome of Walford's educational policy, demonstrated at the heart of patriotic pride. The occasion was a débâcle of considerable proportions. Leigh Henry in his report mentioned only the performance's 'low level of mediocrity.' Perhaps, for once, he was ashamed. Colles, however, was a pained observer of what happened.[61] The length and solemnity of the event seem to have caused a spasm of revulsion in an audience many of whose members must have wished for greater excitement. In response to ebullitions of dissatisfaction and frustration during the performance, Walford made an appeal to his listeners, but was met with a spirited rendering of the Welsh national anthem from the rear of the pavilion in the midst of the *Passion*. Such a crude antiphonal effect had not been part of his plan, and had surely not been prepared by the Society of Musicians as an act of musical disruption.

In any case it was the last flourishing of the anti-Walford movement on a grand scale. Pecking and pouting were to continue; but by 1923 the main lines of his business in Wales were firmly set. For the remainder of his time at the National Council the work of evangelizing and teaching – over the radio as well as face to face – playing and organizing continued unhindered. Even when confronted by increasing financial difficulties and the onset of his own ill-health, Walford's geniality and enthusiasm never cracked.

CHAPTER SEVEN

The Achievement

Walford Davies did not languish under criticism. He too had his agents
and agencies of support. Yet some of his friends spoke on his behalf
so pungently that they reinforced the case of critics who were urging
that he would destroy more effectively than he could create. It was said
that, early in his Welsh career, he was greeted with the remark, 'If you
can conquer our conceit, Doctor, you will do a lot.' His main enemy
was undoubtedly Welsh pride, allied to his own boundless confidence.

Thomas Jones of *Welsh Outlook* – 'its founder, its first Editor and
still its counsellor'[1] – had created the journal in 1914 as a Liberal-
Socialist publication of comment and inspiration for Wales in a new
age. In 1921 'GNP' contributed an article entitled 'The Renascence of
Music in Wales' which must have caused antagonism even among the
most sensible of the 'Nationalists'. He identified as the main cause of
stagnation in Welsh music 'our insular conceit', recalling that Cyril
Jenkins had recently observed that there were more composers to the
square mile in Wales than there had been orators in ancient Athens.
The sum total of accomplishment, however, was 'a mass of froth.'

> The spectacle of powerful streams of unharnessed energy offends the
> sight of the utilitarian, unemployed processions grieve the economist,
> but the greatest form of waste in the universe is genius undeveloped.
> Music is the birthright of the Welshman; his sure sense of intonation is
> sufficient to stamp him unique among the races of Western Europe.
> Desolate Finland can rear occasional giants, whilst Wales abounds in
> myriads of mediocrities.

The National Council of Music, claimed 'GNP', was 'nobly en-
deavouring to create and refine taste in music'.[2] Such praise probably
did considerable damage to appreciation of Walford's work in its early
stages.

From 1918 onwards *Welsh Outlook* consistently acknowledged the
need for the functions of the National Council, in its editorial
comment and commissioned articles. Other opinions had already been
permitted an airing, such as Cyril Jenkins in 1916 on 'Recent Music'

('Wales is isolated from the rest of the world...because she is geographically divided from the largest towns of England, and because she suffers from the lack of that particular kind of social life which demands both music and drama as a necessary part of everyday existence');[3] David Vaughan Thomas, on 'Welsh Music and Modern Tendencies', offered a moderate review. Unlike the more rabid 'anti-Teutons', Vaughan Thomas argued for close study of the achievements of the past – which had been his own course during 'years spent at Oxford' – as well as of 'Scriabine's Poèmes Op 69', Wagner, and Debussy's 'Il pleure dans mon coeur'.[4] He concluded, 'Our young Welsh composers are to be encouraged to make new discoveries, but in the end, the final discovery is that of the eternal amid the changing, the self amid the "non-self", the one amid the many.' That was language not far removed in tone and supplication from Walford's mode of speech.

Walford Davies himself published a series of articles in the journal under the general title, 'The Musical Outlook' in 1925–6. The first of these, devoted to 'Local Music-Making', began with evidence of demand in the form of a letter from 'a humble precentor in a crowded part of South Wales':

> Some of us have been thinking for a long time past as to some means of forming a local musicians' society where we could meet, discuss musical matters, and give musical extracts of ancient and also modern music (by a small party) of selections which are for the most part unsung and unknown, yet treasures... This may be a dream, sir, but do you think such a movement practical?

Of course he did. And by 1925 it had been made even more feasible by the advent of Walford's two great instruments in alliance – Gramophone and Radio. He significantly took as his analogies for this kind of dissemination Baden-Powell's Scouts and the Competitive Festival Movement, the latter begun by Mary Wakefield in Westmorland and patronised by Elgar among others.[5]

Walford devoted his second article to 'The Eisteddfod'. He appreciated the spiritual nature of the festival, and the three functions of its competitions: as concert, as examination, and as general music lesson. But he was critical of the administrative disorder of the Eisteddfod's choral competitions, and thought that the public missed the point of competition as an educational force. What he wanted – enshrined in his classic statement – was to hear choirs singing together and 'pacing each other on the high-road to choral perfection'.[6] Perhaps he was unleashing an excess of optimism when he hoped that, 'however much men love a friendly fight of choirs, a battle of giants, they love still more the fine way they are treading...along the paths of beauty.'

He dealt with the nub of his task in Wales in three articles on 'Music in Training Colleges and Schools'.[7] The educational system, he thought, was caught in a vicious circle, a musical deadlock: training-college entrants were musically unskilled before starting their brief course, and the quality of school music-teaching would therefore improve only as a result of better musical training in schools. He praised the pioneering work in general musical education which he had witnessed at Caerleon Training College, under Mr Lewis, the music specialist, though it had been mainly on the choral side.

His chief lever of encouragement, in relation to school and college work, was the evidence of effort and achievement by inspiring individual teachers and tutors. He instanced the work already undertaken by 'that heroic lady', Beatrice Langley, in the Aberystwyth and Montgomery districts, which, with proper support from LEAs, could be emulated throughout Wales. She had begun with violin classes in Aberystwyth council schools in 1922, helped by Hubert Davies, one of the college instrumentalists; the experiment was extended to Machynlleth, Berriew, Llanfyllin and Caersws. By 1924 a number of school orchestras had been established;[8] at Aberystwyth the Concert Orchestra numbered eighty children between the ages of eight and sixteen, including two clarinets, two cornets and timpani. At another level George Senogles of Menai Bridge Council School wrote describing a violin class he had started, also in 1922, for his own pupils and some from Beaumaris Grammar School, about twenty of them altogether, including flute, oboe and clarinet. Such instances were as yet, perhaps, exceptions; but while they could not be instantly imitated in many of the schools, almost all children were capable of learning to sing and, by means of melody-building exercises, to 'make orderly thoughts audible.' In Scotland, he noted, the Education Authorities in 1924 had made music one of three obligatory subjects in the secondary-school curriculum. He might have added that Scottish music teachers had lately formed their own Association for the discussion of educational principles and methods.[9]

Surveying the Welsh educational scene at a time when the financial bedrock of schooling was crumbling, however, Walford Davies was forced to end on a minor cadence. He reported that the principal of a training college, a musical man, had recently felt obliged to abandon his aim of promoting the musical training of his students because he could not justify 'the general usefulness of music' above the claims of art and handcraft. The time was not propitious for the kind of effort Walford was seeking to promote. The development of Welsh musical education which he was encouraging between 1919 and 1941, in an economic ice age, therefore seems all the more remarkable.

The initiatives taken after 1919 were largely personal and unilateral, the work of dynamic, enlightened enthusiasts. Walford was the chief agent, drawing to himself the energy of others and transforming their efforts into messages of hope delivered to a vast number of individuals. But his activity as receiver and transmitter had to be sustained by material support in a bleak financial climate. Without the philanthropic sympathy of the Davies sisters, the National Council would not have been created in the first place; without their continuing help – supplemented as time went by with aid from public and charitable bodies – it would have withered and disappeared, perhaps even before the end of the 1920s. In the 1990s, when at its very best the funding of higher education errs on the side of parsimony, it is necessary to remember how financially constrained the University of Wales was in the inter-War years. Even in the wake of the Davieses' generosity, and in the context of a system of higher education which had existed for only twenty-five years, the National Council of Music was directly answerable to the Universty of Wales for all it did; and there were Welshmen who could, with some justification, point to contemporary economic and social problems which were more immediately pressing than the need for training in musical sensibility among a people who, crudely, already 'sang' so well. It could be argued that only the power of Walford's personality kept the money flowing and the Welsh mission alive through hard times; but the National Council was more than a one-man band: it was a public organism which had to meet standards of financial and administrative accountability.

By 1921 two distinct funds were being administered by the Council: that provided by the University, the 'Director's Music Fund', which included private gifts for use at his discretion; and the fees earned for services given by the Council to other bodies. Originally the Directorship was completely financed by the Davies Endowment Fund; but as time went on the University made up the difference between the Endowment income and the Director's salary. The University Council determined that the University's grant should be used to cover general administrative costs and the payment of musical staff.[10] In its Report for 1922 the Council noted that they had just appointed a specific Finance Committee and an Accounts Sub-Committee to examine claims and authorize payments.[11]

In the same year, therefore, the Council prepared Estimates of Expenditure for 1922–3, emphasizing that they 'have never been unmindful of the financial position and economic pressure'. There were two main headings under 'Administration' in the Report. The Staff and Establishment charges included Walford's part-time (£500) and MacLean's full-time (£462. 10s.) salaries, with £350 for clerical assistance. The estimate of travelling expenses came to £315. The total of administrative costs – £1,772. 10s. – was covered by the University grant. The Council's publications – a *College Song Book* and the *Choral Festival Book* of 1923 – were estimated at £250, and this cost was borne by the publishers, Oxford University Press. The income expected from the lecture-recitals and concerts provided by the Council for schools and other educational groups was £800. The University grant to the extent of £212 would cover the concerts and recitals given in the constituent colleges and also 'Aids to Students' for the colleges and summer schools.[12] Walford's income probably seemed excessive, particularly to those who envied his holding at least three posts in Wales and London simultaneously. But alongside that legitimate response to his annually published salary should be set a fact which was less widely known or recognized: the Director frequently dipped into his own pocket to pay the fees and expenses of the less financially fortunate students who showed promise.[13] When forced by ill health to appoint a temporary Deputy to undertake his lecture-recital commitments, he likewise paid from his own, rather than the Council's, resources.[14] To that extent, and despite MacLean's meticulous management of day-to-day details first at Aberystwyth and later from the office at the University Registry in Cardiff, the Council was the fiefdom of an enlightened despot, rather than simply an adjunct of University administration.

The idiosyncratic character of the Council's work is explained partly by the powerful charm which Walford exerted over his Executive Committee, but mainly by the nature of its genesis in a private bequest and the gentle bonds which gradually came to bind the Director's mission to the temple of musical culture at Gregynog. The workaday office, with its clerical staff under MacLean's supervision, and the annual meetings and more frequent idyllic rehearsals and concerts at Gregynog were the two poles of the Council's endeavours. Just as the Temple church was Walford's busy sanctuary on his hectic English travels, so Gregynog was a Welsh haven into which he could breathlessly retire, full of enthusiasm and expecting refreshment and tranquility. Throughout the 1920s and 1930s the Davies household, a few miles from Newtown in Montgomeryshire, hummed with the musical and social energy which he generated.

The story of music-making at Gregynog has been variously told in detail by Ian Parrott and John Hywel.[15] From 1921 onwards the annual general meetings of the Council were held in the house, accompanied by a service of dedication complete with orchestral and vocal music. Other important meetings were frequently held there: of the Welsh School of Social Service and of David Davies's League of Nations Union (Welsh Council); but the atmosphere was invariably musical. Music, usually provided by Walford and his friends, created the mood for serious contemplation which was a constant feature of Gregynog in the locust years of Wales between the Wars. There were also moments in which individual lives of public service were celebrated. At the Gregynog Conference of the National Council of Music in July, 1922, Hadow gave one address on the aims of the Council, and another on 'The Ideals and Work of Sir Henry Jones' who had had 'much influence in the formation of the Council'.[16] In 1923, with a choir of delegates from the Montgomeryshire Festival Chorus, an orchestra drawn from Bangor, Cardiff and Aberystwyth colleges, and Charles Clements at the Rothwell organ, in a music room which had until recently accommodated billiards players, Walford conducted a full performance of the *St Matthew Passion*.

In 1923, rather ostentatiously, Walford brought his Temple Choir to Wales. From their Gregynog base they sallied forth in an open charabanc to show the Welsh what could be achieved if only they would listen as well as sing. Walford wrote to his beloved T. J.,

> On Wednesday I go to Gregynog for a fortnight. On the 18th we begin to have a little Mission throughout Wales on *Worship-Music* in Village Churches (and I hope on Village Greens) with 10 Temple boys. It is a venture which will need to be tactfully made, but it seems greatly welcomed so far...[17]

This 'treble' tour probably had a double purpose: in 1921 the newly disestablished Church in Wales had commissioned from the Council of Music a series of service books, published by Novello, which included bilingual settings of psalms, hymns, responses and Magnificat and Nunc Dimittis. These were surely used during the charabanc's Welsh progress.

The involvement of the Davies family in music-making produced an almost inevitable result: the formation of a Gregynog Choir, largely drawn from among local villagers and estate employees. Schooled by W. R. Allen from Aberystwyth, and inspired by Walford, this forty-voice choir gave performances of 'difficult' contemporary works like Vaughan Williams's Mass in G minor and Holst's *Ode to a Grecian Urn*, and even more remarkably, received the plaudits of the composers. The choir epitomized what Walford was striving to achieve throughout Wales. Thomas Jones wrote, 'Perhaps it was as a choir-trainer that Sir Walford was at his best. He made the simplest country singers rich with the wealth of the great composers, shared out amongst them by waving his magic wand'.[18] Singers of the standing of Elsie Suddaby, Keith Faulkner and Steuart Wilson came to sing the solos; the young Adrian Boult was a frequent co-conductor or deputy, and Thalben Ball came from London to play the organ.[19] A constant adornment of the household during the sisters' era was their colleague and helpmeet, Dora Herbert-Jones, whose fine singing voice had earlier impressed Mme Barbier. She was instrumental in drawing the attention of Gustav Holst to the treasures collected by the Welsh Folk-song Society, and was to remain a vital singer of Welsh songs until over seventy years of age.[20]

The nucleus of the Gregynog orchestra would have been the members of the college trios. Their customary performances were chamber music for students, but more significantly the Aberystwyth trio members were the disciples who accompanied Walford's musical sermons during his missionary peregrinations. In the first full year of its operation it was reported that the Aberystwyth trio had visited forty-two county schools and given twenty-nine additional public lecture-concerts 'in village institutes and elsewhere';[21] because of a financial deficit only ninety were given in 1921–2. In 1921 Cardiff and Bangor colleges adopted trios. In all three places the instrumentalists, employees of colleges and Council jointly, were engaged in their extra-mural work during the first part of each week, and in teaching students for the remainder of their time.

Orchestras

The main executive item in Walford's programme, indeed, a chief cause of concern among leading musical Welshmen since the 1880s, was the need to provide frequent opportunities for audiences all over the Principality to hear orchestral performances of good quality. Cyril Jenkins's necessary stopgap, in the form of infrequent importations of the LSO and the Queen's Hall Orchestra, was by the early 1920s deemed insufficient. In the three newly formed college chamber ensembles the Council had the nucleus of a national orchestra, thus foreshadowing Gerard Hoffnung's much later creation, 'The Augmented Allegri Quartet' (consisting of 120 players). With Walford's help, and conducted by T. Hopkin Evans, a 'National Orchestra' was inaugurated in south Wales for several concerts in 1920.[22] The *Musical Times* reported,

> ...the Welsh National Orchestra has not only come into being, but has been launched on its career. Its satisfactory performances give hope for its future. The financial question of the permanent support of the organisation is a matter still to be determined... In any case the National scheme should wield an inspiring influence in the formation of small orchestras in towns and villages...thus fostering the study of instrumental playing.[23]

The brevity of that 1920 experiment and of later initiatives only marginally justifies the recent statement that 'prior to 1928 and the creation of the NOW, there was no symphony orchestra in Wales'.[24] As J. Glynne Evans noted, there were private-enterprise orchestras in Cardiff, and at the north Wales summer resorts during their season. But the main continuous effort before 1928 was the result of the National Council's work. As suggested earlier, in his desire to establish the sweeping novelty of the Council's plans, Walford tended to play down what was already being achieved; this was certainly true of orchestral work, and the Council's subsequent achievements were surely founded on the blossoming local efforts of men like Bumford Griffiths in the Cynon Valley, and Arthur Angle and Herbert Ware in Cardiff. In 1922 the Council sponsored an experimental tour of north Wales by an *ad hoc* ensemble. This led, a year later, to the creation of the Welsh Symphony Orchestra which consisted of players resident in Wales, with occasional additions of outsiders when necessary.[25] Its membership took a favoured tripartite form: teachers; professionals –

that is, the trio players supported by instrumentalists from the theatres; and good amateurs. The Orchestra's personnel, grouped around a permanent core, would vary according to where it played. This new band performed, for instance, at the 1923 Aberystwyth Festival; at the 1924 Pontypool Eisteddfod; at Pwllheli in 1925, and regularly for the Harlech, Cardiganshire and Newtown Festivals.

The first 'full' performance by the WSO was at the Fifth Aberystwyth Festival in June, 1924. Adrian Boult conducted Quilter's *Children's Overture*, the 'Clock' Symphony and a Mozart Serenade, and later Holst's *Fugal Concerto*, Stanford's *Irish Rhapsody*, and Beethoven's Eighth Symphony. On the second day Henry Wood conducted Brahms's Violin Concerto and the Franck Symphony.[26] This was a flamboyantly ambitious beginning. Criticism quickly followed from expected quarters.

At the Pontypool National Eisteddfod later in the summer one of the ancillary sessions was the first annual meeting of the Society of Welsh Musicians, constituted at Mold a year earlier. David Vaughan Thomas was its President, and a guest on this occasion was Sir Richard Terry. The 1924 meeting was addressed by Leigh Henry who said, probably with Walford Davies in mind, that one of the new Society's aims was to save Welsh musicians from the influence of 'pettifoggers'. In particular he thought that it had been injudicious to use the strippling Welsh Symphony Orchestra at the current Eisteddfod. Writing later in the *Western Mail*, he reinforced that opinion:

> ...All thinking musical Wales desires to see a permanent representative national orchestra established and playing at the annual musical festival... Unfortunately, preliminary pronouncements have led public opinion elsewhere to expect something superlative, which, in justice to Welsh musical taste, cannot be allowed to stand unquestioned in view of actual results. To allow the impression to go forth that the orchestra fulfilled Welsh ideals would be to lay Welsh musical discrimination open to serious criticism. Hence, I think, at this stage the title is a misnomer...[27]

Such comments must have been very hurtful to those who were trying to add growing expertise to honest enthusiasm in the Welsh orchestral endeavour. It should be noted that, generally speaking, outside Manchester there were no *British* provincial orchestras to which the Welsh players might have looked for a satisfactory model. The leading English critic, Ernest Newman, on returning from a visit to the USA in 1925, said he had feared the splendid American orchestras would make the London bands sound poor: '...but I was agreeably disappointed. The LSO, I suppose, ranks as our premier orchestra; and I am glad to be able to record that at its concert last Monday it compared not unfavourably with the orchestras in some of the New York picture houses'.[28] Henry Wood was a strict orchestral taskmaster; and Boult was building up a similar, though more gentlemanly, reputation in Birmingham during the 1920s. In Wales, then, Walford Davies could at the very least be seen as bringing about improvement by regularly importing the skills of those two men into Wales for the sake of the WSO's development. What his critics chose to overlook was that, despite the *ad hoc* nature of the new band, the Principality had never possessed a reliable, continuous orchestra of any kind until 1923.

The fortunes of prospective orchestral players were being pulled in opposite directions in the 1920s. On one hand, the proliferation of Newman's picture palaces meant that in the larger silent cinemas there were opportunities to play in quite large ensembles the kinds of music which Carl Davis, for instance, has recently re-created or revived. But such prospects hardly affected musicians outside one or two big towns. Indeed, the rise of cinema tended to limit the chances of hearing live orchestral programmes. One commentator on post-War Welsh musical life was complaining, as early as 1920,

> ...it is becoming increasingly more difficult to secure accommodation suitable for holding concerts on anything like a grand scale... The 'film-fiend' is gradually annexing our halls...

The Albert Hall in Swansea, like the equally fine Park Hall in Cardiff, had recently been acquired for 'super-cinema' purposes.[29] Sunday-evening orchestral concerts in Cardiff in the inter-War years, by the Angle and Ware orchestras, were probably staffed by players some of whom during the week earned wages in local theatres and cinemas.

On the other hand, another medium of mass entertainment, which offered a new fillip to musical education and experience, was increasingly seen by professional musicians as a threat to their livelihoods and to the public habit of going to hear live performances. Moreover, the BBC was a monopoly corporation. It soon became the largest single employer of musicians. By 1935 thirty-five per cent of the Performing Right Society's revenue came from the BBC,[30] and by 1939 the Corporation employed 400 musicians of various kinds, exercising its patronage not simply in the interests of groups offering music of all popular types, but decidedly 'with the deliberate intention of moulding public taste'.[31]

As perhaps the most influential member of the BBC's Music Advisory Committee from its beginning in 1925, and as one who even more importantly gained John Reith's granite-like respect,[32] Walford Davies was in a position to play a leading part in shaping Corporation policy. In 1924 a 'Wireless Orchestra', a small corps of players which could be augmented on occasion, was formed under Percy Pitt. At notable moments in the 1920s, Strauss, Honegger and Bruno Walter came to conduct as many as 150 players at special concerts.[33] The first permanent radio orchestra in Europe started in Copenhagen in 1927.[34] This Danish experiment may have inspired Walford immediately to urge Reith to consider the need for a similar fully equipped permanent orchestra attached to the BBC in London. As Nicholas Kenyon has pointed out, it was not until 1930 that the BBC Symphony Orchestra was created under Adrian Boult, as a band which at first gave only broadcast, rather than publicly attended concerts. But Kenyon, in his comprehensive history of that orchestra, does not mention an interesting provincial anticipation by the BBC of its greater creation.

An essay by J. Glynne Evans[35] recalls that in 1927 the BBC formed a small instrumental ensemble in Cardiff.[36] In February, 1928, it was reported that a symphony orchestra was to be started in the Welsh capital, through the collaboration of the National Council of Music, Cardiff City Council and the BBC:

> The BBC undertakes to support the scheme financially. The Cardiff City Corporation provides the Assembly Rooms at the City Hall on two nights a week, with permission to charge admission at popular prices. These concerts will be given in three seasons – twelve weeks before and twelve weeks after Christmas, with six weeks in the early summer.[37]

Warwick Braithwaite was appointed conductor. There were also to be free lunchtime concerts for city workers in the awful acoustic conditions of the National Museum.

This remarkable experiment in broadcast public concert-giving flourished for a while, though reputedly the free concerts were far better attended than those in the evenings. Beecham, Elgar and Henry Wood came as guest conductors; and the orchestra's repertoire ranged from popular classics to Mahler's Fourth Symphony.[38] But there had been early criticism centring on the fact that very poor wireless reception in many parts of the Principality made the Orchestra a Cardiff, rather than a completely Welsh, possession. The running cost of £12,000 per annum – only £2,000 came from public subscriptions – proved finally too great for the BBC to bear in the straitened financial circumstances of the early 1930s. The orchestra was engaged for the Llanelli National Eisteddfod of 1930; but the Committee of the Bangor Eisteddfod for the following year reluctantly declined to employ it without a guarantee of its continued existence. The *Western Mail* praised the generosity of the BBC, but was otherwise mordantly critical:

> It must be admitted that economic conditions are not at this moment favourable to an exercise of popular generosity, though there seems to be no lack of funds where mass emtertainment in the form of sport is concerned. ...the Welsh National Orchestra is the only orchestra in the country to the funds of which the BBC contributes, apart from its own studio performers...[39]

The orchestra gave its last concert on 6 October 1931. It had been one in a remarkable sequence of efforts by Walford to enlist English support (albeit on this occasion through the agency of a Scottish Director-General) for his Welsh schemes.

Of course Welsh orchestral performance, even to contemporary professional standards, did not end with the demise of the BBC's intervention in Wales. Broadcast concerts, from London, Birmingham and Manchester, were heard frequently and must have systematically encouraged emulation among talented enthusiasts. And the desire to enjoy live performances of the classical repertoire was satisfied, in Cardiff at least, by the extraordinary Herbert Ware. From 1920 until the early 1950s Ware, Cornish by birth, but Welsh by adoption and inclination, did more than any other single figure outside the subsidized ambit of the National Council to promote good orchestral performance in Wales. As a teacher (though the name of his own early violin tutor in the Rhondda is unrecorded) he is reputed to have sent his pupils into every professional orchestra in the British Isles.[40] In 1920 his Cardiff Orchestra carried off the most prestigious prize at the Blackpool Competitive Festival. He adopted Walford's style of lecture-concerts, and in 1923 embarked on a complete cycle of the Beethoven Symphonies in Cardiff, a project which was to take three years for its completion. The lecturers who spoke before each of those concerts included Walford, E. T. Davies and W. H. Reed.[41] Among the soloists who came to perform with his players were Solomon, Myra Hess and the ever-generous Willy Reed. Ware's efforts were truly heroic. One of his colleagues, Ronald Jones, wrote of him in 1973, 'The bald fact is that his love of, and determination to bring, classical orchestral music to the people of Wales were bigger than his purse – which he emptied.' Ware's greatest efforts were made during the Great Depression, before the era of Arts Council grants.

The Council and the Schools

Ware also worked with younger musicians: one of his junior viola-players, who came from the Valleys to rehearse in Ware's Cardiff Junior Orchestra, was Alun Hoddinott. Forging links with the schools was an essential part of Walford's plan; and in this sphere he was supported by outstanding individuals. In May, 1920, the Welsh County Schools' Association held its annual meeting in Aberystwyth. In the chair was Miss M. A. Vivian of Newport High School, a formidable proponent of school music, and, on behalf of her Association, a member of the newly formed National Council. The presidential address was offered by an even more resonant personality whose work on the northern margin of Wales has been insufficiently recognized, except by his pupils. Arthur Lyon had been headmaster of Hawarden Grammar School since 1910. The subject of his 1920 address was 'Music in Its Relation to Education'.

Lyon, an Englishman, advised that, if music was to permeate Wales as a living force, it had to become rooted in the schools' curricula and in university studies. Such progress as had recently been made owed little to processes of formal education; and like Hadow he drew a clear distinction between music's appeal to the educated and the uneducated:

> To the uneducated it was entirely emotional, but an intellectual element was inseparable from music of a higher order, as in every great art, and its growth and development would proceed from education alone, and its connection with general intellectual growth.

Lyon wished all schools to lay the foundations of taste and apprecia-tion of the highest and best in music so that 'the majority of students' would arrive at understanding. As far as he knew, Beethoven's Ninth Symphony had never yet been heard in Wales: and the Welsh would never possess an orchestra and chorus to perform it, or an audience to appreciate it, without the proper nurturing of musical appreciation in schools.[42] He thought that the energetic initiative of the new Council was being received complacently. A letter from Walford to the conference was read in which he pleaded that heads of schools should offer all possible encouragement to any instrumentalists among their pupils, so that they might follow up the visits of the trios with simpler performances of their own. At Lyon's insistence the conference decided to urge the Council of Music to 'rush on' with the publication of the *School Hymn Book* so that it should be ready for the beginning of next term. Out of this and other contacts with Walford Davies came Lyon's close participation in the work of the Council, to the extent of his being commissioned to write its report, *Music in Secondary Schools*, published in 1922.

Lyon exemplified the kind of headmaster Walford must have longed to encounter much more frequently; but in the 1920s he was unique in Wales, perhaps even in Britain. HMI were profoundly impressed by the kind of institution he had created in Hawarden. In 1922 Lyon, a modern linguist, was using a gramophone in Form V to improve French accent and intonation, and had developed science attractively in Form VI, despite poor funding for laboratories. But HMI drew particular attention to music: the school possessed an orchestra of sixteen to eighteen players; periodical concerts were given; again, the gramophone was used as an instrument for developing musical appreciation. In summary,

> There is no doubt that, in this School, the utmost use is made of music as a factor in the education of the pupils... The general atmosphere of the School is of a most stimulating character. There is a wholesome social life and one especially satisfactory feature is the close connection between the old pupils and the School...[43]

A more complete inspection was made in 1929, Lyon's last year in office, by a team under the leadership of D. Vaughan Johnston. Earlier impressions were confirmed. In music the School's range of activities and standards of attainment were 'almost unique'. Most tellingly, musical accomplishment was linked to assessment of the corporate life:

> The social activities of the School are so vigorous and many-sided... The exceptionally distinguished and pioneer work done in Music, however, demands special recognition in this connection in view of the prominent place taken by Music as a vivifying and refining influence throughout the School.
>
> It is safe to say that in no school in the Kingdom had the standard of

musical performance reached a higher level than it has done in this School.

In recent years choir and orchestra had performed the B-minor Mass, *Gerontius*, the Brahms *German Requiem* and *Song of Destiny*, and Parry's *Blest Pair of Sirens*.

> It is sufficient to add that the community spirit so clearly shown in Music pervades the whole atmosphere of the School. ...a truly great School has been built up at Hawarden...special credit is due to the Headmaster (who) may indeed look back with pride and satisfaction that he has maintained high ideals undimmed...[44]

One acidic commentator on the barrenness of Welsh secondary schooling had written, not long before, that the few instances of encouragement given to music had been due to the enthusiasm of individual amateurs: 'Hawarden owes its excellent work in music to its *English* headmaster'.[45] It is interesting also that the prizes for choral sight-singing and for the glee party at the Barry Eisteddfod in 1920 were won by groups from another 'new' Welsh industrial town, Shotton, in Flintshire, within the catchment area of Lyon's formidable School.

Quite evidently Hawarden was untypical. Lyon's report for the National Council in 1922 provides sufficient evidence for that judgement. He began, 'The present position of Music in the secondary curriculum makes one doubt if there exists yet a wide outlook on the part of the authorities in the domain of secondary education.' That was true of Britain generally. Of Wales Lyon said,

> It seems almost incredible, yet it is true, that the majority of youths and maidens in Wales, who are going through a course of higher education, pass some of the most impressionable years of their lives without any, or with the very slightest association with the central art of the Eisteddfod, as far as their life in school and college is concerned... The Central Welsh Board has had a special conference on the subject...but the Board needs to enlist the youthful enthusiasm of the Council of Music to create the necessary quickening.

The time actually spent on music lessons in schools varied widely – from a whole afternoon a week, in one case, to nothing. Such lessons as did take place usually involved singing practice and sight-reading exercises. In twenty schools staff notation predominated; in fifty-seven both notations were used. 'Music cannot be said to have got beyond the elementary stage until the sol-fa system has been swallowed up in the Staff.' The teaching of simple harmony hardly occurred at all. Most school music was in fact confined to the lowest classes. All children should sing throughout all the 'impressionable and golden years of adolescence.' Lyon recommended suitable collections of music and books on appreciation, and use of the best gramophones and records, according to Sir Walford's suggested five-year course: 'Paderewski does not lose all his enchantment in a gramophone record, whatever he does as a Prime Minister'.[46]

Further evidence for Hawarden's uniqueness was offered by the Prime Minister of Welsh Music. In 1928 Walford, who always enjoyed a very positive relationship with the conservative secretariat of the Board of Education, was appointed an 'Occasional Inspector' of Music. He was thus able intermittently to gain firsthand knowledge of the condition of music in secondary schools. In this new role, guided by the experienced HMI Abel Jones, he examined musical provision at a school rather different from splendid Hawarden in March, 1928. The headmaster of Port Talbot County School described to him its musical activities as 'recreative and, to some extent, financial': much money had been raised by school concerts. A musical society had been formed in 1926, and the Cardiff Trio were invited to perform. It was proposed to buy 'a good wireless set', and to found an orchestra. The physics master, Mr Hooper, had written incidental music for a school production of *A Midsummer Night's Dream*; the mathematics master accompanied songs in daily assemblies. However, the only formal music on the curriculum consisted in the singing of hymns, conducted by the headmaster, and one class-lesson per week, but – perhaps a comment on the greater need for physical exercise – 'only if the weather is wet.' Walford found the pupils 'quickly responsive' when he took them through a hymn-tune, and also when they were 'listening to a short address with gramophone illustration.' He recommended that there should be carefully graded music lessons, 'similar to those in use, for example, at Ogmore Secondary School...enabling a ten per cent more musically minded children to rise to the musical matriculation standard', and with the more general aim of encouraging all pupils to read new tunes at sight.[47]

The official offer of an opportunity for revitalizing the whole school curriculum had been implied in the 1918 Education Act, inspired by Lloyd George and planned by H. A. L. Fisher. The Act, progressive in intent and a reflection of the widely felt need to reconstruct a society and economy severely damaged by war, required LEAs to prepare

long-term schemes which might include the initiation of nursery education and the improvement of schooling for senior pupils. The Welsh
Department of the Board of Education's Red Book of *Suggestions for
the Preparation of Schemes* under the Act might have taken its cue
from the recommendations of the Haldane Commission, for it proposed the development of subjects which 'have been neglected, though
Welsh children have an aptitude for them, such as Music, Art, and
Handicraft'; and under the heading 'Peculiar Needs of Wales', special
proposals for music were invited.[48] This was a distinct invitation for
the Council's involvement in the work of the schools. There was then
no specialist Music HMI in Wales, and the Council consequently
seemed to be the body most appropriate for undertaking the task of
determining the new place of musical studies in school curricula.

A sub-committee of the National Council, with Lyon playing a
prominent part, produced an eight-page document in 1921, *Memorandum on Music in Schools, both Primary and Secondary, being Suggestions for a Musical Policy and a sketch for a five-year's Course.* The
Council already had a general guide to a possible course in the form
of Arthur Somervell's contribution to the *Handbook of Suggestions* of
the Board of Education, published in 1904.[49] Anticipating later developments in the overall structure of eleven-plus schooling, this 1921
Committee volunteered a tripartite identification of types of pupils:
first, those with 'no special musical aptitude'; second, pupils who were
'specially apt to sing' and would form the core of a school choir; and
third, the 'outstandingly gifted' who played instruments in a school
orchestra or chamber-music party. But like the later Norwood Committee,[50] the Welsh sub-committee hoped that there would be fluid
movement upwards from one group of pupils to another.

In recommending the appointment of a specialist music teacher for
each secondary school, Lyon added the qualification that such a
teacher, by local arrangement, might be released for part of the time
to supervise musical work in neighbouring elementary schools. This
proposal appealed to Walford who had already described the 'vicious
circle' which bedevilled the production of well qualified music
teachers.[51] Other suggestions reflected the principles he had enunciated
in his Downing Street Cymmrodorion paper: ten minutes' daily choral
singing (preferably in the afternoon, 'when mental effort is hard, and
cheery doings are a God-send'); a weekly forty-minutes' school
concert; and a class lesson in music each week when 'the making,
reading, and writing of simple tunes would be taught to all.' Extra-

curricular activities might include school and house choir practices, instrumental and vocal lessons for the specially gifted, and ensemble work. The small edition of Somervell's *National Song Book*, with its 136 songs of the four nations, was recommended as a text, at least one strongly rhythmic tune being in each daily session. Scholars should as far as possible be used as conductors and accompanists. 'It is highly desirable that schools should write their own topical words to well-known tunes.' Such novelties could be lithographed, or copied out by the keenest pupils; a large enough school might even print its own version, perhaps as part of a school magazine. There should be in each school a music committee, including two pupils, which would draw up a programme of concerts and musical events for each term, including visits by one of the college trios. The weekly school concert had to be a focal point:

> The only indispensable conditions for this weekly concert are that it should be run entirely for the school, preponderantly by the school, and that it should be full of joyous effort and genuine *esprit de corps*.[52]

It is as well to remember that the elementary (primary) and secondary maintained sectors, before 1944, each constituted a separate administrative system: only a very small proportion of elementary-school pupils passed into the grammar schools. This helps to explain what appears to be a point of confusion in the Council's memorandum, which referred to 'Years I to V' in its outlined syllabus. A footnote admitted the probable need for modification:

> It may be necessary greatly to extend the time allotted in Primary Schools. Thus three years may be given to the First Year's Course, and the whole course ultimately re-adapted to suit pupils passing from Primary (Elementary) to Secondary Schools.

The formal adoption of a 'National Curriculum', in continuous detail for all maintained-sector pupils between five and sixteen, was an act of policy for which teachers would have to wait almost sixty years; though it must be said that much of Walford's 'Mother-Tongue' scheme of musical education had to wait an exactly similar length of time for its full, general implementation in State schools.

The five-year-long music syllabus which the Council proposed is represented in an Appendix (p. 183). It will probably now strike music teachers as dry and over-ambitious. Had it been carried into practice in the 1920s, however, music might still have become the most stimulating item in the school curriculum, though it is unlikely whether even Walford considered seriously that run-of-the-mill pupils in his first, and lowest, category, as fourteen-year-olds, would end their school-days by analysing the forms of Beethoven first movements, let alone constructing songs 'in one, two, and three parts without accompaniment.' The memorandum can be added to other voluminous contemporary evidence of that optimism which was activating many educational policy-makers in the immediate post-War years, before freezing gusts of financial constraint blew their schemes awry after 1922.[53] Teachers, as ever, must have thought they knew better than theorists gazing through rose-tinted lenses from ivory towers. In this instance, despite the presence of Lyon on the sub-committee, they would probably have been right. Even in the 1930s, elementary-school classes of fifty and more pupils were by no means uncommon. In such circumstances the only practically appealing section of Walford's plan would have been mass choral singing, not for the pupils' aesthetic development, but rather simply as a means of keeping them under control. One Bristol school-pupil of the era immediately before 1914 remembered that

> ...the kids was either playin' around with bits of paper or throwin' things, chatting, laughing, sniggering quietly, you know, she couldn't put it over. If it was a subject we kids didn't like, the teacher might just as well 'ave closed the book and said, 'Well, I'll tell you a story'. The only time they could control us kids was in singing lessons, 'cos the kids liked singing, so that was alright. Apart from that nobody took no blind notice.[54]

Such scenes of pedagogical desolation were probably not to be found in the rural parts of Wales, but for all the strength of its choral tradition, they must not have been uncommon in some of the elementary schools of the mining valleys. It required something like Walford's Pied Piper necromancy to engage the real listening attention of a whole assembled school.

Nevertheless the hope represented by the memorandum, and in Walford's evangelical approach, was sustained among leading educationists for most of the inter-War years, and particularly in two general reports of the mid-1920s. One of these was *The Education of the Adolescent*, prepared by Hadow's Consultative Committee for the Board of Education in 1926. Its suggestions were more practical, limited and down-to-earth than Walford's scheme; but its emphases in matters of principle were similar. Hadow stated, for instance, that the aim of music teaching in schools should be 'rather the cultivation of taste than the acquirement of proficiency', laying the foundations for intelligent appreciation in later life. He acknowledged the lead given by some city LEAs, in the form of municipal concerts for children, without actually naming the pioneering work of Walter Carroll in Manchester since 1918.[55] As well as listening, pupils ought to sing for ten minutes each day, though Hadow thought the early morning was the appropriate time. In the year of the General Strike the theme of social engineering – with overtones of discipline and patience – crept into the score:

> 'The chief advantage of singing', an eminent Prima Donna once said, 'is that you cannot be out of temper while you are doing it'; and although this may be considered an accessory rather than an essential of the art, it is one which all who have to do with discipline might very well bear in mind.

In addition, weekly lessons should be devoted to sight-singing and musical dictation. A particular element of the Welsh mission's recent achievement was noted:

> Sir Walford Davies has discovered an astonishing capacity for melody among the children of the Welsh schools, and those pupils who have any desire or aptitude may well be started on a very elementary course of harmonisation.[56]

It would appear, from the general drift of the few pages on 'Music' in the report that Hadow's views on musical education had changed little since his 1918 Oxford Barnett paper.[57]

The second official report, issued in 1927, *Welsh in Education and Life*, was the consequence of an increasingly acute anxiety in Wales about the recent marked decline in the use of the Welsh language. The section on 'Music' in the report identified two related problems: the dearth of music set to Welsh words; and the controversy between those who thought the chief aim should be the promotion of music by Welsh composers, and those who believed musical culture in Wales had been starved of hearing and knowing great European music. Welsh composers had not generally responded to the recent renaissance in native literary creativity. On the other hand, the European school of thought in Wales,

> ...who wish to induce the Welsh people to listen to, and learn from the works of the great European composers, have little understanding of

Welsh sentiment, and often through sheer insensibility, succeed in conveying the impression that they despise the native musical culture and wish to substitute for it an entirely new culture based on the knowledge of foreign music.

After this barely concealed criticism of Walford's tactics, the proposed remedy was simple: the Council of Music, 'while doing admirable work for musical education', had achieved little in the way of helping to preserve Welsh linguistic culture; instead of beginning with Bach's music, they should first of all have arranged that 'Bach's words' be translated into Welsh. Walford's sense of chronology was, apparently, topsy-turvy:

> Now that we seem to be advancing from Mendelssohn to Bach, no improvement can be discerned in what is surely vital to all musical knowledge and appreciation, namely the association of the music with words which shall be fully significant to the singer and the listener.

The Council of Music ought immediately to apply itself to the task of providing all its recommended music with Welsh words.[58]

The publishing policy of the Council had in fact been more comprehensive and sensitive than the official comment suggested. Walford often rode roughly indeed over the sensitivity of Welsh-speaking Welshmen, and made only a hasty effort to understand the linguistic principles put forward by David Vaughan Thomas and others in relation to the organic interpenetration of Welsh melodic utterance and native poetry. But the Council, while not promoting the 'Welshing' of European song, had at least pursued a bilingual policy of publication almost from its inception. And Walford was ever willing to respond to pressure exerted through the pages of an official report. It will be clear from a brief selection of the Council's early publications that the indictment by the 1927 Committee was without firm foundation. By the time the report appeared the Council had issued a book of bilingual *St Matthew Passion* selections for use at *gymanfaoedd canu*; five bilingual Church Choirs Festival books; a students' hymnal; *Hymns of the Kingdom* (in English), and the book of music for the Wembley Exhibition Welsh Week.

In encouraging the work of the Welsh elementary schools Walford was often building on already firm, if rather archaic, foundations of enthusiasm and expertise among teachers and pupils. The crucial area in which reform had to take place was the secondary-school sector, from which specialist teachers would inevitably be drawn. Here the barrier of tradition – which took the form of resistance to the idea that music should be a Matriculation subject of sound academic standing – proved to be virtually immoveable. The practical achievements of Arthur Lyon at Hawarden, and all his public pronouncements on the value of music as a secondary-school subject, emphasized the need for a change of attitude. In 1922 the Council set up a temporary committee, consisting of the Director, Lyon and J. Lloyd Williams, to consider ways in which a Matriculation Examination of the University of Wales might be initiated. The committee received advice from Hadow in the form of a specimen syllabus, which was delivered to them by Reichel. Walford's declared aim was to make the examination 'a really practical one... Practical music examinations are now so widely used.' After due deliberation he wrote to the University Registrar, Anthony,[59] noting that he was sending the committee's draft syllabus to Hadow for final comment, 'as I have had some personal talk with him on the whole question of school music'.[60]

The draft syllabus, signed by Walford, Lyon and Williams and submitted in October 1922, certainly broke new ground in Wales. Candidates would be required to satisfy the examiners in practical work, that is, in playing an instrument in a fifteen-minute programme of classical pieces, or in singing two selected classical songs, or by submitting two extended compositions of their own; in sight-reading and ear tests. They would also have to sit papers in musical form and history.[61] The viva voce part of the examination, it was anticipated, would cause financial problems at the very least; and Walford had to explain to Anthony that though

> ...the practical difficulty in arranging for an examination in any instrument may seem great the examiner will examine in their *musical* efficiency on their instrument and not on their technical mastery... The appointed examiner (being a musician) is the impartial judge of the candidate's power to speak music through the instrument...[62]

Remarkably, the first round of the examination took place only a year later, in June, 1924. However, there was only one candidate who, though (perhaps understandably) weak in paper-work, came through the pianoforte 'practical' admirably, demonstrating his 'instant musical grip and intelligence', according to Walford. This revelation of 'the candidate's attitude to music' was likely to be 'a great safeguard in future examinations.' Walford claimed it would be 'disastrous' if Matriculation music should become a 'paper-subject'.[63]

The sub-committee had no power to interfere with the First and Second School Certificate Examinations of the Central Welsh Board, which remained pinned to the dead-level of the English examining boards. Hadow and Somervell, in their Report on School Music Examinations, prepared in 1924 for the Board of Education, noted that, in general, the examining boards offered some variety, but retained 'a comparatively narrow and old-fashioned scheme' which did not reveal 'the musical intelligence of the candidates.' The history of music elements usually called for 'only a string of names of composers.' Some extremes of the statistics Hadow compiled are revealed in the following edited table:

First Examination in Music, 1923

Exam Board	No. of cands.	No. offering music	No of passes credit and +	Distinctions
Oxf and Cantab	4,699	4	2	–
London	9,382	188	136	50
NUJMB	11,587	32	26	–
CWB	3,772	128	118	47

Hadow and his colleagues thought that, even in view of 'the greater musical ability of the Welsh child', the distinction rate of the CWB was 'excessive'. The syllabus was wider than those of the other boards but was still 'formal and old-fashioned.' Their main recommendation was that 'the whole question of musical teaching in schools should be discussed at a conference of music teachers and examiners as soon as possible', and that in particular summer schools should be convened 'by which methods can be compared and standards adjusted and improved'.[64]

Walford's continual perambulations throughout Wales helped him to make contact with a fair number of music teachers; but, in addition, he had already taken up the idea of the summer school. In fact, Hadow's earlier preoccupation with the Holiday Schools of the Home Music Study Union[65] and his visits to Walford's Welsh Summer Schools may have played a part in prompting the remarks made in the 1924 Certificate Report. With the help of Davies funds the first Aberystwyth Summer School 'to instruct Teachers in the Foundations of Music and the Art of Teaching it' took place in 1920, and continued each year till 1941, when the number of participants was 105. From

1926 the summer school was recognized for a Board of Education grant, and from 1928 met at Thomas Jones's new Coleg Harlech. Walford participated as director, lecturer, performer and conductor. Others who came regularly to communicate their wisdom and experience were H. C. Colles (later to become Walford's biographer), Walter Carroll from Manchester, E. T. Davies, David de Lloyd, Hadow, J. Lloyd Williams, Sir Hugh Allen, Percy Buck and Reginald Jacques. On these occasions Walford must have been overwhelmingly impressive in his generosity of time, energy and ideas, many of them his own. In 1926, alongside talks by W. R. Allen on Singing and Choral Technique, by J. Lloyd Williams on Welsh as a singing language, and Charles Clements on the Pianoforte and Organ, Walford weighed in with

> ...a chain of morning lectures om melody (from folk-song to sonata, and from plain-song to church cantatas); intervals, scales, chords, harmony, rhythm, from Bach and his 24 keys, and 'music in harness'...[66]

It was usually possible to raise a decent orchestra from among the teachers with the result that the summer school also assumed the character of a performers' festival.

The lecture-recitals given throughout Wales with the assistance of the trios from the colleges were among the most constantly visible of all the Council's activities. In addition to the chamber concerts which were a regular weekly feature of their work at the colleges during term-time, the members of the trios gave each year a steadily increasing number of itinerant performances throughout the 1920s. Soon after these began the University Council became curious to know how the travelling circus operated. MacLean was asked to prepare a document describing the 'Illustrated Musical Lectures' in 1921. The object of the scheme, he said, was primarily educational, and not financial; though the Council was eager to make the scheme pay for itself. Generally the individual schools receiving the recitals were asked to bear the cost, up to £15; after the daytime concert for pupils, the school might organize an evening lecture-recital for which the Council expected appropriate remuneration. During the 1919–20 and 1920–21 seasons the trios had played in more than 250 places in Wales.[67]

Walford took part in these concerts as often as he could, as lecturer, pianist in the trio, or both. He delighted in communicating his love of music to expectant audiences. In 1924 the Registrar, Anthony, expressed a desire, on behalf of the University Court – which then held its sittings in sequence over a number of towns on a Welsh circuit –

to see him at work: 'There seems...to be such an excellent opportunity at Carmarthen of allowing the Court to see the type of work which is actually being done by the Council of Music.' Anthony had provisionally booked the St David's Memorial Hall in Carmarthen for the occasion. MacLean warned Anthony that Sir Walford's London heart specialist had ordered him to rest completely for several weeks; the proposed concert was therefore in doubt, 'as without the Director it may be a very flat affair.' It would also cost a great deal more than usual – about £24 – since in addition to the trios from Aberystwyth and Cardiff, there would be a small choir. If the Court could not afford that arrangement, MacLean thought that a fit Sir Walford might still consent to put on a one-man show; but this could be dangerous, for the Director 'would probably make a chorus out of the members of the Court!' (Walford had done that very thing during a lecture at Hadow's Sheffield University earlier in the year.)

The concert went ahead on 10 December 1924, with all three trios participating, and a choir from Aberystwyth. The first section of the programme covered Walford's favourite territory: 'From Handel to Beethoven', with overtures, minuets and gavottes, and Mozart piano variations. The second part comprised mainly choral items, including some out of the *Wembley Festival Book*, ranging from works of the Jacobean Welsh composer Robert Jones, to Welsh settings by J. Lloyd Williams. Finally, Joseph Morgan (later to become Professor at Cardiff) played the first movement of the *Waldstein* Sonata, and that was followed by part of Schubert's Quintet in C major, and a group which concluded with a unison setting of Beethoven's 'The Heavens Declare!'[68]

That was a special, august occasion. The 'bread-and-butter' events involving the trios continued to grow in number – except for a slight dip around 1930–31 – well into the second decade of the Council's existence. In 1939 it was reported that the total of trio lecture-recitals from the three colleges had been more than 3,000 over the past twenty years. The earliest concerts came about through isolated, disjointed visits to schools. By the end of the 1930s the process was becoming more sophisticated. E. T. Davies said in 1939 that the Bangor trio had recently been forming the nucleus of local orchestras in lecture-concerts throughout north Wales, by arrangement with the LEAs. In the case of the chamber-music concerts, 'great care is exercised in the preparation of programmes to meet the varying requirments of the numerous schools visited, and co-operation between the visiting players and the staffs of the schools is constantly becoming closer'.[69] In this respect, as in others, Welsh schools had travelled a long way since the publication of Walford's and Lyon's pamphlet in the early 1920s.

Festivals

Festivals were Walford's home ground. Their congeniality and spirituality fitted him perfectly. Joyce Grenfell described an informal episode at the Malvern Festival in 1937:

> One late afternoon the talk turned to the subject of gaiety in music. To illustrate a point Walford got up and went to the piano to play a minuet from a little known opera by Handel. Then Myra (Hess) took over and played the G major Gigue of Bach. It is dance music and was not to be resisted at that moment. Walford, then in his seventies I think, led us into an unpremeditated jig that took us in and out of the chairs and tables all around the room. The jig then turned into a Grand Chain and everyone joined in.[70]

Festivals were also a vital antidote in Walford's cabinet of remedies for the over-emphasis upon bitter competition which the Eisteddfod exemplified. His meeting with Harry Evans in London before the Great War at a session of the Association of Musical Competition Festivals has been recorded earlier;[71] and he was a devotee of the principles of the Competition Festival movement promoted by Mary Wakefield in Kendal (the family base also of Arthur Somervell). In July 1905, W. G. McNaught in the *Musical Times* estimated that 50,000 English singers participated in such festivals annually, in combined performances as well as friendly competition. Apart from the old Harlech Festival, Wales had held aloof from the movement. But in 1920, at Easter, amid organ recitals and services at the Temple, and his new functions in the Principality, Walford found time to pay one of his frequent visits to the Kendal Festival.[72]

Using the Aberystwyth students as a nucleus of performers, he inaugurated a new Festival in the town in the summer of 1920. Its continuing success year by year encouraged the idea of promoting a chain of annual festivals in some of the remoter towns of rural Wales, and these events became among the most powerful forms of regenerative activity. Professor Parrott has described their lively character, particularly that of the Festival at Newtown, whose concerts must

Walford Davies with Aberystwyth students (by permission of Irwyn Walters)

have involved a large minority of the whole population of Montgomeryshire.[74]

The Montgomeryshire Festival was conveniently close to Gregynog and owed its financial security to the Davies family. David Davies had founded and funded the Montgomeryshire County Recreation Association in 1919, and one of its best innovations was the office of County Organizer for Music, whose first incumbent, J. Morgan Nicholas ARCM, was expected to work closely with the National Council. The first Festival, held in a reconstructed aircraft hangar brought from Lincolnshire, took place at Newtown in July 1921, and was, in Ian Parrott's phrase, 'rather like a glorified *Cymanfa*.' The soloists were imported, as were some of the players, from Aberystwyth and Birmingham. But it was a mark of Walford's early influence in this part of Wales that thirty of the string players were 'graduates' of the violin tuition classes which had recently begun in the area.[74] The first climax of the Festival came in 1923 with an almost complete performance of the *St Matthew Passion*. In preparing for this Walford used the strategy of delegation which he was to develop on a grander scale: the conductors, accompanists and two singers each from the nineteen participating choirs met at Gregynog for strict tuition by Walford, then returned to impart the lessons to their local colleagues. In some subsequent years Adrian Boult and Sir Henry Wood acted as the Director's deputies.[75]

In 1924 Walford induced Elgar to attend the fifth Aberystwyth Festival to conduct the *Enigma Variations*, and then took him on to Harlech whose open-air Festival in the Castle was enjoying a temporary revival. The distinguished composer, who had much earlier in his career received the chief melodic inspiration for his Introduction and Allegro for Strings while on holiday on the Cardiganshire coast, now suffered a calamity in Merionethshire some miles to the north. The work he was to conduct, *The Apostles*, was to be performed by sixteen choirs of eager local singers who were, however, inexperienced in such 'modern' music. The result was that Elgar's rehearsal took up time which should have been devoted to practising a work by a Welsh composer; this was consequently deleted from the programme at the last minute. When Elgar approached the rostrum he was greeted by a sustained outburst from a member of the audience who evidently supported the cause of the 'Nationalist' school and had little respect for the reputation of the greatest living British composer. It was said that Elgar, after attempting to quell the disturbance with an abrupt 'Shut up!', continued, and was later taken to Gregynog to recover.

Shepherding away an ageing English composer at the end of his tether was a unique festival experience for Walford. Far more typical of the Council's enterprise were the festivals for musical children at the beginning of their careers. Welsh pupils were used to singing in choirs. At the Barry Eisteddfod in 1920 one of the most pleasurable events had been the massed children's concert organized by W. M. Williams.[76] But a new element was added in the early 1920s which was not entirely due to Walford's intervention: to children's voices instruments were added, particularly strings. In Montgomeryshire and Cardiganshire a host of violin classes sprang up. It was at Aberystwyth that Walford Davies, assisted by Bumford Griffiths, began to mount regular children's concerts as part of the annual Festival. On 29 May 1925, in the University Hall, twenty-one children's choirs, drawn from the rural districts, gave a morning concert accompanied by a children's orchestra.[77]

The violin classes scheme under the National Council initiated the Youth Orchestra movement in Wales. In 1931 the total number of pupils receiving tuition from the Council's sponsored teachers was 736, divided as follows:

Violin Tuition in Wales, 1931

Section	No. of classes	Pupils attending classes	Individual lessons	Total no. of pupils
Aberystwyth	2	32	22	54
Newport	3	20	2	22
Rhondda	13	119	–	119
Aberdare	7	64	–	64
Cardiff	3	34	–	34
Breconshire	19	269	–	269
Bridgend	4	49	–	49
Merthyr	2	34	–	34
Nanyglo	2	33	–	33
Swansea	4	58	–	58
	59	712	24	736

Nineteen new classes had begun in the first half of 1931. The Council held a library of 2,835 tuition scores and books of exercises. In

Montgomeryshire under J. Morgan Nicholas a separate scheme operated, with seventy-one pupils in twenty-one classes.[78] Also, in the Rhondda, at the most unpropitious economic moment of the decade, the Education Committee drew together local initiatives, in the form of classes, to create school orchestras, even dignifying their intention with the title 'School'. The *Western Mail* reported that 'a municipal school of orchestra', with an annual training fee of 2*s*., was proposed, 'indicative of the growing popularity of the orchestra in South Wales.' The experiment was to be conducted in conjunction with the evening continuation classes, under the direction of John Jones B. Mus., a Treorchy organist. Yet even this, it transpired, was not a complete innovation; for, in the years immediately preceding the Great War, 'a very flourishing class' had been established in mid Rhondda, involving thirty young players, and had only foundered with the ending of the Board of Education grant. W. P. Thomas JP, of the Ocean Coal Company, 'one of the staunchest supporters of musical ventures in the valleys', had placed Noddfa Hall, Treorchy, at the disposal of the 1926 venture, with free lighting and coal. The instructor was to be paid, and the scores provided, by the LEA.[79]

The main surge forward in children's mass music-making followed the appointment of Bumford Griffiths, subsidized financially by Gwendoline Davies, as Walford's roving choir-trainer under the Council, after his graduation in 1928. Griffiths was a musician of considerable pedagogical gifts. In June 1931, he presented the first official report on his work to the Council's general meeting. He had been responsible for the close supervision of all the violin classes in south Wales, though some of those in the Rhondda had diminished because of increasing local unemployment. There were eight separate school orchestras in the south Wales coalfield region, spread among Aberdare, Mountain Ash, Mid and Upper Rhondda and Blaenclydach. The children's festival movement was taking up an increasing amount of his time. He had inaugurated the Cardiff Schools Festival in March, 1929: two separate programmes were given by four choirs drawn from forty-six schools, with a juvenile orchestra of sixty players. Griffiths had supervised 123 rehearsals. Fifty-two schools had applied to take part in the 1932 Festival. In the same year ten schools took part in the third Llanidloes Festival; and the seventh Newtown Festival had drawn upon seventeen schools, involving thirty-two rehearsals. Brynmawr started a similar event in 1931, with a choir of 300 and a small orchestra. Plans were afoot for further festivals in Blaina, Brecon,

Bridgend, Llandrindod Wells, Pontypridd and Ystradgynlais. Also the recently created Three Valleys Festival had maintained its popular Children's Day in the Pavilion at Mountain Ash, with a choir of 1,250 and a junior orchestra of 125. The Mountain Ash event demanded very detailed organization and rehearsal, and the areas supplying partici-pants – Dowlais, Merthyr, Troedyrhiw and Penycraig – held district festivals in which the main programme was repeated locally.[80]

It is probable that most of the children who responded vivaciously to the glint in Bumford's eye were at least within Walford's category of those 'specially apt to sing'; but the simple musical achievement, in choral terms, is nevertheless most impressive. The participation of string and wind players in such numbers did owe a great deal to the organizational stiffening provided by the Council's agents; though it may also have been in part a spontaneous rejoinder to the stinging criticism of Wales as a 'non-instrumental' nation in the period up to 1922. Gethin Jones, one of the surviving members of the Aberdare Junior Orchestra, conducted by Bert Phillips, recalls the moment of his recruitment in the 1920s, and the rapid transformation of ignorance into competence by local teachers in chapel schoolrooms; and how the new generation of youngsters soon became chirpily critical of the relative incompetence of a much older local musician who was seen conducting a rehearsal of the LSO for a *Messiah* performance from a tonic sol-fa vocal score.[81]

Arguably Walford's greatest single public festal achievement on behalf of his western province was the Welsh Week – 25 to 30 August – at the British Empire Wembley Exhibition in 1924, which one commentator called 'a galant attempt to uphold the rights of music in that vast fair.' The *Musical Times* reported (perhaps after suitable priming by the Director),

A good deal of Welsh music was heard...but a good deal also of universal music. In fact it was less the native works, and even less the standard of the performances than the excellence of the foreign music chosen, which distinguished the Festival and promised a better future for music in Wales.

Beloved Bach predominated at Wembley, with the *St Matthew Passion* and *Sleepers Wake!* The preparations had involved the hurried super-vision of fourteen delegate-choirs from all over Wales; and Walford even used the novel agency of the BBC to deliver last-minute pep-talks to his scattered cohorts before they marched on London. He was criticized for talking too much during the concerts:

> Sir Walford Davies was always having to make explanatory speeches of one sort or another. Before the St Matthew Passion he 'gave away' that there had been no rehearsal and prophesied a break-down – which only too truly occurred.

The Wembley audience was also introduced indirectly to one of the quaint customs of the Eisteddfod – and to the publicity-seeking traits of politicians – when 'an MP from the Rhondda' interrupted the concert with a long speech expressing the thanks of the promoters for the presence of an audience and reproaching absentees. The final performance, *Messiah*, was a whale of a success.[82]

The instrumental part of Walford's mission could hardly have been blighted by attacks from the 'Nationalists' on the ground that orchestral performances were not offered through the medium of Welsh. But general criticism of Walford's methods and his insensitivity to native feelings persisted. The Director was apparently unperturbed. However, despite the achievements, disagreements – for which, on the Welsh side, there were certainly legitimate causes – continued to harass a true harmonization of the effort to produce a distinctive musical culture firmly rooted in the language, literature and traditions of Wales.

CHAPTER EIGHT
'...us composer-johnnies...'

In a report for the *Musical Times* on the 'First Welsh Orchestral Festival' in Aberystwyth, which took place in November 1923, Alfred Kalisch quoted Walford, who had himself contributed munificently to the guarantee fund, as having called this series of concerts 'a beginning ...a unique event (which) must obviously not remain so'. Walford had been attacked frontally and obliquely for his insistence on the priority of 'foreign' music while ignoring native creative endeavour. The Festival programme in 1923 included work by T. Hopkin Evans (*Brythonic Overture*), David de Lloyd (a group of songs to Welsh words), Hughes Clarke (*A Welsh Fantasy*), Hubert Davies (*Symphonic Allegro*), Kenneth Harding (*Prelude*) and D. Christmas Williams (*Suite in D minor*).

The work on which most critical interest focused was David Vaughan Thomas's *Saith o Ganeuon*, a group of songs to medieval Welsh lyrics for tenor, harp and strings. Kalisch the Druid, observing the Welsh desire to find a distinctive voice in composition, commented that 'a ringing native note' would emerge only when a group of gifted composers wrote with 'fearless directness' and without affectation. He noted that among the group of composers in Aberystwyth, one was a product of the University of Wales, another of the Leipzig Conservatoire; one, at least, was self-taught. He estimated that a generation and more would have to elapse before such different elements could acquire a sense of unity. He asked, speaking patently on Walford's behalf – and noting the apparent influences of Stravinsky and Debussy – whether Wales had yet 'absorbed enough of the classics to appreciate modernity'. It was most unfortunate that Welsh music was riven by 'violent controversies'. But Kalisch emphasized that the Aberystwyth programme contained the names of composers who had hitherto been in opposition to Sir Walford Davies:

> This is a point of no little importance. We cannot help seeing that there is a certain amount of irony in the situation – for here we have a raging tearing campaign against Sir Walford, who is denounced as the enemy

of national music, and we find him making what is perhaps the most significant gesture that has hitherto been made on its behalf...

Of the new works, he thought that Vaughan Thomas's Seven Songs were 'truly national in character...contemporary in spirit...a genuine attempt to exhaust the musical possibilities of the Welsh language in modern musical idiom'.[1]

Vaughan Thomas and Walford Davies were the two leading figures in Welsh musical development between the Wars. Vaughan Thomas's career was bracketed by early exceptional promise and belated reluctant acknowledgement of his worth by the public and the powers that presided over Welsh music. In between, his high aspirations were damaged by lack of consistent opportunity. After a late apprenticeship in the techniques of contemporary European music at Oxford, his brief schoolmastering career ended with a musical appointment at Harrow, whence, in 1906, after marrying, he came back to Wales, taking up permanent residence in Swansea and becoming the leading native composer, pedagogue and adjudicator.

In one respect he had chosen well his moment for returning. After the death of Joseph Parry, his sometime teacher, new ideals were struggling to be born, in literature and politics as well as music. Vaughan Thomas, a member of the Dafydd ap Gwilym Society while at Oxford, further developed his deep scholarly and emotional interest in Welsh medieval poetry. But while his reputation flourished on a national level, he dwelt in a country still marked by strong features of cultural conservatism. Aware of this weakness, he strove for reform by trying to infuse into the stream of musical life the element of appreciation for the lyrical treasures of ancient Welsh literature. He became an intelligent, if somewhat laconic, missionary in his own land: he showed respect for the lore of the tribe, while recognizing impartially – as a man of wide learning – what the world had to offer in the realm of music. After all, his own earliest compositions, like *The Bard*, had owed much to the models of Wagner and Strauss, as well to those of his cosmopolitan life-long friend, Granville Bantock. And his espousal of Skriabin's piano music at a Barry 'miscellaneous concert' has already been noted.[2]

As suggested earlier, Vaughan Thomas's temporary role as Music Inspector for the CWB in 1918 might have encouraged in him the real hope that he would become the first Director of Music for the University of Wales.[3] His disappointment at what he saw as an affront to national, as well as personal, pride coloured the remainder of his career. Having missed a post which seemed perfectly apt for him, he was confined to the role of sniper, albeit with a satisfyingly precise aim. But even from the crow's nest of the National Eisteddfod, to which he became Musical Director in 1925, and from his lively eyrie in Swansea, he never succeeded in shooting down the Walford-bird, whose constantly circling flight was supported by powerful private bequests and by the convected warmth of the great and good.

One of Walford's Welsh roles after 1919 was that of itinerant lecturer. Vaughan Thomas had already trodden similar paths in Wales before the Great War. His notes of acerbity now clash with Walford's genial concords. In 1909, during a lecture on orchestration to a tonic sol-fa conference at Rhymney, Vaughan Thomas offered the following: 'Advice to those about to use the oboe (for the first time), "DON'T. It bites".' And in an undated lecture on 'Canon and Fugue', after devoting most of his time to a defence of tonic sol-fa (noting that Bantock's *Omar Khayyám* and Delius's *Sea Drift* were available from Boosey's in that notation), he concluded by saying,

> Do you seriously mean to say that you want to hear me talk about canons and fugues, when you have volumes you can refer to on these subjects...? I have come to the conclusion that some of you may want to find a short method of adding letters after your names.[4]

The two men conducted an intermittent correspondence, shot through with misunderstanings and a series of false starts to an improvement in what had to be a difficult relationship. Vaughan Thomas was mentioned at the first meeting of the National Council at Shrewsbury in January 1919, as a representative of the University Court.[5] Clearly, however, he must have found the character of the Council's early policies – or the ways in which they were articulated – unattractive, and Walford's exercise of his new leadership overbearing. The new Director wrote to him in April 1920,

> The Council would have warmly appreciated your help and efforts... Now your resignation has been handed to me. May I, before communicating it to the Council, earnestly urge you to withdraw it? I hope and believe you will enjoy giving valuable help in our deliberations. Do reconsider the position.[6]

In a reply which has been lost, Vaughan Thomas must have stated his 'position'. Walford replied,

David Vaughan Thomas (by permission of the Welsh Music Archive)

What you say of your incessant work for fourteen years for Welsh music and Music in Wales and of the meagre financial and moral support is sad and sounds very 'tired of it all'...We are this year the guests of Miss Davies at Harlech. And we always have happy times, heartening and refreshing to hard workers.[7]

Vaughan Thomas indeed worked, and travelled, as hard as Walford; though never at the philanthropic expense of the Davieses. Despite that early rebuff – in the year when the Barry Eisteddfod had set high musical standards – Walford tried again to make fruitful contact early in 1922, inviting Thomas to permit the performance of his new Welsh songs at the Aberystwyth concert mentioned earlier. However, the proud composer made stipulations:

They require an expert in Welsh metres for their correct presentation...I should not care to introduce them to a wider public without the assistance of a truly Welsh singer specially prepared...The nation, I believe, looks for a more charateristic Welsh utterance in its music and to its leaders to supply it. It has taken me many years, begun in my Oxford days..., to arrive at even a tentative solution of the problem, by a close study of Welsh poetry...I am glad the naturalness of the poems appeals to you.[8]

Walford, the monoglot Englishman, did his best, among all other claims on his time, to understand the reasons for Vaughan Thomas's strict performance requirements. But, engrossed in his role as deliverer of Wales from its Adullamite cave, he was still perplexed. It is clear that he admired the other man's gifts; but it is equally evident that there had been opportunities early in the life of the Council for him to deploy Vaughan Thomas in at least a part-time office. When, as noted already,[9] he had been pressed by Thomas Jones and Hadow to appoint someone of substance to direct College activities at Bangor, he seems to have eschewed thoughts of the Swansea candidate altogether, preferring instead to incline towards the impractical choice of Vaughan Williams or Herbert Howells. He met Vaughan Thomas occasionally at *eisteddfodau* and festivals, but those fascinating moments are frustratingly beyond recall. At the Mold Eisteddfod in 1923 Walford seems to have made a new approach, for Vaughan Thomas wrote, later in the year, 'I appreciate your admission of my capabilities, which official musical Wales, however, has failed to acknowledge after twenty years of public work...before the advent of organised effort supported by powers such as have never before been at the service of any Welsh musician...' With a hint of paranoia he spoke of his 'enemies'; with valid percipience he added, 'you will have observed that, in Wales, it is not what a man is, but rather the appointment he holds that commands respect. With all our educational machinery, we have not outgrown that vulgar conception of value'. Realizing, perhaps, that Walford and his alien ilk were not now to be dislodged from powerful posts, he ended,

> Possibly, some day, an explanation may be given for my being discovered *now* a useful asset to organised effort in Wales, not, however, when my enthusiasm was at its highest, but only when it has been replaced by a spirit of indifference. In the meantime I can only follow the path which lies before me, assuring you that I have never, in thought, word or deed, entertained or expressed anything but respect for yourself as an artist. With kindest regards...[10]

By return, Walford strove to show that he had the best interests, not simply of musical Wales, but of Welsh creativity, at heart in constructing the Aberystwyth 'Welsh' concert:

> You must see that I only want to do the right and helpful thing. I had better tell you that I am paying £50 out of my private and, at present, depleted pocket in order to have a *complete* orchestra of the first rank, that not one note of the Welsh MS works shall be handicapped. Here are 800 students ready for anything. Could you have a better audience? Can you really justify a public refusal [for performance of *Saith o Ganeuon*] to a Welsh University College who hold out a hearty and persistent and utterly friendly disinterested invitation to you to come and let them hear your new Welsh songs, with a full orchestra, at the first festival of its kind?[11]

He also offered personally to pay the fees of any Welsh singer Vaughan Thomas might choose for the performance (though in the event Tom Pickering sang). But patronage was not enough for the other proud man: why, he probably asked, in a town like Swansea was there no Music Department attached to the new University College, and no official Director of Music, similar to E. T. Davies at Bangor? In fact, the National Council had made strenuous efforts to attach a Music Department to Swansea. Jenkin James had written to McLean in January 1924, from the University Registry, that a resolution of the University Council had been passed relating to the establishing of such a Department in December, 1923; but that he was required to state that 'there were no funds available'.[12] Nevertheless it must always have appeared to the Swansea candidate for any post which might be created there that progress towards installing an academic department was being mysteriously blocked by the powers that were, and that Walford was probably manipulating those powers.

Over the matter of the Aberystwyth performance, however, Vaughan Thomas capitulated, and sent his songs to Walford, who immediately treated him like a pet student in a composition class:

> I must tell you what enjoyment and relief I have experienced in your happy songs. Their simple directness and natural beauty and the little [sic] happy turns in them (such as the C-sharp bit on p.9) are going to do real good and help to lead our students. I had feared they were going to be a bit more complex!... Give my kindest greetings to your wife, and real gratitude to her (I hope I said nothing hurtful or clumsy in the effort to get things right...)[13]

Morfudd Vaughan Thomas was certainly the staunchest of her husband's supporters: her steadfastness and kindness impressed both Bantock and Leigh Henry, two of many musicians who enjoyed the hospitality of Walter Road, Swansea.[14] But she seems not to have been deceived by Walford. On a number of occasions his brief visits to their villa did not convince her of the transparency of his intentions. He saw the problem. Before the Aberystwyth concert in 1923 he wrote specially to Mrs Thomas, inviting her to stay at his expense in the Queen's Hotel, appending times of trains so that she might be sure of returning soon to her family.[15] When he was imploring Vaughan Thomas to contribute to the 'All Wales' concert at the Wembley Exhibition in 1924, he added a postscript: 'Hearty greetings to your dear wife. Fancy, I am to have a wife too. Thank God for such happiness.'[16] And earlier the same year he had admitted, 'If I could get Mrs Thomas on my side...we would get ahead! So this screed is as much to her as to you, dear man'.[17] Walford, who lived out of a portmanteau, may have seemed to Mrs Thomas to have little understanding, not simply of Welsh music, but of the trying details of domestic life. Vaughan Thomas refused to attend the Wembley concert, which he probably saw as chiefly a glorification of Walford's role in educating Wales. This was despite the offer of first-class rail-fare and accommodation, though the terms in which it was couched seemed almost calculated to offend: 'Ten guineas is official rail and hotel to the singers. I think the same should be available for us composer-johnnies. Please reply quickly, "an thou lov'st me".'[18]

The career of the Swansea man was running in its accustomed grooves: teaching, the encouragement of fellow Welsh composers by performances on his native patch, adjudication and frustration. In 1925, however, the balm of a performance of two songs at one of the Three Choirs Festival chamber concerts momentarily eased the perpetual ache. Yet even that occasion became the source of further misunderstanding. Apparently Vaughan Thomas, Walford and Bantock had strolled in the Gloucester cloisters discussing the future. Walford, worried about his own declining health, spontaneouly offered Vaughan Thomas the opportunity to take over temporarily some of his work as lecture-recitalist in south Wales. From amid the peals of Walford's encouraging words, Bantock seems to have recalled a statement of intent that Vaughan Thomas should soon assume a permanent official function under the National Council. The lecture-recitals took place in Monmouth, Abergavenny, Resolven, Pontycymer, Milford Haven and elsewhere, with the assistance of members of the Aberystwyth trio. Yet even this experiment exploded in the face of the demonstrators.

The difficulty in this case turned on a subject of misunderstanding common among professional musicians: money. At Gloucester that summer Vaughan Thomas had distinctly heard Walford offer him ten guineas a day for the lecture-recital work. When the time for settling accounts came, the fee had shrunk to five guineas; and, humiliatingly, the Council end of the correspondence was dealt with most perfunctorarily by MacLean. For Vaughan Thomas, a freelance man, as for many other piece-work musicians, this contractural blunder marked the end of a relationship: 'I cannot lay myself open to further unsatisfactory experiences'.[19] Walford's compromise of paying forty guineas (again from his own pocket) for six of the Swansea lectures was unacceptable. The Director was appalled: 'In sending this I wish to say that I think your charge for this is surprisingly excessive as between fellow-musicians'.[20]

By the middle of 1926, then, Vaughan Thomas saw no possibility of reaching a mutually satisfactory relationship with the Welsh musical establishment over which Walford presided. This was despite his recent appointment as Musical Director for the National Eisteddfod. At this moment musical England came to his aid, but with help in the form of a dilemma. The Trinity College of Music wished him to take the post of Overseas Examiner. This would involve colonial tours of duty lasting five or six months each year. Vaughan Thomas wrote to

Bantock for advice. That generous man replied wisely, and with a better understanding of the politics of musical Wales than Walford had yet demonstrated: '...you are the first leading musician and composer in Wales. There is no other man of your mental capacity and ability, and our friend H. W. [Walford Davies] knows this.' Bantock believed that, in taking the overseas job, Vaughan Thomas was likely to abandon the chance of 'a belated yet inevitable recognition' of his claims by his countrymen.

> Like Fabius Maximus, or Cincinnatus, you have been living a quiet, modest life, out of the world's affairs, and I certainly think you will lose more than you are likely to gain, if you absent yourself for five or six months from Wales, leaving the way free for bounders to come in and rob you of your rightful inheritance...Moreover, you would lose money if your Eisteddfod adjudications and vacancies created by your absence would be filled up by younger men...I have an idea at the back of my mind that he [Walford] will recommend your appointment to the Chair of Music in Wales when he has tested you and is satisfied of your genuine qualities.[21]

This heartfelt advice was insufficiently convincing. Vaughan Thomas went to lie abroad for a conservative examining body, on one occasion enjoying a tour of South Africa in Bantock's company. His world had been turned upside down. In New Zealand, at Oamaru, in 1929, he sat down, perhaps late at night after an exhausting day's examining, and reflected ironically on the substance of a press report he had read of a lecture in England by his rival, whose failure to use him had indirectly led to his being temporarily marooned on a large atoll. In that particular statement Walford, flying too close to the sun for intellectual comfort, had coined the aphorism, 'A good tune is a part of God'. Auden could hardly have responded more bitingly, and a hundred childhood chapel sermons reverberate through Vaughan Thomas's private rejoinder:

> Our first feeling must surely be akin to regret that the world has not known this before. Every statement which throws a light on the nature of God is a solace and a joy to every true believer. The present generation is fortunate in being privileged to receive a new truth...We must remember that what is hid from the wise is often revealed unto babes...It must be realised that all profound statements are apt to be misunderstood by the average man, or, as Sir Walford would probably prefer to say, by the average listener...In conclusion,it is hoped that all who love

the art of music, our mother tongue, will reflect on the great truth placed before us...In nomine Patri, et Filii, et Spiriti Sancti, Amen, Vates Britannicus, errans...[22]

Two great ironies are revealed in the final English sentences: 'mother tongue' consciously recalls the lecture Walford gave in Downing Street soon after his mission began; the 'average listener' was part of the title Walford gave to his famous broadcasts on music in the 1920s and '30s.

Vaughan Thomas died tragically bearing the white man's examining burden in South Africa in 1934. At the end of his career in Wales he had prepared a talk for the BBC prefaced by what was probably a conscious epitome of his feelings about the altercations of the previous fifteen years: 'Musicians thrive by their discords, in more senses than one. Their lives are frequently one long suspension, which rarely resolves into a nice comfortable concord'.[23]

In the Vaughan Thomas papers at the National Library of Wales there is preserved only one genuine obituary letter, from Granville Bantock:

My dear Mrs Thomas I read in the newspaper this morning the sad and unexpected news of the loss we have all suffered. Your husband was one of my oldest and most cherished friends, and I shall never forget the happy memories of the past... He was the greatest composer that Wales has produced, and this country will soon realise what it owed to his genius and patriotism. His name will live in the annals of Welsh national music, and will occupy an honoured place in the hearts of the people...[24]

There is no note of condolence from Walford. Perhaps it has been lost.

CHAPTER NINE

'Opening a window in a dark room': the National Council and Adult Education

Walford's obituary notices were not written until 1941, but he had much earlier presented signs of his mortality. The hurly-burly of his existence, as Director of Music and Professor in Wales, at the Temple, as Gresham Lecturer in London and frequent occasional lecturer elsewhere, and most of all as weekly broadcaster for the BBC, damaged a physique even as robust as his. As early as February 1920 he had written to Thomas Jones from Hampstead saying that he hoped to be able to spend a short weekend with him and the Davieses at Llandinam discussing the progress of his Welsh mission; but that he was also expected, almost simultaneously, in Oxford where he was lecturing on leisure, in London, and at Barry for an Eisteddfod Music Committee meeting. He would arrive in mid Wales at 5.15 in the morning. T. J. replied, in haste, 'It would not be worth your while to travel down through the night as you proposed...I notice that you are lecturing to others about their leisure. Perhaps you will take some of your own advice to heart!'[1]

Eventually such a strenuous programme took its toll, and an intermittent heart complaint necessitated ever more frequent periods of recuperation. He resigned from the Gregynog Chair in 1926. The *Western Mail* commented that his influence then over British music generally 'and the music of Wales in particular' was 'probably unrivalled in the present day':

> Sir Walford has done remarkable work in inculcating love of music both in the schools and among the communities of Wales, his methods ranging from chatty lectures before all sorts and conditions of men to the spread of instrumental music...[2]

Walford immediately became Organist at St George's Chapel, Windsor. In 1934 he succeeded Elgar as Master of the King's Musick; and he continued his association with the BBC in an advisory, as well as an executive, capacity.[3] Essentially the tone of all his public utterances was, in the best sense, late-Victorian. His vision of the progress of musical creativity in the twentieth century continued to be limited.

When Bartók visited Aberystwyth to play his own music in 1922, Walford is reputed to have turned to a colleague at the concert and said, wistfully, 'Baffling, isn't it!'[4] His friend Hadow, however, for all his public conventionality, strove to understand the very new. As early as 1915, writing on 'modern' music, and commenting on Schoenberg's 'admirable' treatise on harmony and his early piano pieces, Op.11 and 19, he concluded that they gave him 'the impression that they mean something to which I have not yet a clue. They start on a different hypothesis from other music, like Lobatchewski's geometry which started on the principle that the triangle consisted of less than two right angles'.[5] Hadow's attitude was always sufficiently Whiggish for him to wish for the traditions of the past to be linked to the experiments of the present; but his effort to make sense of Schoenberg and to understand the revolutionary artistic tendencies of his own time placed him in a position from which he was better able to exercise a moderating influence on the progress of education in the 1920s and early 1930s. He considered that the real besetting sins of the age were 'intellectual slovenliness' and the fact that 'everybody is half-educated'. Contemporary musical criticism was 'lost in a prevalent fog through which you can hear nothing but the megaphone and see nothing but the electric light'. Walford, too, though he never became a musical progressive, had to accommodate his schemes for musical regeneration in Wales to a new social and political temper after 1919.

Writing in 1935 of the condition of industrial Wales, Dr Thomas Jones was untypically caustic:

> It is Downing Street which is the distressed area. So many remedies have been tried in vain. South Wales has become a bore...Why won't it go to sleep like Dorsetshire? The Commissioner [for Distressed Areas] has turned himself into a Red Cross ambulance and is providing nurses for the sick, hospitals for the dying, and suits, shovels and soup for those who are willing to build swimming pools. Lady Astor comes out of the sky and drops a nursery school. The Carnegie Trust and the Pilgrim Trust and the Society of Friends...scatter libraries, and settlements, and allotments up and down the area. The Prince of Wales, with a mind clear of cant and humbug, keeps on making speeches and touring the area and won't let his friends forget their neighbours and his...The Welsh are a credulous nation...always imagining some new Utopia, reminiscent of harps and angels in white robes. They are like the Greeks in this, and of them it is said that they built their towns to the sound of the lyre.[6]

Even at a slightly more optimistic moment in Welsh development, in 1913, another commentator had drawn attention to the picture palace 'bright and treacherous, pleasing and damning', to the 'consumptive and asthmatic species' which were visible in Welsh industrial communities, and had enquired what parental control was being exercised over their fifteen- to sixteen-year-olds – 'the flapper' – seen out after dark. 'We ask what concern these parents have with literature, art or religion. We want a school for parents as much as for our children'.[7]

The political and cultural energy of pre-War Wales, based perhaps upon false confidence about future development, was severely damaged by the paralysis of her staple industries in the period immediately after the War. Kenneth O. Morgan succinctly says, 'As British capitalism lurched into massive crisis in the years after 1922, the Welsh valleys were foremost among its helpless victims'.[8] In one sense, then, Walford Davies's energy might have been seen to be pouring into an economic abyss which he had approached as if it were simply a cultural desert. Almost from the start of his Welsh campaign musical activity and industrial inactivity were antiphonally conjoined. Even the dispassionately distanced *Musical Times* was commenting in 1920, before the worst of the crisis had begun, 'Despite industrial unrest, signs are not wanting of activity in the various musical centres' throughout south Wales.[9] And it was noted that concerts were a chief means of raising money to alleviate distress. In 1926, Bumford Griffiths's Aberpennar Orchestra gave a series of concerts in Mountain Ash Pavilion 'for the benefit of the distressed of the area', with audiences of about 8,000 on each occasion, and tickets at a penny, twopence and threepence.[10]

The Welsh musical mission began in 1919 on the assumption that it was to be part of the University's programme of providing, from on high, a combination of spiritual elevation and greater social harmony in a discordant society. Progressively, in the 1920s, the work of the National Council of Music became the means of delivering a message of hope throughout the distressed areas and of scattering cultural manna in the form of the best possible musical experience. Walford became very familiar with the lives of those who were suffering financial deprivation in the Valleys. He also came to understand harshness of attitude among those who controlled Welsh capital in this anxious area.

Early in 1926 in the Park Hotel he gave before the members of the Cardiff Business Club a two-hour lecture entitled, 'On the Use of the

Domestic Piano'. He spoke of music as a 'League of Nations language';
of the generosity with which he had seen the best tunes received by the
inmates of jails when he had lectured in those places; of the ability of
children to construct beautiful melody; of Paderewski, Kreisler 'and
Harry Lauder in his great art', as they obeyed the summons of the
angels. He demonstrated his own peculiar skill at the piano, asking his
audience to treat it as a harp which could sing. The vote of thanks was
proposed in a somewhat confused way by Sir William Seager. He was
thankful that Sir Walford had 'shut his ears to the siren' that would
have fastened him to an academic career in the University, and had
freed himself 'to help the people'. Walford, who had just announced
his intention of resigning the Chair at Aberystwyth, while retaining the
Directorship of the Council, was evidently appreciated by the Cardiff
businessmen as a hard-working musician. But Seager made another
point: 'Some of those present this evening were very anxious that the
harmony of the riveting hammer and the rhythms of the rolling mills
should be heard again in Cardiff, for there was music in these things'.[11]
Walford did not become the servant of such attitudes; rather he strove
to change the direction of the Council's endeavours so that at least as
much emphasis was laid on developing its adult activities as on the
important work in the children's schools. In extending its role to that
dimension he had only a limited degree of support from Cardiff and
other leading Welsh businessmen during the remainder of his period
in the Principality.

   Throughout the adult course of his mission he retained undimmed
the Utopian idealism which had charged his initial foray into Wales.
In this he might have looked back to words uttered by a musical
colleague in 1905. Then Arthur Somervell had suggested that 'the
national capacity for getting rich counts for absolutely nothing, as
compared with the consevation of those forces which express themselves in noble art'. He had gone on to say,

> Hooliganism, slum dwellings, mean streets (by which I do not mean the
> slums, but the miles of grey hell in which our respectable working
> classes are condemned to live), the cognate problem of the depopulation
> of the country, the sordid joys of the public-house, and the curse of
> gambling are all directly attributable, in a large measure, to that soul-
> destroying heresy which popular moral teaching has encouraged, in
> confounding the persons, and dividing the substance, of the Eternal
> Trinity of Truth, Beauty and Goodness.

A disciple of Matthew Arnold to the end of his days, Somervell concluded with the words, 'My own belief is that responsiveness to music is the outward and visible sign of an inward sensitiveness to the rhythm in all things'.[12]

The economic and social realities of the 1920s were a hard resistant to those kinds of views. British adult education became, politically and economically, an arena of revolutionary activity. A wide variety of elements in the Labour movement were seen to be struggling for ascendancy; and south Wales was the most militant area of the struggle. Many on the extreme left depicted a conspiratorial alliance, embracing the mild Workers' Education Association, the TUC and the Federation of British Industries, whose aim was to restrain the most radical activists and maintain the status quo. In 1916 *The Times*, commenting on the way the Durham miners had moved away from militancy, attributed that 'change of heart' mainly to 'the University-inspired teaching' whose influence it also detected in south Wales coalowners' plans to establish classes in the 'impartial' study of history and economics under the 'guidance' of properly equipped teachers.[13] In 1923, a leader in the Tory *South Wales Echo* suggested that the WEA 'should receive the strongest support from employers of labour, if for no other reason than that it provides an antidote and a corrective to the mischievous propaganda of the various sorts of revolution in our midst'.[14]

Of course there is no evidence that Walford or Hadow were ever involved in such a conspiracy to use music in adult education as a political palliative. But it is clear, even from the musical journals of the 1920s, that social and political anxieties did occasionally invade the thinking of the musical establishment. Imperial Russia, it will be recalled, had been used by the Haldane Commission as a model for the way in which Welsh musicality might develop.[15] After 1917 English observers were fascinated by the progress of musical education in the Soviet Union. C. D. Graham, writing on 'Music and Communism' in 1922, while pouring scorn on Education Commissar Lunarcharsky's experiments with a Gilbertian system in which 'everybody is some-body', admitted that the Russian experiment with free musical training was interesting; though he did wonder whether, 'with food at famine prices, the Russians would not cheerfully forego "culture" in exchange for benefits of a more tangible kind'.[16] In 1920, after commenting on the 'barbarian' Welsh choral habit of singing from the heart, Gerald Cumberland also recorded the performance at a Welsh concert of works by Skriabin, Rimsky-Korsakov and Borodin, ending with the remark, 'What to us is familiar daily food is to Wales the very Leninism of music'.[17] Whatever his political sympathies may have been in the contemporary political struggle, by the late 1920s Walford's main concern in south Wales was to provide through music some humane alleviation of widespread economic distress. Even before that he had sought to demonstrate that the working-class roots of music-making in Wales were thriving. The *Musical Times* in 1921 had reported on his behalf that in Treharris an orchestral society of fifty players had been formed. Its recent concert had provided 'an indication of the potentialities in instrumental music of a working-class combination with a working miner as conductor'.[18]

The adult education work of the National Council took three main forms. First, there was the provision of classes in musical appreciation and musical instruction; second, the publication of cheap vocal scores for choral groups of the unemployed, and third, the development of sequences of orchestral and choral concerts of a high standard in the distressed areas.

In the aftermath of Fisher's 1918 Education Act the Board of Education began to take a more positive interest in the provision of adult education, establishing in April, 1921, an advisory committee which was expected to prepare a succession of papers on various aspects of the subject. By the Board's definition, 'adult education' was the education of all over school age, not simply Somervell's 'respectable working class'. The committee included the Oxford English scholar, Grace Hadow, sister of Sir Henry, Professor F. B. Jevons, son of Stanley Jevons, Albert Mansbridge, founder of the WEA, Reichel, and R. H. Tawney. In November 1923, the committee presented its fifth report, *British Music*, for which they had been offered evidence by, among others, Sir Hugh Allen, Adrian Boult, Sir Walford Davies, Sir Henry Hadow, Charles MacLean, Secretary of the National Council of Music, Percy Scholes and Arthur Somervell.

In justifying the new status of music among subjects deemed worthy of serious adult study, they quoted Hadow's remark that 'Music is not only a source of noble pleasure...It is a form of intellectual and spiritual training with which we cannot afford to dispense.' Walford reinforced this opinion with the simile, 'The striking of good music upon the ear is not unlike the throwing open of a window in a dark room'.[19] It was admitted that, while the Welsh were not necessarily more inherently musical than the other peoples of Britain, they had given a greater place to music in their national life; though their concentration on choral singing had 'tended to restrict a little the Welsh musical outlook.' Such a weakness was now being eliminated under 'the inspiring influence' of Walford Davies, and the result had been a raising of the standard of music and performance 'in the most remarkable way in a short time'.[20]

In the nation at large, however, there were still undesirable elements to be combatted: 'the Jazz Band in the West End is answered by the cheap gramophone in the East.' Percy Scholes's evidence of having heard a Mozart Trio encored at a horse camp during the Great War was taken as an indication that it was certainly possible to transform public taste. The problem was largely, as Major J. T. Bavin of Kneller Hall School of Military Music saw it, to make sure that good music was not played 'as a sort of solemn ceremonial'.[21] In the matter of instrumental players, it was acknowledged that Walford had found no difficulty in forming an orchestra in the forces during the War. The work of Mary Wakefield's Festival Movement was praised, but the National Council of Music was given special attention. For the time being, it was said, an enlargement of the Council's activities beyond the schools and colleges was inhibited by lack of funds. But the chief hope for the future lay in the close association of the Welsh University with its work. 'We doubt whether it is possible in England to organise such a scheme under University auspices over so large a tract of country, but we feel that coucils on much the same lines might be organised in certain areas by the co-operation of the University, the Local Education Authorities, and voluntary associations'.[22]

The committee also took its lead from Walford over the importance of gramophones in the progress of music at all levels, having expressed surprise at 'the unanimity of our many witnesses in regard to the value of the gramophone and the possibility of using it for educational purposes.' They had been convinced by Walford's visit to the Committee bearing a gramophone and later illustrating his mode of teaching.[23] In the matter of university extension lectures they instanced Walford's having delivered a series of talks at the Mold Eisteddfod as a preliminary to the performance of Bach's *St Matthew Passion*. But with his special gifts in mind, they warned that, for lectures delivered to audiences consisting largely of 'musically half-trained people', it was essential that musical illustrations should be abundantly provided.[24]

In discussing the parallel method of the university tutorial class, the Committee offered its only caveat. HMI thought that the tutors were uniformly competent; but that 'greater care was requisite in the selection of students; there was apt to be too great a distance between the best and the weakest students to form a sufficiently homogenous class'. Such extended tutorial-class courses, they thought, were at present only practicable 'in rare instances'. The secretariat at the Board of Education were to maintain their suspicions about the quality of tutorial classes to all for the remainder of the 1920s, until the pressures for open entry imposed by large-scale unemployment forced a gradual change of administrative attitude. The opening up of adult education, after all, raised potentially embarassing questions about access to selective schools at eleven-plus, at a time when only a small proportion of children were seen to deserve secondary-school places. Nevertheless the generally sympathetic report of the 1923 committee presented an opportunity for developing what became the most important area of activity for the National Council.

In 1925 the Council applied to the Board of Education for recognition under the Adult Education Regulations as an 'Approved Association' for offering one-year and terminal classes in music. This new phase began formally in the following year.[25] These terminal classes became a permanent feature of the Council's work, and were the outcome of the original recommendations of the Haldane Commission.[26] In November 1926, Walford was unable to attend a meeting in Shrewsbury of the University Extension Board, and so he sent to the Registry a memorandum on 'One-Year Classes in Music' which provides a detailed account of the aims of the new venture. The detail of the memorandum was partly the consequence of the closer proximity between Welsh HMI, the WEA, the YMCA and the Walford's staff which had occurred after the removal of the Council's offices from Aberystwyth to Cardiff in 1926, on Walford's resignation from the Gregynog Chair.

The memorandum took as its theme a remark made in *The Times Literary Supplement*, 9 October 1926, about the choral tradition of the crowded Valleys of south Wales: 'What is perhaps most needed at present is the organisation of the untutored enthusiasm for music which now prevails.' These words Walford considered to be his 'marching orders'.[27] The main limit on the immediate expansion of the Council's work was the shortage of tutors. It was therefore its first aim to find suitable teachers and co-ordinate their work. Walford foresaw that both the Board of Education and the University might wish to impose uniformity on adult education. He argued the tutor should have 'entire freedom to develop the class in each district in ways which seem to him most suited to the needs of that district.' For instance, if the singing were strong, and the sight-reading poor, the tutor ought naturally to devote most of the first term's work to intensive score-reading; in another district the human resources might suggest the development of orchestral and instrumental work as the basis of practical activity. Three principles of action ought to underpin all the efforts: '...each week's work should enable the class to *hear* music, to *make* music, and, under guidance, *try to understand* it'.[28]

This new policy for action was already being shaped by new forces.

Only a few years ago it would not only have been a counsel of perfection, but almost a counsel of despair to say that every class in every part of the country, however remote, should every week hear good music. Now this is no longer so, owing to wireless and the gramophone, for, however mixed the fare of these two inventions, not only are strides being made with amazing rapidity in good transmission and good recording of the greatest music of the world, but this means that the hearing of music is within the reach of every district.

The Council's plans therefore ran 'in happy consonance' with the Board's new policy for adult education classes, begun on 29 April 1926. The supply of gramophones was a temporary problem: Walford was already arranging that machines should be supplied by the Council, and that local groups should be able to purchase them if they wished at wholesale rates, through the Council's agreement with the Gramophone Company. By his intimate contact with the BBC he was also negotiating the supply of 'an ideal specimen wireless' for those who wished to purchase a set. In this way, even outside formal class time, in listening groups students would be able to hear the best music 'every night of the week'.

Within four years, against an unpromising economic background, all these optimisitic plans had been implemented under the direct guidance of the Council and assisted by the Board of Education Grant. In the year 1929–30 there were seven one-year tutorial classes, in Britton Ferry, Caernarfon, Mold, Penllwyn (Cardiganshire), Pontypool, Tŷ-croes (Llanelli) and Waenfawr (Caernarfonshire), whose tutors included Tom Pickering from the Aberystwyth Music Department, T. Osborne Roberts and A. Haydn Jones. Moreover, these classes seem to have been well equipped: at Penllwyn, for instance, from the Council's permanent stocks the class had used twelve records, ten sets of miniature scores, one handbook (for broadcasts), fifteen copies of Bach Chorales, and a gramophone. The number of students in each class ranged from fifteen in Britton Ferry to thirty-two each at Penllwyn and Pontypool. There were also one-term classes in twenty-one centres scattered throughout Wales from Tanygrisiau through Tregaron to Cardiff, with an average of twenty students each. In all the Council of Music had 563 students on the books of its adult classes and 539 scores and 401 gramophone records in circulation. In addition it provided equipment for nine other classes conducted by the WEA, though in a number of cases, those tutors were also employed by the Council in its classes.[29] By 1932–33 there were fifty one-year and terminal classes, with 855 adult students,and 176 sets of orchestral parts in circulation.[30]

Receipt of the Board of Education grant entailed the intervention of HMI who kept an eye on standards of teaching and attendance. There is evidence that some of the inspectors were still conventionally sceptical of the seriousness of, even the necessity for, music in the higher curriculum of adult studies. In 1928 one HMI turned in a report on the tutorial class conducted at Melindwr Penllwyn, near Aberystwyth, by Tom Pickering. Apparently Pickering had committed the dreadful sin of keeping the class register open for fifteen minutes after commencement. MacLean, on behalf of the Council, offered an explanation. He stressed that, despite the delay, two hours' full tuition had been given (the lesson had finished at 9.15 pm). Also the local secretary of the class, Mr Jones, who was responsible for the keeping of the register, wrote to the Board of Education offering similar information and, in the process, describing neatly the character of a large music class in a rural area:

> ...in an agricultural district like ours ten minutes margin is not enough to meet our local difficulties re attendance. More than half our Class are farm servants, whose hours of work are not as regular as those of collieries, factories or quarries; those workmen finish at the same stated hour every day, but a farm servant has to depend on exigencies of weather and calls for attention which cannot be regulated by a clock. And moreover by the time they change clothes and get themselves ready for class and then walk three quarters or [*sic*] a mile to class: it ought to be clear to the Education Authorities that hard and fast rules cannot be applied to a rural district as they can to an industrial area.
>
> To have secured such faithful attendance as we had last session is a sufficient testimony to the keen interest taken in Mr Pickering's music

lessons: and it should prove more than ample compensation for the trifling request of an extra 5 minutes before closing the Register. But apart from that concession – if concession it be – I can assure the Board that no abuse of the Regulations took place. Not always were the 15 minutes wait for the arrival of pupils always [*sic*] necessary and, even then, the Classes were not finished till 9.15.; *so the members were never wihout their two hours' tuition.*

I trust the above explanation will meet the requirements of the Board, and that in consequence we shall not be discouraged in our efforts to provide a music cultural study [*sic*] for the young people of this sparsely populated rural district, by too literal adherence to a regulation...

The Board's officials continued to debate this weighty matter among themselves in Whitehall. Finally, however, Mr T. Owen HMI came out in support of Jones, saying that he did his 'thankless' job exceedingly well: '...the success of the class was due as much to his enthusiasm and enterprise as to the Tutor's teaching ability.' On one appallingly wet night when Owen had paid a visit, there were thirty students present out of a possible thirty-two, and on that occasion, he had been so impressed by the attendance and punctuality, and by 'the very interesting manner in which the class was conducted that I'm afraid I paid little attention to the details of registration...I am prepared to take the whole responsibility for any misunderstanding'.[31]

Those tutorial classes had as their main aim, not the enlightening entertainment of local groups, but the rigorous infusion of proper understanding of music and of the acquisition of a high degree of technical competence by the students. As has been shown, they made their mark in this manner among rural and urban populations. However, the dark cloud which descended upon south Wales in the mid-1920s gave to the National Council a rather different adult-education task, in which humanitarian values were seen to transcend mere academic standards in the provision of opportunities for the enjoyment and understanding of music. In taking upon itself this much broader duty the National Council truly entered the dignified realm of social work among the unemployed and the spiritually bereft. Thus far in his endeavours for Wales, Walford Davies had relied heavily on the munificence of the Davies family; but in order to pursue musical and extra-musical aims in the mining areas he was to enlist the support of those who had placed him at the head of the Welsh musical establishment in 1919. It was as if his coterie of influential friends had been waiting in the wings until, at a pre-arranged cue, they rushed on stage to save a stricken heroine.

If Walford Davies was gifted with the ability to diversify in musical activity, Sir Henry Hadow was positively polymathic. Throughout the 1920s and early 1930s he used his capacity for comprehensive administration as Vice-Chancellor of Sheffield University, while at the same time devoting his energy, powers of inquiry and summative talent at the Board of Education as chairman of a sequence of consultative committees on important educational topics between 1924 and 1933. In addition he chaired the Music Committee of the Carnegie Trust. In that voluntary office he at first guided the dispersal of large amounts of money towards the encouragement of new music and gentle local music-making. In 1919 Mary Paget had established the Village and Country Town Concerts Fund, in the belief that 'the love of good music was not confined to those who had frequent opportunities of hearing it.' The movement grew, to the extent that in 1922, with the help of a financial rescue operation by the Carnegie Trust, the organizers arranged 417 concerts in the course of thirty tours through twenty English counties.[32] Hadow also handled the Trust's sponsorship of the Tudor Music scheme, the scholarly rediscovery and publication, under Terry and Fellowes, of the glories of English choral music. This he described as 'the most exciting thing that has happened in the world of music since Sir George Grove and Sir Arthur Sullivan went and discovered the lost Schubert manuscripts in Vienna'.[33] Later the Trust paid for the publication of works like Vaughan Williams's *A London Symphony* and Warlock's *The Curlew*.

In 1921 Hadow wrote a report for the Carnegie Trust which was a survey of the present condition and future prospects of British music. He commented on the progress of musical education in the specialist schools and colleges of Ireland and Scotland. In Wales the problem was more concentrated: there was an intense love of music, and probably no conservatoire was needed since 'the new Music Council is already taking very successful measures for organising the forces of musical education throughout the Principality'.[34] Incidentally, the following remark of Hadow in 1921 may have been the source for one of Walford's Welsh ideas:

At the National Welsh Eisteddfod...the Welsh hymns are sung not only by the competing choirs but by the entire assembly, many thousands in number. It is not too much to hope that we may some day close a festival with a performance of the *St Matthew Passion*, the choruses sung by the massed choirs, and the chorals by the audience.[35]

Thomas Jones, who had been chiefly reponsible for mobilizing the resources of the Davies sisters in aid of Welsh musical education in 1918, retired from the Cabinet Office in 1930. At Stanley Baldwin's suggestion he moved immediately to become Secretary of the Pilgrim Trust, which was designed to dispense the bequest of a wealthy American, Edward Harkness. Jones told his new employer in New York that the London office of the Trust would not need to be staffed with specialists for education, hospitals, churches and so on. 'If only somehow I could be made a member of the Athenaeum Club, where at midday is gathered more queer knowledge to the square table than anywhere else in the Kingdom, I could secure whatever advice I needed on every sort of appeal...'[36] The Carnegie and Pilgrim Trusts were to reinforce the funds of the Davieses and of the University of Wales when Walford's Welsh mission reached a critical stage in its evolution. Thomas Jones was intervening even more directly in the development of adult education in Wales during the 1920s. Having been frustrated in his desire to become Principal at Aberystwyth, even while he was at the Cabinet Office he undertook the all-consuming effort of creating a Welsh equivalent of Ruskin College, arranging for the purchase of a mansion at Harlech for the purpose. Coleg Harlech survives to this day as a memorial to Thomas Jones and as a thriving institution whose service to thousands of aspiring working-class Welsh men and women is incalculable.[37] From the moment of its founding in September 1927, the new College became one of the chief bases for the adult work of the National Council of Music. For instance, the Aberystwyth Summer School was re-located there in 1928.[38] Walford followed the growth of the Harlech scheme with interest from its inception, and probably contributed much to its discussion. In January 1927, he wrote to T. J., 'I hear, to my delight, from Miss Davies, that you will be at Gregynog over the weekend, and we shall be able to thrash out things in that ideal atmosphere at some leisure, though I fully expect you to be divinely obsessed with "Coleg Harlech".'[39]

In March 1929, a new epoch in the life of the National Council of Music was inaugurated. The Welsh School of Social Service, which deployed aid to the most depressed inhabitants of the coalfield during the Depression, and held its annual meetings at Gregynog – with music presented by Walford and his colleagues – asked the National Council of Music to organize the systematic provision of music in the south Wales mining valleys. Through the association of Walford Davies, Thomas Jones and Henry Hadow, a grant of £1,100 was made for the purpose by the Carnegie Trust. Immediately the Council set in motion a scheme for providing concerts, visits of conductors for courses in combined singing, the extended use of lecture-recitals, and the planting of listening clubs for local people. In the spring and summer of 1929 alone, 161 free concerts were given in forty-six places, with audiences totalling approximately 72,500. The Council provided free song-books for the choirs who sang at eighty-nine singing meetings that summer, attended by 5,800. Wirelesses were donated to workmen's halls and institutes; the listening clubs were provided with records and gramophones. Through Walford's long professional association with the Gramophone Company, 1,000 HMV records were given free for circulation. This considerable administrative achievement was rewarded in the next year by an increased grant of £2,000.

Many groups of musical enthusiasts already existed; but the main importance of the Council's work was that it could identify needs and help to satisfy them in materially useful ways. It created a substantial network of spiritually necessary nourishment at the darkest time in the history of modern Wales. In 1930 seventy-six concerts were given and ninety-two singing-meetings held, attended by 32,000 people. The number of listening clubs increased to forty.[40] These activities were truly a fulfilment of Hadow's confident hope in 1921: '...music is permeating the entire land and becoming the possession and delight of the whole people'.[41] But it would not be too wide of the mark to suppose that behind the warm cloak of benevolence extended to cover those in need, extra-musical factors were being considered: Hadow had also written that 'we are again beginning to permeate our education with music, and by its means to teach our young people a love of beauty and *a reverence for law*' (my emphasis).[42]

The establishment of a listening club and its possible consequences were described in the cases of those at Cilfynydd and Porth: '...we started with Concerts which led to a Gramophone Listening club, then a Terminal course, and now a Choral society is to be formed in readiness for the next [Three Valleys] Festival.'[43] Again, however, the needs of such groups could be diverse. One might ask for copies of Negro spirituals and sea shanties, another for symphonies and concertos with minature scores. The Council acted as a sort of schools library service, packaging representative and graded sets of records, consisting of symphony, string quartet, solo-vocal and choral specimens. In 1930–31 the listening clubs were accepted in some cases as recognized courses by the Board of Education. The attendances during a year could be massive. At Pontypridd YMCA, for instance, in 1930–31 there were thirty-one meetings attended by over 1,200; at Burry Port thirty-six with 873; at Abergorky Hall, thirty meetings with 750. This was a positively successful use of largesse.

This part of the musical campaign continued to take music to the people throughout the 1930s without intermission. But it was not always certain that Walford's failing health would tolerate the strain. His brother, Harold Davies, an academic physician, had emigrated to Australia. During a visit to England in 1928 he was prompted to offer a filial second opinion on Walford's heart condition. Writing to Thomas Jones from his brother's lodging in Windsor Castle Cloisters, Harold Davies said,

> I have been much concerned to find him so over-pressed with work and resposibilities which, it seems to me, he cannot continue to carry without gravest risk...To me the issues are clear, and to Walford himself I have put them this way – 'What is your life worth, not merely to Margaret and yourself, but to the cause of music? Do you want to survive at most for 2 or 3 years, or do you wish to perpetuate your usefulness it may be for another 10 or 15 years?...' As I see it, he should give up Wales at the earliest moment. Through the BBC his tremendous influence can still be exerted with the least expenditure of physical energy... If I can leave England feeling that his best friends are conspiring to shield him (even from himself) I shall be happier...[44]

To complicate matters further, siren-songs were being sung from other rocks: in 1927, Walford had written to Thomas Jones outlining the invitation which had been offered him to start a new College of Music in Scotland. This he refused on the grounds that 'the rest of my working days should be given to making music rather than organising and distributing it'.[45] But in Wales, of course, Walford was undertaking all three tasks, though with the help of MacLean and his office staff.

He had already shed the not very considerable teaching and the more onerous administrative work associated with the Gregynog Chair at Aberystwyth. Commuting between the Home Counties and the Cardiff office after 1926 was less taxing. But matters reached a crisis in 1930. Since 1927 there had been murmurs of dissatisfaction from some members of the University Court about the administrative and financial procedures of the National Council of Music and Walford's unusual standing as a non-professorial person. In July 1930, while recuperating from illness, Walford informed Jenkin James, the Secretary of the University Council, of his intention to resign the post of Director:

> I feel it has been a great privilege to serve the University and country generally as their first Director of Music; and it has been an unforgettable happiness to have been a fellow-worker with the Members of the National Council of Music, during its first decade, in the cause of the spread of musical happiness and study throughout the country... The work has grown organically, and lately alarmingly owing to the new possibilities now opening up in the needy areas of South Wales. But I feel I am leaving it ready for extension...because of the efficiency of the Secretary and staff...[46]

This decision was felt as a body-blow by his supporters inside and outside Wales. Without Walford the National Council might become a tinkling cymbal. Immediately the University initiated a committee of inquiry. Its terms of reference were straightforward: to review the constitution, duties and powers of the National Council. But its central functions were to consider the legally doubtful area of the University's contribution to elements of the Council's work which were not of university standard. Hadow became chairman of the Committee which included Gwendoline Davies, Reichel, Sir Percy Watkins, J. Lloyd Williams and Miss M. A. Vivian, all of whom were Walford's devotees. They recommended that, on his departure, the title 'Director', as suggested by the Haldane Commission, should be retained. The tricky question of Walford having latterly served as Director while not holding an academic post within the University was resolved: in future the Director ought to be a Professor at one of the constituent Colleges. In the matter of the standard of work undertaken in adult education by the Council and supported financially in part by the University, the Committee recommended that 'it does not appear advisable to differentiate too closely between activities which are of a University standard and those which are not. A reasonable amount of discretion...must be left to the Council of Music...'[47] Such a recommendation was clearly in line with the wide powers originally envisaged for the Council by the Haldane Commission, of which Hadow had been a member, in 1918.[48]

Convalescing at Windsor, Walford expressed 'unmixed delight' on reading the 1930 'Hadow' Report.[49] He withheld execution of his resignation until late in 1931 when Thomas Jones informed the Pro-chancellor, the Hon W. N. Bruce, 'I have good reason for believing that, if Sir Walford Davies were invited by the University to continue in the Directorship until the end of the Session 1932–3, he would be prepared to accept the invitation'.[50] And so he did, continuing in office until his death in 1941.

The years 1930 and 1931 were otherwise a watershed in the Council's affairs. The journal *Y Cerddor*, edited by W. S. Gwynn Williams, had valiantly struggled on through most of the 1920s; but its financial resources were over-stretched and its circulation not large. It had never been, even formally, the friend of the National Council. In 1929, with the original journal in abeyance, the Council decided to take it over, and revive it under the same title. Henceforward it became the mouthpiece of the Council, but also the means of co-ordinating the activities of an informal society of music and musicians throughout Wales, Cymdeithas Ceredigion Cerdd. J. Lloyd Williams, the new editor of the journal, reported in 1931 that, after its first year of publication, *Y Cerddor* was maintaining a circulation of about 850, 200 more than its predecessor.[51]

In June 1930, Professor Maurice Jones, of Lampeter College, chairman of the Cymdeithas executive committee, published a letter outlining the aims of the Society, which were, 'to provide mutual help, guidance, and comradeship in music, and to secure effectual lines of communication between music lovers, be they amateurs or professionals.' He wished all Welshmen, 'for the love they bear towards their country and its culture, and more particularly on its musical side, to join in their thousands'.[52] The connections between the cells of the new society were not, however, to be tangible in the ordinary way. At the first conference of the society, at Cardiff in the summer of 1930, Walford brought John Reith of the BBC as a guest and physical embodiment of the fact that the wireless was to be the chief agent of the further progress of musical appreciation in Wales. At the Cardiff meeting of the new society Reith said,

...The days of great Patrons are over. The arts are now in care and keeping of the common people...And the future of music must lie with 'amateurs' in the broadest sense of the word...The BBC is out to help you; and you must help the BBC...The BBC wishes you every success...

He promised Welsh music-lovers that, despite the peculiar 'orographi-cal contours of Wales', they would get two high-powered stations which would deliver good music to them wherever they were. The BBC also provided high tea for the members of the society.[53] That meeting, Walford's broadcasts, the new society, the listening clubs in the Valleys, the publications of the Council and the temporary BBC Orchestra in Cardiff together represented the wide extent of the Director's inexorable influence over the development of musical sen-sibility in the Principality. In spite of ill health, the wave of his enthusiasm was unstoppable, and drowned earlier serious discussion of the survival of Welshness in music in the face of outside forces.

Walford's was one of the best-known wireless voices. In Britain generally it is for his pioneering broadcasts that he is now most often remembered. But in south Wales there are still those who recall the remarkable efforts he made to translate the principles embodied in his programes of education for the distressed areas into a festival which would raise the spirits of the jobless, and give those who sang a leisure occupation, and those who wished to play professionally a chance to sustain their careers locally.

Until the recent creation of St David's Hall in Cardiff, Wales had no purpose-built permanent concert hall. There was, however, in the Cynon Valley a phenomenon of staggering proportions which was used to tremendous advantage in the ten years before the Second World War. In 1901 a consortium of Mountain Ash business people (known locally as 'the forty thieves') had proposed to build the largest hall in Wales. At first their Pavilion was a market-hall, but the failure of that enterprise led to its use as a boxing and roller-skating venue and also as a concert hall, which, it was found, could accommodate up to 15,000 people. In the winter months it housed Studt's Indoor Fair or Bostock & Womble's Menagerie – a lion cub was born there in 1912.[54] Walford Davies found an even more extraordinary use for the Pavi-lion. With the local musician Bumford Griffiths, and in what was by tradition the most musically energetic of Welsh communities, he created the Three Valleys Festival whose concerts became the high points of music-making in Wales during the penurious 1930s.

In 1927 Bumford Griffiths and his Aberpennar Orchestra had given a series of concerts in aid of the Mountain Ash (Coal Strike) Distress Fund in the Pavilion 'to a crowded audience'.[55] That served as the model for the series of Festivals which began in May, 1930. The *Musical Times* heralded the event somewhat inaccurately by announc-

The Executive Committee of the Three Valleys Festival at Mountain Ash, 1932, with Malcolm Sargent seated fourth from right, J. Charles MacLean seated far right and C. W. Dixon (Walford's assistant) standing third from right in the middle row (by permission of Cynon Valley Public Libraries)

ing that it was 'designed to yoke together the musical potentialities of the Rhondda coal-mining area'.[56] Walford himself described it as 'a wholesome companion-event to the National Eisteddfod itself'. A purely musical festival of such magnitude, he said, 'established as an annual fixture in the heart of our populous districts, must prove a boon, not only to the mining areas themselves, but to the whole country'.[57]

In the programme of the first Festival, Walford thanked the BBC for all their help, particularly in permitting the National Orchestra of Wales – augmented with local instrumentalists – to play at the main concerts; in addition the Columbia Gramophone Company had sent engineers to record some parts of the programmes. The National Council provided the administrative expertise. Funds came from private donors, businesses and public bodies: Gwendoline Davies; the Ely Brewery; Sir Percy Watkins; Lord Aberdare; Boots the Chemists; Hodges and Sons (Clothiers); Mr and Mrs Charles MacLean; Walford himself; Aberdare and District Co-operative Society; the Countess of Bradford; local Directors of Education; the National Union of Teachers; Principal Maurice Jones of Lampeter, and Lord Jersey. Part of the cost of printing the Festival programmes was borne by advertisers: 'In the interests of public health this building is disinfected with SANITAS'.[58]

A *cymanfa ganu* was the beginning of each Festival. In 1930 thirty chapel choirs took part. At first there was a children's concert, with 2,500 singers assembled together, and a junior orchestra of 200 players. All the amateur performers were drawn from the area which stretched from Merthyr Vale in the east to the two Rhondda Valleys in the west. The *Messiah* became an annual feature, with a choir comprising sixteen to twenty choral societies. The Male Voice concert usually had 1,500 singers. In the 1930s the vocal soloists were regularly Elsie Suddaby, Muriel Brunskill, Parry Jones, Tom Pickering from Aberystwyth, Horace Stevens, Dora Labette, Walter Glynne, Stiles-Allen, Heddle Nash, Frank Titterton, Olive Gilbert and Gladys Ripley. Walford and Bumford undertook some of the conducting, but another feature of the Festivals from the beginning was the quality of imported conducting talent. Henry Wood appeared alongside Sargent in 1930, and even came again in his jubilee year, 1938. Apart from traditional oratorios, there were orchestral concerts with interesting programmes. The young Mansel Thomas was soloist in Grieg's Piano Concerto in 1930 in a concert which included Strauss's *Till Eulenspiegel* and

Brahms's *Alto Rhapsody*. The B-minor Mass inevitably appeared, along with Verdi's *Requiem* (the *Dies Irae* with a choir of 1,500 must have been terrifying in its effect). Morgan Jones, Parliamentary Secretary at the Board of Education, came to preside on Children's Day in 1930.

If Walford had been in poor health at the end of the 1920s, the huge effort he made in bringing the Three Valleys Festival into being and participating in almost every one of its concerts seemed to revive his spirits. Each year he delivered a typical homily in the official programme. He usually thanked the BBC, who continued to send players from Bristol even after the demise of the Cardiff Orchestra; and he was publicly grateful to the Carnegie Trust and the National Council of Social Service for their financial contributions. There was also technical advice of a characteristic kind: 'Let every single singer look at the beat! Look with your *eyes*! and listen with your *eyes*! Give and take the whole time!'[59] He repeatedly emphasized the social implications of the venture. In 1931 he wrote, 'If only we can, with united good-willing work, make the event an annual fixture, it must prove a boon, not only to this district, but to the whole country. It may even call out to our friends (and fellow-sufferers from the trade depression) in Northumberland and Durham, "please copy" for their need and courage for such an undertaking are doubtless as great as ours.' When Wood could not appear in 1931 he leaned upon a military metaphor: '...many people date winning the War from the gloomy day in April, 1918, when all our forces were united under Marshal Foch; so we have gone for unity of command for the whole week under Dr Malcolm Sargent.'

As the Festival established itself, his social message was expressed ever more powerfully: 'It is team-work that is our strength. Everyone in his station must feel it. From our big men like Horace Stevens (the bass), down to the humblest choralist or steward, we are in pursuit of great music, and in strong, friendly determination to be one family in our joy and in our united task. Heaven bless the Three Valleys with happier times...' He dipped into the vast quantity of letters he received from wireless listeners:

> At the time of writing this, a chance letter from a perfect stranger reached me and lies on my table before me now, a scribble on a stray sheet of an exercise book. It is about listening to a music broadcast, and I cannot but quote it here, coming as it does from a lonely working man:

> 'I am a hawker, and I am afraid a very ignorant one; and I looked upon

"this classical stuff" with all the prejudice the illiterate have to things they do not understand...I gradually found, opening before me, like a new and unexplored Eden, a wonderland of new and wider pleasures...'

And in contrast Walford added that the Prince of Wales had written the following message: 'I send my good wishes for the success of the Three Valleys Festival, which I am glad to hear is celebrating its fifth anniversary year – Edward P.' Walford acted as a hawker himself: 'Does your daughter play the piano? Take care she comes to hear Mr Clifford Curzon!' This genial admonition was possibly based on his awareness of the continuing Welsh resistance, even in the Cynon Valley, to purely instrumental music: Gethin Jones remembers that, during Walford's playing in Beethoven's First Piano Concerto in 1931, the audience chattered quite happily before settling down to enjoying quietly a later choral item.[60] The Three Valleys Festival was perhaps the most remarkable spontaneous phenomenon of its kind during the inter-War years in Britain. Its vitality as a social event lightened the gloom of the distressed areas, and served to combine musical enthusiasms and skills of many kinds. In the programme for 1935 Walford wrote, 'Musical power is as invisible as electric power; it is as real and infinitely more important, more human too, and more spiritual.' GWR trains brought audiences from all over south Wales; chapel vestries were transformed into temporary cafés, with tea at a penny a cup and jam sandwiches at 3*d.* each; crowds lined the streets of Mountain Ash to cheer the charabancs of 'their' choirs and to greet David Lloyd George on his visit in 1934. Like the festivals in Newtown, Aberystwyth and Harlech, the Three Valleys involved large numbers of people in music-making, not merely in listening; and that, behind the screen of his rhetoric, was always Walford's main intention.

The National Eisteddfod, with its local off-shoots, continued to thrive as a popular gala throughout the 1920s and 1930s. In its musical activity, it was reluctant to respond to the kind of lead which Walford set. Then, as now, one of its legitimate and necessary functions was to sustain memories of the past, rather than to encourage the pursuit of change for its own sake. The Bangor Eisteddfod of 1931 was attended by the travel-writer H. V. Morton who perhaps consciously echoed the awe of previous English visitors: 'I have seen nations in mourning and in times of popular rejoicing. I have seen crowds as big as this Welsh crowd whipped up into a dervish frenzy about sport; but never have I seen a crowd which represents all the lights and shades of an entire

Group picture taken at Deep Duffryn Colliery, Mountain Ash, during the Three Valleys Festival, 1932. Malcolm Sargent fifth from the left; Bumford Griffiths second from right (by permission of Cynon Valley Public Libraries)

nation gathered together to sing, play musical instruments and to recite verse.'[61] But in the following year, even one of its central figures expressed the view that the Eisteddfod was 'disintegrating through Philistinism and parochialism, and that it was high time to rebuild it on a strong and proper national basis.'[62] Also, W. J. Gruffydd resumed his scholarly tirade in the journal *Y Llenor*: 'The National Eisteddfod is quickly drawing to its end, and the fact that some of us have been prophesying this for some time will not ease the blow when it falls.'

Although those remarks were directed mainly at the literary activity of the Eisteddfod, criticism of its musical standards also continued. The disaster of the *St Matthew Passion* at Mold had set the tone. Choral triumph and tragedy in competition still dominated popular attention. Despite the fair prospect which had been offered particularly by the Barry and Ammanford *Eisteddfodau* after the Great War, musical activity became moribund. Walford continued to attend and conduct, though he must have been somewhat bewildered by Bantock's remarks as adjudicator at Holyhead in 1927: he appealed for a 'more modern and less Welsh outlook', while at the same time, perhaps thinking of his friend Vaughan Thomas, admonishing the Welsh for not listening to 'their Welsh advisers' and for leaning too heavily on the help of 'the mere Saxon'.[63] By this time the militant tendency in Welsh music, led by Leigh Henry, had folded its tents; and David Vaughan Thomas was about to embark upon his examining work abroad. At Liverpool in 1929 Walford's influence over the evening concert programmes was strong. There was a 'Welsh' evening, including a performance by Holbrook of his Piano Concerto *Gwyn ap Nudd*, and a survey-concert of music from Elizabethan times to Vaughan Williams, 'a Welsh composer, of course, for these purposes'.[64]

But the sentimental attachment of many Welsh people to the arid music of the past would not, it seemed, be dissolved simply by the inclusion of selected improving musical examples in annual *Eisteddfodau*. The National Council's work of attempted transformation was therefore more subtle, and more clearly a part of its broad adult-education policy. It chose to work through the smaller local *eisteddfodau* which were centres for most of the amateur music-making in Wales, rather than the grand annual event. In its report for 1928 the Council noted that its plans to help with local 'self-reform' had been taken up enthusiastically as a result of conferences held throughout Wales under its aegis. 'The local keenness shown justifies the hope that such long-standing evils as low standard of test-pieces, absence of high musical aim, and unpunctuality, will be effectually met and dealt with by the whole musical will of the country.'[65] The immediate constitutional result was the formation of Undeb Eisteddfodau Cymru, the Federation of Welsh *eisteddfodau*, with a list of Vice-Presidents which included David Lloyd George, Maurice Jones, Sir William Jenkins MP, Lord Howard de Walden, Gwendoline Davies and the Archdruid, the Revd J. O. Williams (Pedrog).

The tangible effect of the implementation of this policy came in the form of publications by the Council. The first of these was *Hints and Suggestions*. This included a statement of aims, among which was the fostering of Welsh music through the selection of test-pieces, by the introduction of folk-dancing competitions according to Cecil Sharp's principles, the addition of instrumental classes at local *eisteddfodau* alongside traditional vocal events, and the insertion of literary competitions involving research into aspects of Welsh musical history.[66] Charles MacLean had appealed in *Y Cerddor* for assistance in the compilation of the pamphlet, requesting particularly from local secretaries of *eisteddfodau* 'pieces you feel you can recommend, including your own compositions'.[67] MacLean suggested heads – Chief Choral, Tenor solos (sacred), Two-part for Schools, etc. – under which suggestions could be offered. *Hints and Suggestions* subsequently contained a wealth of appendices listing suitable test-pieces, with their publishers.

The work of the National Council in connection with *eisteddfodau* was of a piece with the broad pattern of its activity in the realm of adult education. The achievement was immense. Despite his powerful qualities as a popular communicator, Walford's conception of the Council had been that it should be an inspirer and co-ordinator and, as far as possible, never didactic or over bearing. Fifty years after his death it may seem to the casual observer of the development of Welsh music that, because the Council has not been frequently celebrated as a bearer of gifts to the people of Wales, its work now deserves little acknowledgement. Judging by what Daniel Jones had to say at Swansea in 1951, the Council would seem to have achieved very little.[68] But acceptance of Jones's remark as a judgement on the Council would be misleading.

Epilogue

The years between 1919 and 1941 saw many large achievements; much of what the Haldane Commission had expected in 1918 was accomplished under Walford's direction. He contrived to mobilize financial and human resources in ways which his straitened predecessors in Welsh music would have envied. The wealth and sympathy of the Davieses, the strong encouragement of Thomas Jones, Hadow, Reichel and Percy Watkins, among others in influential places, had provided him with a confident platform from which to plan and execute his campaign. In his day he was a figure of great eminence whose utterances were listened to with more respect than any British musician may command in the 1990s. The leading English critic Fuller Maitland, as early as 1929, could reflectively estimate that, in the work of training the general public, 'no activity has been more important and fruitful than that of Sir Walford Davies'.[69]

Walford had not identified the 'problem' of Welsh music through his own investigations: the Haldane Commission, in the person of W. H. Hadow, had done that before he had ever conceived of Wales as a sphere of profitable activity. Though he was a man of strong and elegantly delivered opinions and possessed by genius as a teacher, Walford was not particularly original as a thinker on musical topics. In 1918 he entered upon work in a country which was not entirely populated by the heathen. The Welsh – or, rather, a small minority of Welsh musicians – had begun to dismantle their own musical myths before 1914. Frederick Griffiths from his desk in the Covent Garden pit, David Vaughan Thomas after experiencing the best that metropolitan and Oxford music could offer, Mme Barbier with her French connections, organizational energy and Gallic aplomb, D. Emlyn Evans exercising a rational kind of sensitivity, and Harry Evans realizing the need for a broader perspective on music-making, had all burnt trails of criticism along which Walford was later to stride. Daniel Lleufer Thomas, not a musician, offered a wider social perspective. Arthur Lyon, from his eccentric enclave at Hawarden, provided a prior model for what secondary schools might achieve in unpropitious circumstances; and the gifted W. M. Williams lent a vertebrate quality to possibilities in elementary-school music. Local orchestral pioneers, like Angle and Ware in Cardiff, Sims in Newport and Harold Lewis in Milford Haven, were already showing that parts of Wales could react to the kinds of criticism offered long before by Fred Griffiths. From the remarkable Cynon Valley cauldron of musical activity Bumford Griffiths emerged to exercise his exceptional talents on Walford's behalf. The depiction of Wales by the Haldane Commission as a musical morass was based partly upon ignorance of these already emerging elements in regional culture.

And there were those, too, from within and without Wales, who had proposed schemes for improvement which were not so different from those which Walford strove to implement after 1918. The greatest of these was Hadow, who had relied very heavily for information on his contact with Reichel and J. Lloyd Williams, who both spoke from from a direct experience which was nevertheless largely limited to the hinterland of Bangor University College. It is possible to guess that Hadow, like Walford, mainly received his picture of Welsh music through the pages of annual reports of *eisteddfodau* in the *Musical Times* and contact with stunned adjudicators returning to their metropolitan academic complacency. More philosophical observers, like Somervell, probably considered that the phenomenon of Wales was little different from regional deserts in the English provinces. The work of Mary Wakefield and her supporters in the English Festival movement presaged much of what Walford achieved so flamboyantly in Wales, in reaction to the Eisteddfod's aggressive tradition. In school music in England, Walter Carroll, for instance, was already using the potentialities of the new local education authorities for creative educational efforts in mass music-making at Manchester. Walford's work, then, was hardly original in its detailed conception.

In the execution of his eclectic policies, however, he supplied an overview, rhetorical energy, varied experience, and the power of an uncomplicated mind. These qualities were electrically connected to his confidence as one of the greatest twentieth-century mass communicators: he knew instinctively that most members of his audiences were waiting to be awakened; and he had the gift of always effectively administering the Sleeping Beauty kiss. His other chief qualities in Wales were an ability to identify unerringly those who were best equipped to serve his musical aims, and the seemingly simple administrative magic which enabled him to draw together amateur and professional musicians who, according to the conventional view of a Welsh inherent inability to co-operate, were otherwise at loggerheads. The conductors' seminars he arranged for hundreds of Welsh choirmasters, with the assistance of Adrian Boult, in the 1930s, must have had an immeasurably large effect on the developing technique of choral direction in subsequent generations.

His work in relation to the schools is equally unquantifiable. The pamphlets of advice produced by the Council in the early 1920s, coupled with the impact of Walford's frequent visits to many elementary and secondary schools, as inspector and inspirer (perhaps in the impressive guise of 'the man on the wireless'), must have had a profound influence on attitudes as well as methodology among teachers. That part of his and the Council's work has become buried under subsequent developments. The Welsh LEAs were slow to evolve their own policies of musical education and ideas about music in the curriculum in the 1920s and early 1930s.

In 1936 W. P. Wheldon, Permanent Secretary, Welsh Department, Board of Education, fashioned a neat Preface to his Department's pamphlet, *Suggestions for the Teaching of Music*, in which he acknowledged that little had been done in Welsh schools during the early part of the twentieth century to nurture musical skills. With the coming of the wireless, however, interest in school music, he claimed, had been renewed. In the years immediately prior to 1936 'it is pleasant to record the notable advances that have been made, stimulated largely by the National Council of Music for Wales, in the formation of school orchestras and schools festivals, and, as far as work outside schools is concerned, in Adult Education.'[70] For the first time, in this instance, Wheldon put pressure upon Directors of Education to make sure that *every* school purchased a copy of the music pamphlet.[71] In addition, Irwyn Walters, a former B. Mus. student of Walford at Aberystwyth, was appointed as the first full-time specialist Music HMI in Wales. His influence on music-making in Welsh schools after the Second World War has been incalculably great.[72] The inspirational and pedagogical work of Bumford Griffiths and J. Morgan Nicholas in training thousands of children for public performances of a high standard needs to be recognized, particularly in an age when such efforts are to some extent unwarrantably taken for granted. Their immediate heir was Dorothy Adams Jeremiah in Monmouthshire, who achieved outstanding results as a motivator of teachers and pupils after 1936.[73] Every school which participated in Walford's and his lieutenants' enthusiasm could be sure that, if they requested it, the National Council would provide the best available resources of equipment, supported, perhaps, by lecture-recitals by the Council's players. Its publications were also essential elements in the improvement, not only of juvenile performances, but of the quality of singing and playing in churches, chapels, *eisteddfodau* and the adult education singing meetings.

It was in adult education that the Council achieved its greatest success. Walford Davies was the protégé of Thomas Jones and Hadow, was financially supported by the Davieses, and was admired and encouraged by such influential figures as Percy Watkins and Harry Reichel. He thus became locked comfortably into well-meaning, high-minded attempts to deliver industrial south Wales from despair. In this he may well have been the innocent agent of forces which had been propounding policies of social control in an age of potential political and social revolution. But his avuncular guidance of musical activity in distressed areas surely earns him a place on the Welsh record of relatively unselfish public endeavour. It is surely too easy to criticize the groups which met regularly in pastoral Gregynog as soft liberals in search of an excuse. Walford, at least, worked strenuously, and for no financial reward, during the 1930s on behalf of the economically dispossessed in south Wales. Like his eminent co-workers in the public interest, but with less clarity of political intent, he strove to keep the beasts of incipient Bolshevism and spiritual impoverishment at bay.

Walford Davies and the National Council provided a necessary bond for musical activity in Wales during the 1920s and 1930s. It still seems incredible that, in such otherwise unencouraging times, an organization with such large resources and for such a purpose should have come into existence and continued to thrive. In his specifically Welsh work Walford relied on the Davies money and the University's less effusive financial support; later this was supplemented by donations from private trusts which Hadow and Thomas Jones were able to facilitate, and grant-aid from an otherwise penny-pinching Board of Education.

However, the most potent feature of Walford's campaign, particularly in its later confident stages, was substantially the universal network of communication which was spun from his BBC broadcasts. In many respects Walford remained a Victorian – in his musical tastes and in those idiosyncracies which Gerald Cumberland had pilloried in such a self-indulgent way before the Great War. But he seized upon the

Walford Davies rehearsing a group of schoolchildren for a radio broadcast, April 1941 (by permission of the BBC)

new medium of broadcasting with a vigour which was unequalled even among much younger contemporaries in the 1920s. What Percy Scholes and Stewart Macpherson systematized in a scholarly way in the field of musical appreciation Walford had delivered as one of the most effective popular communicators from the very beginning of BBC transmissions. Many of his later wireless broadcasts reached thousands of listeners in Wales; and in the stead of 'Y Doctor Mawr' in the Welsh musical psyche, 'Syr Walford' finally emerged a popular cultural hero.

Above his obituary notice in *The Listener* for 20 March 1941, there is a photograph of Walford conducting a choir of children in the studio 'last month.' Reith's successor, F. W. Ogilvie, wrote the notice (which had earlier been broadcast on the Home Service). In it he claimed that, at any committee meeting, Walford 'stood out at once as the most vital and the most delightful person in the room.' Such testimony may help to explain how he could work his magic on an eminent academic like Hadow, on a worldly wise civil servant like Thomas Jones, or a forbidding administrator like John Reith. Ogilvie ended with a statement which ought to become classic in our 'media'-dominated age:

> People sometimes say that broadcasting 'made' So-and-so; but Walford Davies, with his seventeen years at the microphone, is one of those by whom broadcasting itself has been made.

Alec Robertson, another celebrated musical broadcaster – whose only obvious connection with Wales consists in his having been the lover of Ivor Novello – commemorated Walford's communicative skills in this anecdote:

> Once he found himself at a rather rowdy men's dinner. The usual near-bawdy stories were told, and the Walford [*sic*] was asked to say something. As he was talking he edged up to the piano and got the lid open. Soon he had his audience singing. That, perhaps, was not very remarkable: but he ended up by playing a Beethoven slow movement and getting the reception of the evening. I know of no one else who could have done that in such company.[74]

While he used the air-waves to dispense his love of Beethoven, Walford knew that the detested 'jazz band' – an object of hatred he shared with David Vaughan Thomas – was, like the popular cinema, distracting his British audience from the best. In Wales, however, he must have finally exulted in the kind of conservative native obsession with 'good music' some manifestations of which he had been sent to eliminate in 1918.

It is impossible to estimate his overall effect upon Wales in any except the most heterogeneous way. The unnecessary battles he fought against the musical 'Nationalists' in the 1920s are now of almost antiquarian interest. In the biographies of Daniel Jones, Alun Hoddinott, William Mathias and David Harries he scarcely, on the face of it, deserves a footnote. But to the last meeting of the National Council which he attended he could report with some pride, as an agent of the BBC, that although, because of the onset of war, the Welsh wavelength had ceased to be, 'an orchestral work by Miss Grace Williams, which had been commissioned before the war, would shortly be broadcast by the BBC orchestra...'[75] She, Mansel Thomas and Arwel Hughes were leading examples of Welsh creative musicians who, having grown up in Wales bathed in Walford's optimisim (if not his direct influence), benefited from the way in which he had turned the wireless towards the service of much that was best in musical activity.

His real bequest to musical Wales consists in the kinds of subsequent achievement which he would have most relished: not the composition of ephemerally popular works, but rather the evidence of a broadening musical awareness in the mass of the people. This is represented even today in memories of the post-War work of Russell Sheppard as founder of the Glamorgan County Youth Orchestra; in the festivals of Urdd Gobaith Cymru, where Walford would have been in his element; in the schools and community projects of the Welsh National Opera, at which he might at first have turned up his nose; in Irwyn Ranald Walters's National Youth Orchestra, and in all those junior instrumental and orchestral classes which meet on weekday evenings and Saturday mornings and produce players who understand what is best in musical endeavour through the devotion of tutors who are in many cases no longer paid for such extra-curricular enthusiasm. BBC broadcasts on music are now commonplace, and the generation which came up after 1945 saw the transformation of CEMA (which Walford helped to inaugurate) into the Arts Council, which continued his policy of taking music to the people. The University trios have become a largely unnoticed casualty of the latest Conservative 'educational' policies. But even in the current GCSE there are reminders of the Director's obsession with 'melody-building' and an emphasis on the practical side of music-making. Walford Davies ought to be remembered in Wales as an imperial interloper who, in his inmost heart, appreciated noble savagery and provided a means of collecting and co-ordinating its energy. It can be argued that, without his galvanic presence, a leading contemporary Welsh composer, Mervyn Burtch, would not have been able to write, soon after the premiere of Daniel Jones's Ninth Symphony in 1974,

> ...a Welsh composer has written nine symphonies. We now have a wide repertoire of Welsh symphonies available in Wales, and this situation contrasts most forcibly with the situation in our country only 25 years ago. We are producing a basic repertoire of Welsh works, which are not only of intrinsic value now, but will be the launching pad for new generations of Welsh composers. We are still only at the beginning of our professional musical history, and, in modern terminology, we are, musically speaking, one of the 'emerging nations'.[76]

In a simple, magisterial way Walford Davies had striven to achieve two compatible, but distinct, objectives: the realization of the highest creative musical potential, and the development of the greatest common denominator in general musical appreciation. Wales's standing as an emerging musical nation owes a great deal to his work during two decades of its development. However, it is surely likely that, were he now to re-visit Wales, he would be appalled by one aspect of contemporary 'reform': the financial culling of the adult education movement, with its specially deleterious effects upon the teaching of music.

NOTES

Prologue

1. W. H. Hadow, *Collected Essays*, London, 1928, 67.
2. *South Wales Evening Post*, 18 September, 1951, 'Swansea Composer Tells of Poverty of Welsh Music'.

Chapter One

1. Lewis Thorpe (ed.), *Gerald of Wales; The Journey through Wales and The Description of Wales*, London, 1978, 242.
2. John Parry, *Antient British Music* (1742); Edward Jones, *Musical and Poetical Relicks of the Welsh Bards, with a General History of the Bards and Druids, and a Dissertation on the Musical Instruments of the Aboriginal Britons* (1784).
3. Percy Scholes, *The Great Dr Burney: His Life – His Travels – His Works – His Family and Friends*, Oxford, 1948, II, 200.
4. Quoted by Frank Kidson, in 'Welsh Music', *Grove's Dictionary of Music and Musicians*, 3rd edition, 1928.
5. Quoted in Alwyn Tudur, 'Mendelssohn's Visit to Wales', *Welsh Music*, IV, 4, 1974, 43–9.
6. John Parry (Bardd Alaw), *A Trip to North Wales, containing Much Information Relative To That Interesting Alpine Country, and the best mode of viewing its Sublime and Magnificent Scenery...*, London, 1840.
7. Charlotte Moscheles, *Life of Moscheles, with selections from his diaries and correspondence, by his Wife*, London, 1873, I. 289.
8. R. T. Jenkins and Helen Ramage, *A History of the Honourable Society of Cymmrodorion and of the Gwyneddigion and Cymreigyddion Societies, 1751– 1951*, London, 1952, 123.
9. See below, Chapter Two.
10. J. Cuthbert Hadden, *George Thomson, Friend of Burns, His Life and Correspondence*, London, 1898, 124–7.
11. Edward Gray, *Cambrian Mirror, or A New Tourist Companion through North Wales*, 3rd edition, London, 1848.
12. Maria Jane Williams, *Ancient Airs of Gwent and Morganwg: being a collection of original Welsh Melodies, hitherto unpublished...*, 1844.

13. *Athenaeum*, 1 November 1873, 568.

14. *Journal of the Welsh Folk-song Society*, I, 1909–12, 91–2.

15. Welsh Folk-song Society, *Papers Read at Caernarvon, August 22nd, 1906, on Folk-Song by A. P. Graves, Esquire, and Principal H. R. Reichel, MA, LL.D, with Draft of Constitution, Rules, etc., of the Society*, Caernarfon, 1906.

16. Ibid, 9.

17. Ibid, 19.

18. Osian Ellis, 'Welsh Music: History and Fancy', *Transactions of the Honourable Society of Cymmrodorion*, Session 1972–3, London, 1974, 91.

19. Ibid, 93.

20. Quoted in D. E. Parry Williams, 'Music and Religion', in Peter Crossley-Holland (ed.), *Music in Wales*, London, 1948, 49.

21. Quoted in D. E. Parry Williams, op. cit., 54.

22. *Musical Times*, 1 November 1926, 1001.

23. Information taken mainly from D. E. Parry Williams, op. cit.; and from the *Dictionary of Welsh Biography*.

Chapter Two

1. John Curwen, *The Teacher's Manual of the Tonic Sol-fa Method, dealing with the Art of Teaching and the Teaching of Music*, 8th edition, London, 1900.

2. Gareth Williams, '"How's the Tenors in Dowlais?": Hegemony, Harmony and Popular Culture in England and Wales, 1600–1900', *Llafur*, 5, 1, 1988, 77; Williams quoted from 'FTSC', 'The Relation of Wales to the Tonic Sol-fa College' in *Wales*, I, 1911, 273–5.

3. *Western Mail*, Wednesday 9 August 1922.

4. Jenkins and Ramage, op. cit., 125.

5. *Two Essays on the Subjects Proposed by the Cambrian Society in Dyfed...at the Eisteddfod, held at Carmarthen in July, 1819: to which is added An Account of the Proceedings at the Eisteddfod*, Carmarthen, 1822, 93.

6. *Grove's Dictionary of Music and Musicians*, 3rd edition, 1928.

7. For an account of the Beaumaris meeting, see John Parry (Bardd Alaw), *A Trip to North Wales*, 1840.

8. Letter to *The Times*, 'Welsh Nationality', 31 August 1864.

9. See *Transactions of the National Eisteddfod of Wales, Aberdare, 1885*, Cardiff, 1887, x-xii.

10. *Transactions of the National Eisteddfod of Wales, Wrexham, 1888*, Liverpool, 1889, xxiv.

11. *Western Mail*, Thursday, 29 August 1889, '...Grand Welcome to Madame Patti; She Sings Several Songs'.

12. Frederick Griffiths, *Notable Welsh Musicians of Today*, London, 1896, 164–5.

13. Thomas Jones, *Rhymney Memories*, Newtown, 1938, 129.

14. See above, in reference to Llandudno.

15. W. R. Lambert, *Drink and Society in Victorian Wales, c.1820–c.1895*, Cardiff, 1983, 8.

16. A. C. Davies, *Aberdare, 1750–1850: A Study in the Growth of an Industrial Community*, unpublished University of Wales MA thesis, 1963, 316.

17. Lambert, op. cit., 18.

18. Thomas Jones, op. cit., 21.

19. See particularly, E. H. Fellowes, *Memoirs of an Amateur Musician*, London, 1946, 196–8, for his experiences as an adjudicator at the Llanelli Eisteddfod of 1930.

20. *Musical Times*, 1 September 1883.

21. *The Times*, 11 August 1883.

22. *Musical Times*, 1 September 1903, 599.

23. *The Star*, 13 April 1889, 'The Popular Musical Union'.

Chapter Three

1. *Tonic Sol-fa Register*, 1872.

2. E. L. Ellis, *The University College of Wales, Aberystwyth, 1872–1972*, Cardiff, 1972, 41.

3. Ibid, loc. cit.

4. Ibid, 55.

5. Copy in the Salisbury Library, University of Wales College of Cardiff.

6. *Western Mail*, Tuesday, 8 July 1890.

7. Ibid, Wednesday, 23 July 1890.

8. Ibid, Friday, 1 August 1890.

9. W. H. Sonely-Johnstone, *History of the Cardiff Festival, 1892*, London and Cardiff, n.d., 2.

10. *Western Mail*, 12 April 1892.

11. Sonely-Johnstone, op. cit., 94–5.

12. *Grove*, 3rd edition, 1928: 'Cardiff Festival'.

13. *Daily Telegraph*, 28 August 1913.

Chapter Four

1. *Transactions of the Liverpool Welsh Nationalist Society*, Liverpool, 1893, 109–121.

2. Griffiths, op. cit., xi-xvi.

3. Joseph Bennett, 'Music in Wales', *Transactions of the Honourable Society of Cymmrodorion*, Session 1896–7, London, 1897, 1–13.

4. *Musical Times*, 1 August 1907, 526.

5. Ibid, 1 August 1907, 520–4.

6. *The Competition Festival Record*, 1 August 1909, 1–3.

7. *Western Mail*, Friday, 6 September 1912.

8. Ibid, Wednesday, 4 September 1912.

9. Granville Bantock, 'A National College of Music for Wales', *English Review*, April 1913, 58–63.

10. *Musical Times*, 1 February 1912, 114.

11. Cyril Jenkins, 'Music in Wales' *Wales*, III, 3, March 1913, 163–4.

12. *Western Mail*, Monday, 9 December 1912, 'Musical Entente in South Wales'.

13. See below, Chapter Six.

14. *Daily Telegraph*, 27 August 1913.

15. Ibid, 28 August 1913.

16. Quoted in Martha Stonequist, 'Music in Aberystwyth 1909–1915', *Welsh Music*, IV, 7, Summer, 1974, 76–84.

17. *Musical Times*, Wales Report, 1 April 1920, 323.

18. Ibid, 1 June 1914, 410.

Chapter Five

1. Royal Commission on University Education in Wales, Final Report, 1917, 34–5.

2. Ibid, loc. cit.

3. Ibid, loc. cit.

4. D. Lleufer Thomas, 'University tutorial Classes for Working People', *Transactions of the Honourable Society of Cymmrodorion*, Session 1914–15, London, 1916, 69–135.

5. Ibid, 115.

6. See above, Chapter Four.

7. P. C. Buck, J. H. Mee, and F. C. Woods, *Ten Years of University Music in Oxford, Being a Brief Record of the Proceedings of the Oxford University Musical Union, during the years 1884–1894*, Oxford, 1894.

8. Hubert J. Foss, 'William Henry Hadow', *Music and Letters*, XVIII, 3, 1937, 236–8.

9. See above, Chapter One, 1.

10. W. H. Hadow, *Studies in Modern Music*, Oxford, 1892, 12.

11. *Music and Letters*, loc. cit.

12. British Museum ADD MS 55240, Macmillans Correspondence, letter 4 November 1911.

13. *Musical Times*, 1 October 1912.

14. Barnett House Papers, No 3: 'the Needs of Popular Musical Education' by Sir W. Henry Hadow, D. Mus, Principal of Armstrong College, Newcastle-

upon-Tyne, with a Foreword by the Rt. Hon. H. A. L. Fisher, D. Litt, President of the Board of Education, Oxford, 1918.

15. Ibid, 12.

16. Minutes of the Committee of Council on Education, 1840–1, 47.

17. Bernarr Rainbow, *The Land Without Music*, London, 1966, 123.

18. H. A. Bruce (Lord Aberdare), *An Address Delivered at the Swansea Musical Festival, December 28th, 1864*, London, 1885, 205–210.

19. W. Stanley Jevons, *Methods of Social Reform and other Papers*, London, 1883, 1–26.

20. Revd H. R. Haweis MA, *Music and Morals*, London, 1871, 486, 500.

21. Report of the Commission of Inquiry into Industrial Unrest during the War: No 7 Division, London, 1917, 38–9.

22. Sir Henry Hadow, *The Place of Music among the Arts*, The Romanes Lecture Delivered in the Sheldonian Theatre, 31 May 1933, Oxford, 1933, 10.

23. British Museum ADD MS 55240, Macmillans Correspondence: a sequence of letters, 2 March–2 May, 1919, relating to an anti-Bolshevist publication produced by a Mr Beckhofer, a Ukrainian refugee with a Welsh mother.

24. See above, (end of) Chapter Four.

25. *Musical Times*, 1 September 1914, 575.

26. National Library of Wales, J. H. Davies MSS, letter of L. J. Roberts, 4 September 1916.

27. See below, Chapter Six.

28. See Colles, op. cit., 69 ff.

29. Thomas Jones, *Leeks and Daffodils*, Newtown, 1942, 168–177.

30. National Library of Wales, Dr Thomas Jones CH Collection (henceforward, T.J. Coll), Class J Vol II, letter to T.J., 23 March, 1916.

31. Ibid, Class J, Vol III, typescript 'Musical Education in Wales – Notes of Dr Hadow's Conversation', 27 April 1917.

32. Ibid, letter of Gwendoline Davies, 18 May 1917.

33. Ibid, letter of Hadow, 24 June 1917.

34. Ibid, letter of Percy Watkins, 29 June 1917.

35. Ibid, letter of Hadow, 3 July 1917.

36. Ibid, Class J Vol IV, letter of Walford Davies, from Temple Church, 20 March 1918.

37. Ibid, 17 April 1918.

38. Ibid, confidential letter to T. F. Roberts, 17 April 1918.

39. Ibid, letter of Roberts, 23 April 1918.

40. Ibid, letter to T. F. Roberts (copies to others), 23 July 1918.

41. Colles, op. cit., 116.

42. T. J. Coll, Class W Vol IV, T. J. to Walford at Air Ministry, 15 July 1918.

43. For T. J.'s role before Versailles, see Stephen Roskill, *Hankey: Man of Secrets*, III, 1919–1931, London, 1972, 42, 47, etc.

44. University of Wales Registry, Papers of the National Council of Music (henceforward Reg Co), File H498.

45. T. J. Coll, Class X Vol V, letter of H. W. D., 9 October 1919.

46. Ibid, Class W Vol V, November 1918.

47. Ibid, Class X Vol V, letter of Hadow, 9 October 1919.

48. Ibid, 10 October 1919.

49. Ibid, 9 October 1919.

50. Ibid, 9 October 1919.

51. Colles, op. cit., 118.

52. T. J. Coll, Class X, Vol V, letter of Walford, Queen's Hotel, Aberystwyth, 6 November 1919.

53. Ibid, 12 November 1919.

54. Ibid, 12 November 1919.

55. *Cambrian News*, 21 November 1919.

56. T. J. Coll, Class X, Vol V, 10 November 1919.

57. For Coleg Harlech episodes, see Peter Stead, *Coleg Harlech, The First Fifty Years*, Cardiff, 1977.

Chapter Six

1. Quoted in Thomas Jones, *Leeks and Daffodils*, Newtown, 1942, 177.

2. Colles, op. cit.

3. Sir Walford Davies, *The Pursuit of Music*, London, 1935; 'Dedicated by His Majesty's Gracious Permission TO THE KING'.

4. See above Chapter Five.

5. Davies, op. cit., 381.

6. Gerald Cumberland, *Set Down In Malice: A Book of Reminiscences*, London, 1919, 28–31.

7. Ibid, 354–5.

8. Colles, op. cit., 120–1.

9. Cyril Jenkins, 'Dr Parry from the point of view of recent music' in E. Keri, MA, Evans, *Cofiant Dr Joseph Parry*, Cardiff and London, 1921.

10. H. Walford Davies, 'Our Mother-Tongue: A Musical Policy for Wales', *Transactions of the Honourable Society of Cymmrodorion*, Session, 1921–22, London, 1923, 1–9.

11. See above, Chapter Five.

12. For a detailed account of Somervell's preparation of this chapter, see PRO (Kew) Files ED24/233 and 237.

13. For the general significance of Somervell's educational achievement in England, see Gordon Cox, '"Sensitiveness to the Higher Rhythms": Arthur Somervell and His Vision of Music Education', a Paper read to the Society for Research in Psychology of Music and Music Education, 4 March 1990, Roehampton Institute of Higher Education, London.

14. Edward Lyttelton, *Schoolboys and School Work*, London, 1909, 31.

15. Donald Leinster-Mackay, *The Educational World of Edward Thring*, Brighton, 1987, 71–2; 110, etc.

16. Central Welsh Board, *Report on the Teaching of Music in Welsh Intermediate Schools*, Cardiff, 1918, 1–3.

17. Ibid, 7–8.

18. Ibid, 4.

19. National Library of Wales, David Vaughan Thomas Papers, File 30, items 11 and 12.

20. *Western Mail*, 3 June 1919.

21. *Who's Who*.

22. *Western Mail*, 26 July and 7 August 1919.

23. Ibid, 14 and 21 April 1920.

24. Ibid, 27 May 1920, 'Cardiff and Sir Edward Elgar: a Sublime Symphony and Empty Seats'.

25. Ibid, 26 April and 3 May 1920.

26. Ibid, 29 September 1919, 'Strike Scenes in South Wales'.

27. *Musical Times*, 1 September 1919, 472–6.

28. Ibid, 1 July 1919, 347, 'Dr Walford Davies on "The Musical Outlook"'.

29. Donald Moore (ed.), *Barry: the centenary book*, Barry, 1984. See especially Peter Stead, 'The town that had come of age: Barry 1918–1938', 367–427.

30. Conversation between the late Leslie Tusler and the author, recorded in Penarth, 9 September 1988.

31. *Musical Times*, 1 June 1921, 442.

32. Leslie Tusler, 'The Romilly Choirs', *Welsh Music*, 8, 1, 20–23.

33. *Western Mail*, 26 January 1920.

34. *Musical Times*, 1 September 1920, 622–3.

35. Ibid, 637.

36. Reg Co Files: applications for the post of Secretary to the Director of the Council, as at September 1919.

37. National Library of Wales, D. V. Thomas Papers, letter to Walford, April, 1920.

38. T. J. Coll, Class W Vol IV, letter of Walford to T. J., 26 April 1919.

39. *Musical Times*, 1 September 1920, 637.

40. T. J. Coll, Class W Vol IV, letter of Walford to T. J., 15 May 1920.

41. *Musical Times*, 1 November 1920, 776.

42. David Morgans, *Music and Musicians of Merthyr and District, Together with a List of Eisteddfodau to the Year 1901*, Merthyr Tydfil, 1922, 188.

43. *Transactions of the National Eisteddfod at Cardiff, 1883*, Cardiff, 1884, 442–3.

44. Gwilym P. Ambrose, 'The Aberdare Background to Y Côr Mawr', *Glamorgan Historian*, 9, Cowbridge and Bridgend, n.d., 191–202.

45. The author's conversation with Mr Gethin Jones, former deputy-headmaster of Vaynor and Penderyn County Secondary School, 7 June 1990.

46. J. Gwynfor Jones, *The Caernarfon County School: A History*, Gwynedd County Archives and Museums, 1989, 198.

47. W. H. Reed, *Elgar as I Knew Him*, London, 1936, 22–29.

48. Author's conversation with Mr Gethin Jones, ibid.

49. For W. J. Gruffydd's criticisms, see below

50. *Western Mail*, 11 August 1922.

51. Parrott, op. cit., 97–98.

52. *Musical Times*, 1 July 1919, 347.

53. *Y Cerddor*, I, 3 March 1922, 1.

54. Ibid, I, 3 May 1922, 2.

55. Ibid, I, 4 June 1922, 1–2.

56. *Western Mail*, Thursday, 10 August 1922.

57. See letter in NLW DVT Papers, of Leigh Henry, from School Lane, Liverpool, 1 February 1913.

58. *Western Mail*, Thursday 10 August 1922.

59. Leigh Henry, 'London Letter: Bartok and some Nationalistic Considerations for Wales', *Y Cerddor*, I, 3, May 1922, 74–5.

60. Leigh Henry, 'The National Eisteddfod', *Y Cerddor*, II, 19, September 1923, 175–7.

61. Colles, op. cit., 121–2.

Chapter Seven

1. *Welsh Outlook*, July 1922, 154.

2. Ibid, October 1921, 285.

3. Ibid, 341–2; NB, Jenkins mentions Lord Howard de Walden as librettist for Joseph Holbroke's *Dylan*.

4. Ibid, 218–9; NB, at a miscellaneous concert in Barry in 1912, David Vaughan Thomas played Skriabin's third Piano Sonata (NLW D.V.T. Papers).

5. Ibid, June 1925, 146–7. See also below, this Chapter.

6. Ibid, August 1925, 202–3.

7. Ibid, November 1925, 286–7; December 1925, 314–6; January 1926, 6–8.

8. See below, this Chapter.

9. *Musical Times*, 1 July 1933, 646–7, records the twentieth year of meetings of the Scottish School Music Association.

10. University of Wales, University Council of Music, *A Review of the Activities of the Council of Music, 1919–1941*, Cardiff, n.d., 9. (Copy in the Welsh Music Archive, UWCC, Cardiff.)

11. University of Wales, *Report of the National Council of Music*, July 1922, Cardiff, 1922, 3.

12. Estimates of Expenditure of the National Council of Music, University of Wales, For the Year from 1 July 1922, to 30 June 1923.

13. Conversation with Leslie Tusler, 9 September 1988.

14. See below, Chapter Eight.

15. Ian Parrott, op. cit.; John Hywel, 'Music in Gregynog', in Glyn Tegai Hughes, Prys Morgan and J. Gareth Thomas (eds.), *Gregynog*, Cardiff, 1977, 69–87.

16. *Musical Times*, 1 April 1922, 584. Sir Henry Jones, (who had died two months before, after a long, painful illness), in his early career as a schoolmaster in Brynaman, had demonstrated great expertise as a teacher of tonic sol-fa to his pupils. See, Sir Henry Jones, (ed. Dr Thomas Jones), *Old Memories*, London, 1923, 112–116.

17. T. J. Coll, Class W, Vol VI, 31 July 1922.

18. Hywel, op.cit., 77.

19. Michael Kennedy, *Adrian Boult*, London, 1987, 160–1.

20. Obituary of Dora Herbert-Jones (by Lindsay Evans), *Welsh Music*, Vol IV, No 6, Spring 1974, 103–4; see also, A. E. F. Dickinson, 'Gustav Holst and Welsh Folk-Song', ibid, 71–6.

21. *Report of the National Council of Music, to be presented to the Council at its meeting on July 15th, 1920.*

22. See above, Chapter Six.

23. *Musical Times*, 1 June 1920, 422.

24. J. Glynne Evans, 'The National Orchestra of Wales (1928–1931)', *Welsh Music*, Vol 6, no 2, 1979, 49.

25. University of Wales, University Council of Music, *Review of the Activities of the Council of Music*, 1919–1941, 15–16.

26. *Musical Times*, 1 August 1924, 747.

27. *Western Mail*, 12 August 1924, 'National Eisteddfod in Retrospect', by Leigh Henry.

28. *Sunday Times*, 29 March 1925.

29. *Musical Times*, 1 November 1920, 775.

30. A. Peacock and R. Weir, *The Composer in the Market Place*, London, 1975, 81.

31. Cyril Ehrlich, *The Music Profession in Britain since the Eighteenth Century*, Oxford, 1985, 212.

32. Asa Briggs, *The History of Broadcasting in the United Kingdom: II The Golden Age of Wireless*, Oxford, 1965, 121–184.

33. Nicholas Kenyon, *The BBC Symphony Orchestra*, London, 1981, 10–13.

34. *Grove's Dictionary of Music and Musicians*, 1980, III, 'Broadcasting', 315.

35. J. Glynne Evans, op. cit., 49–56.

36. BBC Annual Report for 1927, London, 1928, 3.

37. *Western Mail*, Saturday, 11 February 1928.

38. J. Glynne Evans, op. cit., 53–4.

39. *Western Mail*, Thursday, 5 March 1931.

40. Ronald Jones, 'Herbert Ware (1885–1955): An Appreciation', *Welsh Music*, Vol IV, No 4, 1973, 68–71.

41. *Musical Times*, 1 January 1924, 73: 'The First Symphony was played by Mr Ware's Orchestra of 50 performers on November 24 (1923); Sir Walford Davies gave textual notes.'

42. *Western Mail*, 17 May 1920, 'Music and Education: A Weak Link in Welsh Organization'.

43. PRO, ED109/7966, Reports on Welsh Schools: Hawarden County School, 24 January 1922. (Signed 'W.E.')

44. PRO ED109/7967, Full HMI Report on Hawarden County School, 23 October 1929.

45. G. Perrie Williams, *Welsh Education in Sunlight and Shadow*, London, 1918, 62–3.

46. University of Wales, National Council of Music, *Music in Wales: Report on Music in Secondary Schools, by Arthur Lyon*, Cardiff, 1921.

47. PRO ED109/8241, Secondary School Music Inspections: Port Talbot Secondary School, Report of a Visit paid to the School with HMI Mr Abel Jones, on Wednesday, 22 March 1928.

48. Welsh Department, Board of Education, *Suggestions for the Preparation of Schemes under the Education Act*, London, 1919, 36.

49. See above, Chapter Five.

50. Board of Education, *Curriculum and Examinations in Secondary Schools*, London, 1941, 3.

51. See above, this Chapter.

52. University of Wales, National Council of Music, *Memorandum on Music in Schools, both Primary and Secondary, being Suggestions for a Musical Policy and a Sketch for a Five Year's Course*, Cardiff, 1921, 2–4.

53. Brian Simon, *The Politics of Educational Reform, 1920–1940*, London, 1974, 37. Simon explains the cuts in educational spending which were made after Lloyd George's appointment of a Committee on Public Expenditure under Sir Eric Geddes in 1921.

54. Quoted in Stephen Humphries, *Hooligans or Rebels? An Oral History of Working-Class Childhood and Youth, 1889–1939*, Oxford, 1981, 28.

55. Percy A. Scholes, *The Mirror of Music, 1844–1944*, II, London, 1947, 634.

56. Board of Education, Consultative Committee, *The Education of the Adolescent*, London, 1926, 238–241.

57. See above, Chapter Five.

58. Board of Education, *Welsh in Education and Life, Being the Report of the Board of Education to Inquire into the Position of the Welsh Language and to Advise as to its Promotion in the Educational System of Wales*, London, 1927, 293–6.

59. Captain Anthony, the Registrar, was, fortunately for Walford, a reputable

amateur of music. The *Musical Times*, 1 April 1925, 360, noted that in February 1925, Anthony had addressed the Cardiff Societé Franco-Anglaise on '"The Old Songs of Brittany", with musical and lantern-slide illustrations, pointing out the similarity between Breton and Welsh folk-music.'

60. Reg Co, letter of H. W. D. to Anthony, undated, but evidently written during the summer of 1922.

61. Ibid, letter to Anthony, 9 October 1922, with appended draft Syllabus.

62. Ibid, H. W. D. to Anthony, 25 May 1923.

63. Ibid H. W. D. to Anthony, 7 December 1924.

64. PRO ED12/253, School Cetificate Examinations in Music: Report of the Investigators, W. H. Hadow, M. D. Brock, and A. Somervell HMI.

65. See above, Chapter Five.

66. *Musical Times*, 1 August 1926, 1035.

67. Reg Co Files, typewritten statement over MacLean's signature, September, 1921.

68. Ibid, letters between MacLean and Anthony, 4, 11, 17 November 1924; with printed Programme of the University Court Concert at Carmarthen, 19 December 1924.

69. University of Wales, National Council of Music, Minutes of the 48th Meeting... October 20 1939, at the University Registry, Cathays Park, Cardiff, 875–6.

70. Joyce Grenfell, 'Julia M', in Denise Lassimone (ed., with an Introduction by Howard Ferguson), *Myra Hess by her friends*, London, 1966, 60–1.

71. See above Chapter One.

72. Colles, op cit, 123.

73. Parrott, op cit, Chapter Seven.

74. See above, this Chapter.

75. Kennedy, op cit, 98, 104, 105.

76. See above, Chapter Seven.

77. *Musical Times*, 1 July 1925.

78. National Council of Music, Minutes of 31st Meeting, Gregynog Hall, 10–13 July, 1931, 531–3.

79. *Western Mail*, Monday, 11 January, 1926; see below, Chapter Nine, for further discussion of music in adult education.

80. National Council of Music, Minutes of 31st Meeting..., 540–2.

81. Interview with Mr Gethin Jones, now of Hirwaun, 9 June 1990.

82. *Musical Times*, 1 October 1924, 936–7.

Chapter Eight

1. *Musical Times*, 1 January 1924, 66.

2. See above, Chapter Seven.

3. See above, Chapter Two.

4. National Library of Wales, David Vaughan Thomas Papers.

5. Ibid, File 1701, list of members.

6. Ibid, File 30, 24 April 1920.

7. Ibid, 10 May 1920.

8. Ibid, 5 January 1922.

9. See above, Chapter Two.

10. NLW, D.V.T. Papers, 28 October 1923.

11. Ibid, 31 October 1923.

12. Reg Co, letter of Jenkin James to MacLean.

13. NLW D.V.T. Papers.

14. Ibid, letter of Leigh Henry to D.V.T., 19 August 1926.

15. Ibid, 4 November 1923.

16. Ibid, 31 July 1924; Walford married the daughter of the Rector of Narbeth, Pembrokeshire, in 1924.

17. Ibid, 19 April 1924.

18. Ibid, 31 July 1924.

19. Ibid, 29 April 1926.

20. Ibid, 28 May 1926.

21. Ibid, 1 February 1926.

22. Ibid, Box 28.

23. See above, Chapter Four.

24. NLW D.V.T. Papers, BBC lecture script, 'The development of a School of Welsh Composition'.

25. Ibid loc cit.

Chapter Nine

1. T. J. Coll, Class W Vol IV, 20 February 1920.

2. *Western Mail*, 17 June 1926.

3. See below, this Chapter.

4. Parrott, op. cit., 77.

5. W. H. Hadow, 'Some Aspects of Modern Music', *Musical Quarterly*, Vol I, No 1, January 1915, 60.

6. Thomas Jones, *Leeks and Daffodils*, Newtown, 1942, 99–100.

7. A. H. Harries, 'Needs of Welsh Nationalism', *Wales*, February, 1913, 69.

8. K. O. Morgan, *Rebirth of a Nation: Wales 1880–1980*, Oxford, 1981, 210.

9. *Musical Times*, 1 October 1920, 709.

10. Ibid, 1 September 1926, 1031.

11. *Western Mail*, Friday, 8 January 1926.

12. Arthur Somervell, 'The Basis of the Claim of Music in Education', *Proceedings of the Musical Association...*, 31st Session, 1904–5, London, 1905, 149–151; 153.

13. Reported in *Plebs*, June, 1921.

14. Quoted in Brian Simon (ed.), *The Search for Enlightenment: The Working Class and Adult Education in the Twentieth Century*, London, 1990, 37.

15. See Chapter One above.

16. *Musical Times*, 1 July 1922, 481–2.

17. Ibid, 1 July 1920, 477–8.

18. Ibid, 1 April 1921, 291.

19. Board of Education, *British Music: A Report by the Adult Education Committee on the Development of Adult Education through Music...*, London, 1924, 1–2.

20. Ibid, 5.

21. Ibid, 7.

22. Ibid, 20.

23. Ibid, 44.

24. Ibid, 49–50.

25. National Council of Music, *Review*, op. cit., 11.

26. See above, Chapter Two.

27. Reg Co Files, A Short Memorandum to the University Extensions Board on One-Year Classes in Music (typescript), n.d., 2.

28. Ibid, 5.

29. Reg Co Files, Extra-Mural Classes in Music, 1929–30 (typescript).

30. University of Wales, Annual Report of the National Council of Music, Presented to the Academic Board, the University Council, and the University Court, Session 1932–3, 21.

31. PRO ED73/44, Welsh National Council of Music, a sequence of documents, 31 May–25 July, 1928.

32. *British Music* (1924), 36–7.

33. The Carnegie Trust, 7th Annual Report (for the Year ending 31st December, 1920), Edinburgh, 1921, 44.

34. *British Music: a Report upon the History and Present Prospects of Music in the United Kingdom, perpared at the request of the Trustees of the Carnegie UK Trust, by Sir Henry Hadow...*, Dunfermline, 1921, 9–10.

35. Ibid, 12.

36. Thomas Jones, *A Diary with Letters 1931–1950*, Oxford, 1954, xl-xli.

37. Baroness White of Rhymney (Eirene White), *Thomas Jones CH: founder of Coleg Harlech*, Printed for Coleg Harlech at the National Library of Wales, Aberystwyth, n.d.

38. Peter Stead, op cit, 78–9.

39. T. J. Coll, Class X Vol V, 11 January 1927.

40. Reg Co Files, Short precis of the Activities and Organization of the University Council of Music (typescript), n.d., but probably 1931.

41. Hadow-Carnegie, *British Music*, 1921, 7.

42. Ibid, 10.

43. University of Wales, National Council of Music, Minutes of the 31st Meeting, at Gregynog Hall, 10th to 13th July, 1931.

44. T. J. Coll, Class X, Vol V, letter of Professor E. Harold Davies, to T. J., 20 February 1928.

45. Ibid, 11 January 1927.

46. Reg Co Files, letter of Walford, from The Cloisters, Windsor Castle, 26 June 1930.

47. University of Wales, Report of a Committee appointed to review the constitution, duties and powers of the Council of Music, together with the observations of the University Council thereon, 15 November 1930.

48. See above, Chapter Five.

49. Reg Co Files, letter of 21 November 1930.

50. Ibid, letter of T. J. from the Pilgrim Trust in London, 25 November 1931.

51. University of Wales, National Council of Music, Minutes of the 31st Meeting, July, 1931, 556.

52. *Musical Times*, 1 June 1930, 648.

53. Y *Cerddor*, 2nd series, November, 1930, 293–4.

54. Bernard Baldwin MBE, *Mountain Ash Remembered*, Cowbridge, 1984, 94–5.

55. *Musical Times*, 1 February 1927, 168.

56. Ibid, 1 July 1930, 650.

57. University of Wales, Annual Report of the National Council of Music, 1930–31, Presented to the Academic Board, the University Council and the University Court, 12.

58. Information selected from the sequence of Festival programmes held in Mountain Ash Public Library.

59. 1930 Festival Programme, Foreword.

60. Conversation with Mr Gethin Jones, Hirwaun, 9 June 1990.

61. Quoted in Dillwyn Miles, *The Royal National Eisteddfod of Wales*, Swansea, 1978, 91–2.

62. Ibid, 94.

63. *Musical Times*, 1 September 1927, 843.

64. Ibid, 1 September 1929, 842.

65. University of Wales, Annual Report of the Council of Music... September, 1928, 8–9.

66. Undeb Eisteddfodau Cymru, *Hints and Suggestions No 1*, The National Council of Music, The Law Courts, Cardiff, n.d., 9–11.

67. Y *Cerddor*, 2nd series, February, 1930, 29; circular letter of MacLean, 16 January 1930.

68. See above, Chapter One, 1.

69. J. Fuller Maitland, *A Door-Keeper of Music*, London, 1929, 296.

70. Welsh Department, Board of Education, *Education in Wales: Memorandum No 4. Suggestions for the Teaching of Music*, London, 1936, 4–5.

71. PRO ED22/225, Memorandum to HMI in Wales, from Wheldon, 9 March 1937.

72. Beryl Bowen James, 'Irwyn Ranald Walters HMI and the National Youth Orchestra of Wales', Unpublished M. Ed. thesis, University of Wales, 1990. Ms James is preparing for publication a monograph on the National Youth Orchestra of Wales.

73. Megan Mansel Thomas, 'Dorothy Adams-Jeremiah (1903–1988): a tribute', *Welsh Music*, Vol VIII, No 10, 1989, 49–51.

74. Alec Robertson, 'Sir Walford Davies', *Music Review*, Vol II, 167.

75. University of Wales, National Council of Music, Minutes of the 41st Meeting, University Registry, Cardiff, 20 October 1939, 884.

76. *Welsh Music*, Summer, 1974, Vol 4, No 7, 125.

Appendix

From *Chords that Matter*, a guide to eight keyboard talks by Walford Davies broadcast on BBC radio, April–June 1935.

VII. SYNOPSIS OF TALKS

A Quorum of Chords

I. A beautiful chord is observed and enjoyed much in the same way as is a beautiful countenance; tones or features are unified at a glance. And a chord, like a face, may be described as 'featureless' or else disfigured (by a missing or a painfully prominent feature). A graceful or euphonious melody, on the other hand, is enjoyed as a graceful or harmonious gesture may be enjoyed. Both these are perceived *in process, in time*; then realized as a whole. And just as it is possible to observe and enjoy both a countenance and a gesture simultaneously, so music requires us to take in both chord and melody together, and to do our best to appreciate them simultaneously. It is good that both are based in all cases on the same fundamental relatings (of fifths, fourths, thirds, and so on) which are a listener's root-concern till they are completely mastered, merely in order to be forgotten.

II. Dr. Johnson defines a *quorum* as 'such a number of officers as is sufficient to do business'. This definition is here adapted as 'such a number of chords as is sufficient to do musical business with Bach or Beethoven'. No listener to great music (or to little music of distinction and beauty) can for a moment afford to rest content till he knows our present quorum of four chords by their sound in every possible guise, loudness, and position, throughout the audible compass of the keyboard. And no listener who has an ear that can distinguish between two such sounds as e.g. *let* and *lit* in a poem, need doubt his own ability (with but very little steady practice) to master the distinction between these chords.

III. Here is the proposed classical quorum, built upon a given note, middle C:

Ex. 5

And here they are in their simplest terms, in their most natural and 'expectable' places in the so-called natural, or white-note, scale:

Ex. 6

IV. The major common chord is undoubtedly the most popular chord in existence; there are three to be found in every natural scale, and these have been together dinned into the ears of the world so systematically, that it is no wonder if we have become *blasé* or rebellious about them. Here is a mercilessly hackneyed major-chord formula:

Ex. 7

This has been used in every order of music from Beethoven's Appassionata Sonata Slow Movement (which shows in its first few solemn bars a typical classical use) and Pelham Humfrey's so-called Grand Chant (which shows a notable sacred use) to the commonplace banjo and brass-band uses of it, which are legion. An escape back to its primal values may perhaps best be found by quietly weaving for oneself *all twelve* major common chords into thoughtful succession in other and various ways at the piano. Having done this, the best way to get to know both the major and the minor common chords by sound, instantly and beyond risk of confusion, is to pick out perfect fifths on the keyboard, and fill them respectively with a major third, then a minor third. This done, in every pitch and position (always *pianissimo*, with the help of the sustaining pedal), the harmonic atmosphere will begin to clear.

V. For accustoming the ear to the other two chords, the dominant seventh and diminished seventh should in their turn be used to 'show up' one another, till the ear is fairly sure to recognize and distinguish them at an aural glance.

Thus, take any diminished fifth: ![Ex.8] and first

Ex. 8

superimpose upon it a perfect fifth, measured downwards

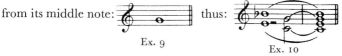

from its middle note: ![Ex.9] thus: ![Ex.10]

Ex. 9   Ex. 10

Then substitute a diminished fifth for the perfect, thus:

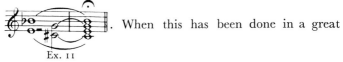

. When this has been done in a great

Ex. 11

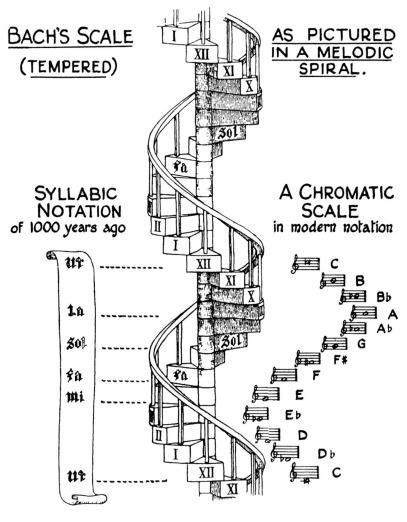

ALL THE NOTES THERE ARE:
THE MELODIC SPIRAL STAIRCASE

number of different positions and pitches on the keyboard (not too low in the bass region or it is apt to sound murky and confused), the ear is ready to listen for both in well-known contexts and examples. For instances of the dominant seventh, Beethoven's Introduction to his First Symphony, the tune called 'Cwm Rhondda', almost any military march, and Wagner's Prelude to the Third Act of *Lohengrin*, are recommended. Examples of the diminished seventh in use are legion. Bach's Chromatic Fantasia is full of it. Wagner's Fire Music in *The Ring* exemplifies it vividly. Beethoven makes striking use of it in his Tenth Sonata for Piano and Violin, and in the Introduction to the ' Pathetic ' Sonata.*

BIBLIOGRAPHY

Primary Sources

Report of the Commission of Inquiry into Industrial Unrest during the War: No 7 Division (Wales), 1917.

British Museum, ADD MS 55240, Macmillans Correspondence.

National Library of Wales, J. H. Davies Collection.

National Library of Wales, Dr Thomas Jones CH Collection.

National Library of Wales, David Vaughan Thomas Papers.

University of Wales Registry, Cathays Park, Cardiff, Collected Papers of the National Council of Music (uncatalogued).

Central Welsh Board, Report on the Teaching of Music in Welsh Intermediate Schools, Cardiff, 1918, (Copy in NLW, Aberystwyth).

University of Wales Council of Music, A Review of the Activities of the Council of Music, 1919–1941. (Copy in the Welsh Music Archive, Department of Music, University of Wales College of Cardiff.)

University of Wales: Annual Reports of the National Council of Music, 1919–1941. (Copies in University of Wales Registry, Cardiff.)

PRO, ED109: various Reports (HMI) on Music in Welsh Secondary Schools (Public Record Office, Kew).

PRO ED12: School Certificate Examinations in Music: Report of the Investigators.

PRO ED73, Welsh National Council of Music: a sequence of documents.

PRO ED22/225, Memorandum to HMI in Wales, 1937.

Board of Education, British Music: A Report by the Adult Education Committee on the Development of Adult Education through Music, London, 1924.

Board of Education, Curriculum and Examinations in Secondary Schools, London, 1941.

Board of Education, Consultative Committee, *The Education of the Adolescent* (The Hadow Report), 1926.

Board of Education, *Welsh in Education and Life, being the Report of the Board of Education to Inquire into the Position of the Welsh*

Language and to advise as to its Promotion in the Educational System of Wales, London, 1927.

Welsh Department, Board of Education, *Education in Wales: Memorandum No 4, Suggestions for the Teaching of Music*, London, 1936.

University of Wales, National Council of Music, *Memorandum on Music in Schools, both Primary and Secondary, being Suggestions for a Musical Policy and a Sketch for a Five Years' Course*, Cardiff, 1921.

The Carnegie Trust, 7th Annual Report for the year ending 31 December, 1920, Edinburgh, 1921.

The Carnegie Trust, *British Music: A Report upon the History and Present Prospects of Music in the United Kingdom*, prepared at the request of the Trustees of the Carnegie UK Trust, by Sir Henry Hadow, Dunfermline, 1921.

Undeb Eisteddfodau Cymru, *Hints and Suggestions No 1*, National Council of Music, Cardiff, n.d.

Secondary Sources

P. C. Buck, J. H. Mee, and F. C. Woods, *Ten Years of University Music in Oxford, Being a Brief Record of the Proceedings of the Oxford Univeristy Musical Union, during the years 1884–1894*, Oxford, 1894.

H. C. Colles, *Walford Davies*, London, 1944.

Peter Crossley-Holland (ed.), *Music in Wales*, London, 1948.

Gerald Cumberland, *Set Down in Malice: A Book of Reminiscences*, London, 1919.

H. Walford Davies, *The Pursuit of Music*, London, 1935.

E. L. Ellis, *The University College of Wales, Aberystwyth, 1872–1972*, Cardiff, 1972.

E. Keri Evans (ed.), *Cofiant Dr Joseph Parry*, Cardiff and London, 1921.

Frederick Griffiths, *Notable Welsh Musicians of Today*, London, 1896.

W. H. Hadow, *Collected Essays*, London, 1928.

W. H. Hadow, *Studies in Modern Music*, Oxford, 1892.

W. H. Hadow, *The Place of Music among the Arts*: The Romanes Lecture, Oxford, 1933.

H. R. Haweis, *Music and Morals*, London, 1871.

Glyn Tegai Hughes, Prys Morgan and J. Gareth Thomas (eds.), *Gregynog*, Cardiff, 1977.

R. T. Jenkins and Helen Ramage, *A History of the Honourable Society of Cymmrodorion and of the Gwyneddigion and Cymreigyddion Societies, 1751–1951*, London, 1952.

W. Stanley Jevons, *Methods of Social Reform and other Papers*, London, 1883.

Thomas Jones, *Leeks and Daffodils*, Newton, 1942.

Thomas Jones, *A Diary with Letters, 1931–1950*, Oxford, 1954.

W. R. Lambert, *Drink and Society in Victorian Wales*, Cardiff, 1983.

K. O. Morgan, *Rebirth of a Nation: Wales 1880–1980*, Oxford, 1981.

David Morgans, *Music and Musicians of Merthyr and District*, Merthyr Tydfil, 1922.

Ian Parrott, *The Spiritual Pilgrims*, Narberth and Tenby, 1964.

Bernarr Rainbow, *The Land Without Music*, London, 1966.

Percy A. Scholes, *The Mirror of Music, 1844–1944*, I and II, London, 1947.

Brian Simon (ed.), *The Search for Enlightenment: The Working Class and Adult Education in the Twentieth Century*, London, 1990.

W. H. Sonely-Johnstone, *History of the Cardiff Festival, 1892*, London and Cardiff, n.d.

The Baroness White of Rhymney, *Thomas Jones CH, founder of Coleg Harlech*, Aberystwyth (National Library of Wales) n.d.

INDEX